The Complete Guide to Operational Auditing

The Complete Guide to Operational Auditing

Harry R. Reider

John Wiley & Sons, Inc.
New York • Chichester • Brisbane • Toronto • Singapore

This text is printed on acid-free paper.

Copyright © 1994 by John Wiley & Sons, Inc.

All rights reserved. Published simultaneously in Canada.

Reproduction or translation of any part of this work beyond that permitted by Section 107 or 108 of the 1976 United States Copyright Act without the permission of the copyright owner is unlawful. Requests for permission or further information should be addressed to the Permissions Department, John Wiley & Sons, Inc., 605 Third Avenue, New York, NY 10158-0012.

This publication is designed to provide accurate and authoritative information in regard to the subject matter covered. It is sold with the understanding that the publisher is not engaged in rendering legal, accounting, or other professional services. If legal advice or other expert assistance is required, the services of a competent professional person should be sought.

Library of Congress Cataloging in Publication Data:
Reider, Harry R., 1940–
    The complete guide to operational auditing / Harry R. Reider.
      p.   cm.
    Includes index.
    ISBN 0-471-59419-9 (cloth : alk. paper)
    1. Auditing, Internal. 2. Auditing. I. Title. II. Title:
Operational auditing.
HF5668.25.R45 1993
657'.458—dc20   93-24896

Printed in the United States of America

10 9 8 7 6 5 4 3 2 1

SUBSCRIPTION NOTICE

This Wiley product is updated on a periodic basis with supplements to reflect important changes in the subject matter. If you purchased this product directly from John Wiley & Sons, Inc., we have already recorded your subscription for this update service.

If, however, you purchased this product from a bookstore and wish to receive (1) the current update at no additional charge, and (2) future updates and revised or related volumes billed separately with a 30-day examination review, please send your name, company name (if applicable), address, and the title of the product to:

Supplement Department
John Wiley & Sons, Inc.
One Wiley Drive
Somerset, NJ 08875
1-800-225-5945

Preface

The objective of this how-to guide is to help you understand the basic principles involved in planning and conducting an operational audit. In addition, it will provide the information and fundamentals you must know to use operational audit concepts effectively. This book is designed to meet your needs, regardless of whether or not you have any prior experience in operational auditing. Both basic knowledge for those with no previous hands-on experience, and reinforcement and additional learning for those who already have some prior operational audit experience are provided.

Questions that will be answered include:

1. What is an operational audit?
2. When should I perform an operational audit?
3. How can I perform an operational audit effectively and efficiently?
4. How can I effect positive change as a result of an operational audit?
5. How can I use operational audit tools and techniques to maintain operations in an economic, efficient, and effective manner on an on-going basis?

The materials presented in this book can be used by internal auditors and others to perform operational audits for their employers, and by external auditors to serve their clients. In addition, the tools and techniques presented can be used by anyone to maintain operations in the most economical, efficient, and effective manner.

PREFACE

Purpose and Objectives

In today's many-faceted and multidisciplined economic environment, organizational management has placed increasing emphasis on evaluation of the economy, efficiency, and effectiveness of the organization's operations. The operational audit is the tool used to perform such an evaluation. This book presents the basic principles of planning and conducting such an operational audit, as well as the fundamentals of which the auditor must be aware, to understand operational auditing concepts.

The objectives of this manual are as follows:

To increase understanding of operational auditing concepts and the ability to use them effectively.

To increase understanding of the purpose and mechanics of conducting operational audits or reviews.

To help identify the relationship and differences between operational audits and financial audits.

To increase the skills and abilities needed to conduct operational audits or reviews.

To increase awareness of operational audit opportunities and to help in their identification.

To improve the auditor's capability to perform operational audits or reviews in his or her present situation.

In many organizations today, top management is grasping for ways to become competitive and maintain market position—or merely to survive. Managers have sensed that many of their organizational systems are detrimental to progress and so have held them back. These are the very systems that are supposed to be helpful; for example:

1. Planning systems, long- and short-term, that resulted in documented plans but not in actual results.

2. Budget systems that became costly in terms of allocating resources effectively and controlling costs in relation to results.

3. Organizational structures that created unwieldy hierarchies, which produced systems of unnecessary policing and control.

4. Cost-accounting structures that obscured true product costs and resulted in pricing that constrained competitiveness.

5. Management systems that produced elaborate computer systems and reporting without enhancing the effectiveness of operations.

Operational auditing is a tool to make these systems helpful as intended and to direct the organization toward its goals. Theoretically, organizations should operate in an economic, efficient, and effective manner at all times. If such were the case, operational audit techniques would be applied on an ongoing basis. However, with the passage of time, good intentions and initially helpful systems tend to deteriorate. Operational audits or reviews are then necessary to get the organization back on track by pinpointing operational deficiencies, developing practical recommendations, and implementing positive changes. Although management should embrace operational audit concepts and apply them as they proceed, this is rarely the case. More typically, management needs to be sold on the value of operational auditing. In selling the benefits of conducting operational audits, it is important to stress that, unlike financial audits which cost time and money for financial statements and an unqualified opinion, operational audits pay for themselves. In effect, the operational audit environment becomes a *profit* center instead of a *cost* center. Although there are no guarantees, a successful operational audit should result in at least three to four times its cost in annual savings. These are not one-time savings, but ongoing—that is, savings year after year. With the success of an operational audit, management may quickly realize that the more operational audits done and the more recommended economies and efficiencies implemented, the greater the savings and results. In addition, the residual capability for performing operational audits remains in the area under review, so operations personnel can continue to apply operational audit concepts on an ongoing basis.

Keep in mind that the intent of the operational audit is not to be critical of present operations, but to review operations and develop a program for positive operational improvements by working with management and staff personnel. This can be accomplished most effectively by working with client personnel in areas where they recognize deficiencies and are willing to cooperate. The concept of operational auditing should be sold as an internal program of review directed toward improved economies and efficiencies that will produce increased operational results.

Who Is the Operational Auditor?

An operational audit can be performed by anyone with the appropriate skills. However, financial auditors (internal and/or external), because of their knowledge of the operations and their analytical skills, are typically requested to perform such services. In some organizations, a separate operational audit or review unit trained in operational audit concepts is established. The most effective way in which to implement such procedures is to assign overall responsibility for implementing organization-wide operational auditing procedures, which would include the performance of operational audits as well as training operations personnel in implementing these techniques in their areas.

The progress and ultimate success in achieving the benefits of operational auditing depend greatly on the auditors' skills and what management and others think of them. Auditors assigned to an operational audit engagement must possess the ability to audit financial, management, and operational areas. The attributes of an effective operational auditor include the following:

- Curiosity (imagination)
- Analytical ability
- Persuasiveness
- Good business judgment
- Common sense
- Objectivity
- Communication skills
- Initiative to develop techniques in such areas as work measurement, flow charting, cost-benefit analysis, organizational analysis, data processing, etc.
- Independence
- Confidence

Beyond those previously listed, the successful operational auditor should possess the following attributes:

1. The ability to spot the trouble areas—to look at a given situation and quickly determine what's getting in the way.

2. The ability to identify the critical problem areas, so as to avoid chasing mice when one should be chasing elephants. The application of the 80/20 rule states that operational auditing requires 80 percent common sense and 20 percent technical expertise, and that 80 percent of the trouble areas cause 20 percent of the problems, and that 20 percent cause 80 percent of the problems.

3. The ability to place oneself in management's position, to analyze the problem and ask questions from management's perspective. This is sometimes difficult, as many times the auditor has never been in an operational-related management position. Even when this is not true, the auditor may have difficulty understanding the constraints under which the manager must work—in effect, what they can and cannot do.

4. The skill to effectively communicate operational audit results. The success of your operational audit is measured by the degree with which your recommendations are implemented—and implementation is a direct by-product of effective communication. A rule of thumb in operational auditing is that you have been successful if you can convince management to adopt more than 50 percent of your recommendations.

Operational Audit Skills and Abilities

Although the attributes described above would also be helpful to a financial auditor, they are vital to an operational auditor. While financial auditors should have analytical ability, they use it primarily to perform repetitive tasks. Operational auditors, on the other hand, use these skills and abilities to assess a client's situation and recommend positive operational improvements.

The difference between required attributes for financial and operational auditors is similar to the difference between the left brain and the right brain. The left brain, which controls thinking and calculation processes, is more important to the financial auditor; whereas the right brain, which controls creativity and perceptual skills, is more critical to the operational auditor. Basically, the operational auditor needs a good balance of both, yet with a greater emphasis on the creative and perceptual side. The financial auditor would need just the opposite. This is why the best financial auditor does not always make the best operational auditor.

To render effective services, the operational auditor must have substantial knowledge of the total environment of the organization being examined and a high degree of skill and experience with the analytical techniques and tools needed to solve problems. The operational auditor should also have sensitivity to, and understanding of, the values and goals of all the various people that make up a going concern.

Someone trained in auditing procedures need not spend many years learning new methods before engaging in operational auditing—the basic techniques are the same. They mainly need to sharpen the audit, problem-identification, and analytical skills they already possess. Operational auditing can be viewed as 80 percent practical analysis and common sense and 20 percent technical know-how.

The operational audit requires the auditor to possess a number of varied audit tools and techniques, many of which can be used in both financial and operational audits. The following are included among these audit techniques:

- Cost analysis
- Preparation and analysis of systems flowcharts
- Development and/or analysis of computer systems and programs
- Evaluation of data processing procedures and results
- Statistical sampling procedures
- Development and understanding of forecasts and projections
- Interviewing skills
- Organizational planning development and analysis
- Creation of goals and objectives and other performance standards of measurement
- Development and analysis of organizational structures
- Verification of the accuracy of data
- Determination of compliance with laws and regulations
- Use of sophisticated analytical techniques such as matrix analysis, linear regression correlation, PERT, and critical path method
- Cost versus benefit analysis
- Communication skills, both oral and written.

Success as an effective operational auditor is based on what is accomplished—that is, recommendations made to management that are subsequently implemented. Operational auditing should be fascinating and rewarding to the auditor. The individual's stature as an auditor, credibility of the entire audit staff, management's and others' positive regard of the audit staff—all will increase in proportion to the degree of success attained in operational auditing.

PREFACE

Because of the number of different types and complexities of operational audits and the varying skills required, supporting functional disciplines are often necessary to supplement the regular audit staff's skills and abilities. However, it is not always practical to maintain personnel with all of the required skills on the operational audit staff. Thus, one should consider the skills that are necessary for the successful conduct of each operational audit, and either make sure that such skills are available on staff or contract for needed outside expertise.

Contents

Chapter 1 Overview   1

1.1	Introduction	1
1.2	Professional Standards	3
1.3	Economy, Efficiency, and Effectiveness	4
1.4	Definition	7
1.5	Terms	8
1.6	Financial Versus Operational Auditing	9
1.7	Why Perform an Operational Audit?	10
1.8	Components	11
	(a) Financial	13
	(b) Compliance	13
	(c) Economy and Efficiency	13
	(d) Effectiveness	14
1.9	Specific Objectives	14
	(a) Financial and Accounting	14
	(b) Adequacy of Internal Controls	14
	(c) Procedural Compliance	15
	(d) Organizational Efficiency	15
	(e) Operational Results	15
1.10	Specific Purposes	16
1.11	Benefits	16
1.12	Phases	20
	(a) Planning	20
	(b) Audit Programs	21
	(c) Field Work	21

	(d) Development of Audit Findings and Recommendations	21
	(e) Reporting	21
1.13	What Functions to Audit	22
1.14	The Budget	24
1.15	The Initial Survey	25
1.16	Engagement Development	26
	(a) Recognize and Define the Problem	26
	(b) Gather Appropriate Data	29
	(c) Evaluate the Situation	29
	(d) Proposal Letter	29
	(e) Perform the Operational Audit	41

Chapter 2 Planning Phase   **45**

2.1	Introduction	45
2.2	Information to Be Obtained	47
	(a) Laws and Regulations That Apply to the Activities Being Reviewed	47
	(b) Material on the Organization	48
	(c) Financial Information	48
	(d) Operating Methods and Procedures	49
	(e) Management Information and Reports	49
	(f) Problem Areas	49
2.3	Sources of Information	50
	(a) Effective Interviewing	50
	(b) Organizational Data	50
	(c) Financial Data	51
	(d) Policies and Procedures	51
	(e) Operating and Management Reports	51
	(f) Physical Inspection	51
2.4	Identification of Critical Problem Areas	52
	(a) Identification of Key Activities	52
	(b) Use of Management Reports	53
	(c) Examination of Audit Reports	53
	(d) Physical Inspection of the Activities	53
	(e) Discussions with Responsible Personnel	54
2.5	SAS 55: Consideration of the Internal Control Structure	54
	(a) Control Environment	54
	(b) Accounting System	55
	(c) Control Procedures	55

2.6	Review of Administrative and Operational Controls	56
	(a) Organization	57
	(b) Policies and Procedures	57
	(c) Accounting and Other Records	57
	(d) Performance Standards	57
	(e) Information Systems and Internal Reports	57
2.7	Planning-Phase Audit Program	58
2.8	Financial Statement Analysis	58
	(a) Comparisons	66
	(b) Trend Percentages	72
	(c) Common-Size Statements	72
	(d) Financial Ratios	76
2.9	Use of Graphics	84
2.10	Identifying Critical Areas	86
2.11	Planning Phase: Example Company	87
	(a) Information to Be Gathered	88
	(b) Organizational Philosophy	88
	(c) Operational Audit Objectives	89
	(d) Scope of Operational Audit	89
	(e) Illustration: Example Company	89
2.12	Conclusion	103

Chapter 3 Audit Program Phase — 105

3.1	Introduction	105
3.2	Benefits of the Operational Audit Program	106
3.3	Operational Audit Program Standards	107
3.4	Who Develops the Audit Program	108
3.5	Audit Program Work Steps	109
3.6	Audit Program Development Procedures	111
3.7	Sample Audit Program	112
3.8	Operational Audit Engagement Budget	119
3.9	Assignment of Staff	125
3.10	Operational Audit Management	126
3.11	Operational Audit Schedule Control	130
3.12	Engagement Control	131
3.13	Example Company Audit Program Phase	137
3.14	Conclusion	137

Chapter 4 Field Work Phase   147

4.1	Introduction	147
4.2	Field Work Considerations and Tasks	148
4.3	Factors in Reaching Conclusions	149
4.4	Field Work Techniques	150
4.5	Specific Field Work Techniques	151
	(a) Interviewing	153
	(b) Systems Flowchart	160
	(c) Layout Flowchart	172
	(d) Ratio, Change, and Trend Analysis	181
4.6	Field Work: Example Company	185
	(a) Function and Authority	186
	(b) Cost to Process a Purchase Order	186
	(c) Sample of Small Purchases	191
4.7	Other Techniques	193
	(a) Tests of Transactions	193
	(b) Performance Versus Plans	194
4.8	Workpapers	194
	(a) Use	195
	(b) Identification	195
	(c) Sample Table of Contents	196
4.9	Evidence	197
	(a) Types	197
	(b) Attributes	197
	(c) Evidence in the Workpapers	198
4.10	Conclusion	198

Chapter 5 Development of Audit Findings   201

5.1	Introduction	201
5.2	Attributes	203
	(a) Statement of Condition	204
	(b) Criteria	205
	(c) Cause	209
	(d) Effect	211
	(e) Recommendations	212
5.3	Audit Findings Development	214
5.4	Identifying Attributes	215
5.5	Approach to Developing Audit Findings	215
5.6	Audit Finding Development: Example Company	221

5.7	Development of Audit Findings: Examples	222
	(a) Employee-Leased Automobiles	222
	(b) Low Dollar and Local Purchases	222
5.8	Developing Recommendations	226
5.9	Conclusion	230

Chapter 6 Reporting Phase — **231**

6.1	Introduction	231
6.2	Interim Reporting	233
6.3	Oral Reporting	234
6.4	Written Report	235
6.5	Characteristics of Good Reporting	236
	(a) Significance	236
	(b) Usefulness and Timeliness	237
	(c) Accuracy and Adequacy of Support	238
	(d) Convincingness	238
	(e) Objectivity and Perspective	239
	(f) Clarity and Simplicity	240
	(g) Conciseness	240
	(h) Constructiveness of Tone	241
	(i) Organization and Positiveness	241
	(j) Summary	242
6.6	Reporting Audit Findings	242
	(a) Statement of Condition	244
	(b) Criteria	245
	(c) Effect	245
	(d) Cause and Recommendations	245
	(e) Inclusion of All Attributes	246
6.7	ABCs of Effective Report Writing	249
6.8	Sample Reports	253
6.9	Conclusion	274
6.10	Afterword	274

Index — **277**

CHAPTER ONE

Overview

1.1 INTRODUCTION

This chapter provides an overview of operational auditing concepts, principles, and terminology. Internal and external auditors (CPAs) have traditionally provided financial audit services to their employers and clients. Now, however, in an ever-changing economic and competitive environment, management looks for more than historical financial data. Managers need and request information about the internal operations of their organization and seek recommendations as to how they can manage and operate more economically, efficiently, and effectively. The operational auditing process is most helpful and beneficial in the following instances:

- Identifying operational areas in need of positive improvement.
- Pinpointing the cause (not the symptoms) of a problem.
- Quantifying the effect of the present situation on operations.
- Developing recommendations as to alternative courses of action to correct the situation.

This chapter will:

1. Introduce operational auditing concepts and principles.
2. Provide an update of the current status of operational auditing.

OVERVIEW

3. Increase understanding of the applicable standards related to operational auditing.

4. Familiarize the reader with commonly used operational auditing definitions and terms.

5. Identify differences between financial and operational audits.

6. Identify the purposes and components of operational auditing.

7. Increase understanding of the benefits of operational auditing.

8. Introduce the phases in which an operational audit is conducted.

External auditors (CPAs), with the assistance of internal auditors, have traditionally been responsible for auditing accounting and financial records for the purpose of rendering an opinion as to whether the financial statements produced present fairly the financial position of the organization. As part of the financial audit process, they reviewed the system of internal accounting controls to determine whether they could rely on such controls or whether they would have to increase the scope of the audit.

Although the organization's external CPA firm was primarily responsible for performing the financial audit, in many cases its internal auditors (if any) would also get involved in such audit procedures. Quite often it was the internal audit group who reviewed and monitored the organization's internal accounting controls, and its compliance with such controls, during the year. Accordingly, both external and internal auditors spent considerable time reviewing organizational operations from an internal accounting control viewpoint, but not necessarily from an *operational* viewpoint. What do we mean when we say "from an operational viewpoint?" We mean that operations are viewed with an eye as to whether they can be improved so as to be performed more efficiently, effectively, or economically.

Given today's increasingly varied and competitive economic environment, management places ever more emphasis on the evaluation of the economy, efficiency, and effectiveness of the organization's operations. Since accountants and auditors, both internal and external, have the fact-finding and diagnostic skills needed to perform such operational audits, they are frequently asked to do so. In some organizations a separate unit is formed strictly to perform operational audits.

For many years, auditing has been considered an integral part of accounting. However, the traditional checking, verifying, reconciling, and confirming procedures are no longer adequate to ensure that management is performing satisfactorily. Operational auditing got its start when the financial auditor stopped being concerned solely with verifying the accuracy of information, and started wondering why a transaction was made in the first place and if there was a better way to do it. Operational auditing is the process whereby the auditor determines whether management is using the resources entrusted to them in the most economical and efficient manner to achieve the most effective results of operations.

What are some of the reasons an operational audit should be performed? The focus and scope of many audits in both the public and private sectors have changed in recent years. Management has increased demands for more relevant information on the conduct of its operations and related results than can be found in financial statements. Both business and government management seek more information with which to judge the quality of operations and make operational improvements. This is why operational auditing techniques are needed to evaluate the effectiveness and efficiency of operations.

1.2 PROFESSIONAL STANDARDS

What standards currently govern or relate to operational auditing? The initial U.S. General Accounting Office (GAO) *Standards for Audit of Governmental Organizations, Programs, Activities, and Functions* (sometimes called the "yellow book") published in 1972 was the start of what has become the operational audit concept. Since issuing these standards, the GAO has issued other publications explaining and supplementing the standards and demonstrating how auditing can improve the efficiency and effectiveness of government operations and programs. In 1981 these standards were revised to expand upon the concepts of

- Examination and evaluation (field work) and reporting standards of Financial and Compliance Audits.
- Examination and evaluation standards of Economy and Efficiency Audits and Program Results Audits.
- Reporting standards of Economy and Efficiency Audits and Program Results Audits.
- Auditing computer-based systems: the auditor's role during system design and development (as an appendix).

In July 1988, the GAO again revised its *Government Auditing Standards* to incorporate the auditor's responsibility for continuing education and revised professional standards. In this revision, the GAO refers to operational auditing as "performance auditing."

Several state and local audit organizations officially adopted these standards, and in 1978 the Institute of Internal Auditors issued *Standards for the Professional Practice of Internal Auditing*, which were compatible with the GAO standards. The GAO standards were also reviewed by an AICPA Committee on Relations with the GAO, whose report in 1973 stated:

> The members of this committee agree with the philosophy and objectives advocated by the GAO in its standards and believe that the GAO's broadened definition of auditing is a logical and worthwhile continuation of the evolution and growth of the auditing discipline.[1]

In addition, the AICPA's Committee on Operational and Management Auditing report, *Operational Audit Engagements*, in January 1982 defines operational audit engagements, but does not set standards or introduce new concepts.

1.3 ECONOMY, EFFICIENCY, AND EFFECTIVENESS

The GAO standards introduced the concept of auditing for economy, efficiency, and effectiveness. The following is a brief description of each of the "three E's of operational auditing."

1. *Economy* (or the cost of operations)
   Is the organization carrying out its responsibilities in the most economical manner—that is, through due conservation of its resources? In appraising the economy of operations, and related allocation and use of resources, the operational auditor may consider whether the organization is:
   - Following sound procurement practices,
   - Overstaffed as related to performing necessary functions,
   - Allowing excess materials to be on hand,
   - Using equipment that is more expensive than necessary, or
   - Avoiding the waste of resources.

2. *Efficiency* (or methods of operations)
   Is the organization carrying out its responsibilities with the minimum expenditure of effort? Examples of operational inefficiencies to be aware of include:

---

[1] AICPA, *Committee on Relations with the GAO*, 1973, p. 12.

1.3 ECONOMY, EFFICIENCY, AND EFFECTIVENESS

- Improper use of manual and computerized procedures,
- Inefficient paperwork flow,
- Inefficient operating systems and procedures,
- Cumbersome organizational hierarchy and/or communication patterns,
- Duplication of effort, or
- Unnecessary work steps.

The GAO standards state that economy and efficiency are both relative terms, and that it is not possible for an auditor to express an opinion on whether an entity has reached the maximum practicable level of either. "Generally, at the completion of a performance audit the auditor does not express an opinion on the overall level of performance. Therefore, these standards do not contemplate that the auditor will be called upon to give such an opinion. Rather, the auditor would report findings and conclusions on the extent and adequacy of performance, and on specific processes, methods, and internal controls that can be made more efficient or effective. If potential for improvement is found, the auditor would recommend appropriate corrective actions."[2]

3. *Effectiveness* (or results of operations)
   Is the organization achieving results or benefits based on stated goals and objectives or some other measurable criteria? The review of the results of operations includes:
   - Appraisal of the organizational planning system as to its development of realistic goals, objectives, and detailed plans;
   - Assessment of the adequacy of management's system for measuring effectiveness;
   - Determination of the extent to which results are achieved; and
   - Identification of factors inhibiting satisfactory performance of results.

Although it is management's continuing responsibility to assess the results of operations, its objectives and measurement criteria are not always clearly defined. Without such clarification, the auditor cannot meaningfully evaluate the results of operations. If management has not done so prior to starting the operational audit, the auditor should work with management to (1) state the objectives, (2) establish measurement criteria, and (3) establish methods for accumulating the data necessary to measure achievement of operational results.

---

[2] United States General Accounting Office, *Government Auditing Standards*, 1988 Revision, pp. 2–5, par. 9.

FIGURE 1.1 Operational audit triangle: The three E's.

The relationship of economy and efficiency and their impact on results can be seen as a seesaw; that is, there is an attempt to balance them to achieve just the right amount of each. In a perfectly balanced situation, the *cost* of operations would be maintained at the lowest possible level without sacrificing efficiency (or the methods of operations) and effectiveness (or the results of operations)—thus effecting *economy*. At the same time, the *methods* of operations would be performed at the least possible cost without sacrificing results—thus producing *efficiency*. Can you see, then, why economy and efficiency are normally reviewed together as part of the operational audit procedure?

The three E's—economy, efficiency, and effectiveness—as well as the seesaw effect between economy and efficiency—are shown in Figure 1.1.

1.4 DEFINITION

Operational auditing is a widely used term. However, no uniform, commonly recognized definition has been unanimously accepted. The definitions that have been given for *operational auditing* include the following:

1. An extension of the audit function into all operations of a business.

2. The application of internal auditing to operations rather than financial controls.

3. The identification of opportunities for greater efficiency and economy, or to improve effectiveness in carrying out operational procedures.

4. A control technique for evaluating the effectiveness of operating procedures.

5. Nothing more than a review of controls, now including nonfinancial controls.

6. Audits of activities other than those pertaining to examination of financial statements.

7. Audit technique that involves evaluating the efficiency and economy with which resources are managed and consumed.

8. Auditing with a management viewpoint.

9. Audits made for internal management, not for external third parties, with the results circulated internally rather than externally.

10. Combination of economy and efficiency auditing and effectiveness or program results auditing.

Combining these definitions, it could be said that operational auditing is an audit of operations performed from a management viewpoint to evaluate the economy, efficiency, and effectiveness of any and all operations, limited only by management's desires.

1.5 TERMS

In recent years various terms have been used interchangeably with *operational auditing* to describe this audit approach. Examples include:

1. Program audit
2. Management audit
3. Performance audit
4. Performance review and evaluation
5. Departmental audit
6. Nonfinancial audit
7. Compliance audit
8. Cost-benefit audit
9. Economy and efficiency audit
10. Effectiveness or results audit
11. Functional audit
12. Full scope audit
13. Responsibility audit
14. Comprehensive audit

Although the term *audit* is generally used to describe these procedures, as in the examples just mentioned, it is often a good idea to avoid the connotation of the term *audit*, which may have a negative impact on the organization. To this end, *review* may be substituted, which may be a better term to use with specific organizations. Often, the particular name given the operational audit procedure enhances management's trust and willingness to work with the auditors, which is vital to the success of the operational audit.

1.6 FINANCIAL VERSUS OPERATIONAL AUDITING

To illustrate the differences between financial and operational auditing, using operational audit concepts, the auditor is *less* concerned with determining whether purchase requisitions and orders and suppliers' invoices reflect proper approvals, as in a financial audit, but *more* concerned with such things as whether

1. The materials were really needed,
2. Quantities used or purchased were reasonable,
3. There was avoidable waste and exposure to damage or loss, and
4. Requisitioners exercised undue influence on procurement by designating sources of purchase.

For example, a typical *financial* audit step could be to determine whether vendor purchase requisitions and invoices have been properly approved. However, when looking at the *operational* aspects of vendor purchases, the auditor might ask:

1. Were materials really needed?
   For example, were materials mistakenly ordered that could not be used owing to changes in production specifications, because the product specifications unit failed to communicate with the purchasing department?
2. Were quantities used or purchased reasonable?
   For example, assuming the materials were usable, were goods bought for inventory above calculated safety stock levels because of the fear of incurring a stock-out?
3. Was there avoidable waste and exposure to damage or loss?
   For example, were steel components and parts that were susceptible to rust bought and stored in an outside yard, owing to an overcrowded inside storeroom?
4. Did the requisitioner exercise undue influence by stating specific sources or brands?

For example, did the requisitioner specify an IBM microcomputer or a Xerox copier when a less expensive brand would do just as well?

Some of the other differences between a conventional financial audit and an operational audit are summarized in Table 1.1.

TABLE 1.1. Financial Versus Operational Auditing

Characteristic	Financial Audit	Operational Audit
1. Purpose	Express opinion on financial condition	Analyze and improve methods and performance
2. Scope	Fiscal financial records	Business operations
3. Skills	Accounting	Interdisciplinary
4. Time orientation	To the past	To the future
5. Precision	Absolute	Relative
6. Audience	Stockholders, public	Internal management
7. Necessity	Legally required	At option of management
8. Standards	GAAP, GAAS	GAO standards, economy, efficiency, and effectiveness
9. Opinion	Required	Not required
10. Audit results	Opinion and financial statements	Recommendations to management
11. Focus	Financial statements presented fairly	Operational positive improvements
12. Viewpoint	Financial	Management
13. Success	Unqualified opinion	Management adoption of recommendations

1.7 WHY PERFORM AN OPERATIONAL AUDIT?

What are some of the reasons an operational audit should be performed? The focus and scope of many audits in both the public and private sectors have changed in recent years. Management has increased demands for more relevant information on the conduct of their operations and the related results than can be found solely in financial statements. Both business and government management seek more information with which to judge the quality of operations and make operational improvements. That is why we need operational auditing techniques to evaluate the effectiveness and efficiency of operations.

Auditors (both internal and external) are being asked more frequently to evaluate an organization's operations. Although this is not a new service for auditors to provide, requests for such specific services have increased due to the greater emphasis on the economy, efficiency, and effectiveness of operations and the related results. The technical skills auditors possess, particularly those of analysis, fact finding, and reporting, make them excellent choices for performing such operational audits.

An operational audit involves a systematic review of an organization's activities in relation to specified objectives. The general purpose of the engagement as stated in *Operational Audit Engagements*, published by the AICPA in 1982, may be to:

A. *Assess Performance.*
Any operational audit involves an assessment of the reviewed organization's performance. To assess performance is to compare the way an organization conducts its activities with: (1) objectives established by management or the engaging party, such as organizational policies, standards, goals, and objectives and (2) other appropriate measurement criteria.

B. *Identify Opportunities for Improvement.*
Increased economy, efficiency, or effectiveness are the broad categories under which most improvements are classified. The practitioner may identify specific opportunities for improvement by analyzing interviews with individuals (whether within or outside of the organization), observing operations, reviewing past and current reports, studying transactions, making comparisons with industry standards, and exercising professional judgment based on experience or other appropriate means.

C. *Develop Recommendations for Improvement or Further Action.*
The nature and extent of recommendations developed in the course of operational audits vary considerably. In many cases, the practitioner may be able to make specific recommendations. In other cases, further study, not within the scope of the engagement, may be required, and the practitioner may simply cite reasons why further study of a specific area may be appropriate.[3]

1.8 COMPONENTS

Operational auditing is considered to have four major components, which are displayed in Figure 1.2: financial, compliance, economy and efficiency, and effectiveness.

---

[3] AICPA, *Operational Audit Engagements*, 1982, p. 3.

FIGURE 1.2. Scope of audit work.

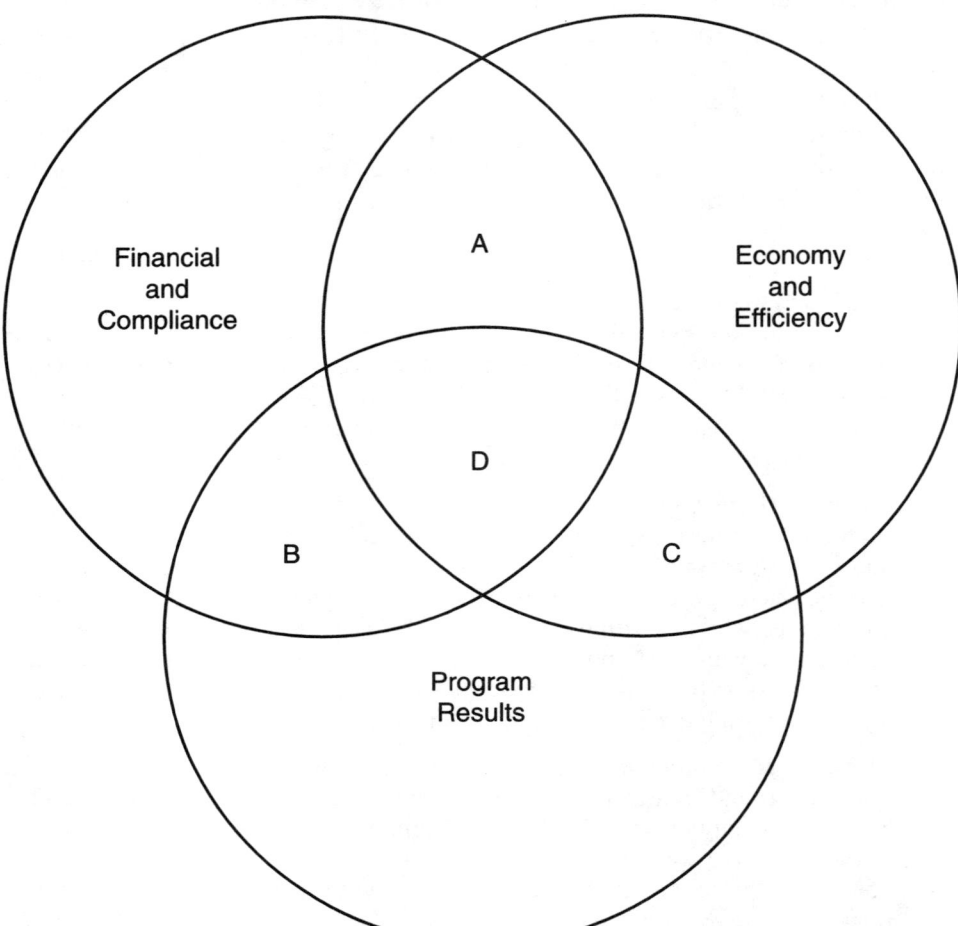

A. Economy and Efficiency Audit
B. Program Results Audit
C. Operational Audit
D. Comprehensive or Full Scope Audit

1.8 COMPONENTS

(a) Financial

This component primarily focuses on proper and adequate accounting and reporting procedures, and is basically the same as a conventional financial audit. The major difference when performed as part of an operational audit is that the financial audit may be but one element in a review that branches out into many additional areas.

(b) Compliance

Normally performed together with the financial component, compliance is concerned with adherence to rules expressed in applicable laws and regulations, and to internal policies and procedures. It is the extension of a compliance review that would be performed as part of a conventional financial audit. However, it may not involve only financial-type rules, but can also apply to rules, procedures and policies governing operations.

(c) Economy and Efficiency

This component is concerned with achieving the optimum balance between costs and results. In performing this component, the auditor evaluates cost minimization, emphasizing reduction of costs, but not to the point where results are not accomplished. In addition productivity maximization may be analyzed, but not to the point where the costs become excessive. In evaluating economy and efficiency, the auditor analyzes the use of resources—people, facilities, equipment, supplies, and money. For example, an auditor might analyze the following:

- Allocation of responsibilities and authority within the organization structure.
- Physical deployment or distribution of resources.
- Scheduling of resources—when people work, when facilities are used.
- Segmentation of tasks into logical groupings.
- Match between skill level, capacity, performance capability, etc., and the way a resource is used.
- Prices paid.
- Charges levied.

- Rate at which tasks are performed.
- Number of tasks completed.

Within the economy and efficiency concept, the auditor does not ask whether the function is worthwhile in terms of what it accomplishes. The auditor accepts that the function exists and asks whether this is the most economical and efficient way to get it done. Results are considered in the effectiveness component.

(d) Effectiveness

This component is concerned with results and accomplishments achieved and benefits provided. In evaluating the effectiveness of operations, the auditor asks whether the activity is achieving its ultimate intended purpose. Analysis is qualitative rather than quantitative.

1.9 SPECIFIC OBJECTIVES

There are many reasons that management might desire to have an operational audit or review of their operations performed. Some of these reasons are listed below. Keep in mind that management may be looking for a single objective (i.e., operational efficiency), a combination of objectives (i.e., procedural compliance and internal controls), or their own specific agenda (i.e., achievement of results on the basis of cost versus benefits).

(a) Financial and Accounting

- Adherence to financial policy.
- Performance of accounting procedures.
- Procedures performed by individuals with no incompatible functions.
- Adequate audit trail exists.
- Procedures can be observed.

(b) Adequacy of Internal Controls

- Accounting controls.
    Safeguarding of assets.
    Reliability of financial records.

System of authorizations and approvals.
Separation of duties.
Physical controls over assets.
- Administrative controls.
    Operational efficiency.
    Adherence to managerial policies.
    Adequacy of management information and reporting.
    Employee competency and training.
    Quality controls.

(c) Procedural Compliance

- Laws and regulations; federal, state, and local.
- Adherence to administrative policy.
- Performance of authorization and approval.
- Evidence of action to achieve stated goals and objectives.
- Adherence to long-range/short-term plans.
- Achievement of management objectives.
- Effective recruiting and training.
- Evaluation of organizational policies.

(d) Organizational Efficiency

- Clear understanding of responsibilities and authority.
- Logical nonconflicting reporting relationships.
- Current job/functional descriptions.
- Separation of duties.
- Staffing levels compared with those of similar operations.

(e) Operational Results

- Organizational planning: goals, objectives, and detail plans.
- Detail plan development and implementation; considering alternatives, constraints, cost-benefit, and resource allocation.
- Evaluation of operational results.
    Appropriateness of measurement criteria.
    Feedback on success or failure.
    Adjustment of goals, objectives, strategies.

1.10 SPECIFIC PURPOSES

In conducting an operational audit or review, the auditor should be aware of the purpose for which the review is being performed. Prior to the start of the operational audit, the auditor should communicate clearly his or her understanding of the purpose(s) to appropriate management personnel. There should be a mutual agreement as to operational audit purpose in the beginning. For example, the purpose could be one or more of the following:

1. To review and evaluate the adequacy of the accounting system and related internal accounting controls (including both accounting and administrative controls).
2. To analyze systems and controls as related to internal controls, functional operations, and legal compliance.
3. To analyze the capability to accomplish agreed upon stated goals, objectives, and results in management's approved plan.
4. To compare actual accomplishments/results with the goals established in management's plan for the period, and to determine reasons that established goals were not met.
5. To analyze and explain cost overruns or high unit costs for each function/activity for which such data can be quantified.
6. To assess and evaluate compliance with federal, state, and local laws and regulations, ensuring at least minimal compliance.
7. To identify and report deficiencies and areas for improvement and to provide technical assistance and follow-up where necessary.

1.11 BENEFITS

Depending on its scope, an operational audit can be of significant benefit to top management and staff in some or all of the following ways:

1. *Identifying problem areas, related causes and alternatives for improvement.* This is a major purpose of operational auditing. Although often aware of a problem, management cannot always define exactly its dimen-

sions. The auditor's third-party, objective viewpoint helps to achieve the proper focus on operational problems.

To define a problem in some instances, an auditor need merely talk to operations personnel and then share their viewpoints with management. Keep in mind that people working in operations are usually more aware of problems and their causes than management personnel.

The auditor's role is also to identify the actual causes (not the symptoms or believed causes) of problems, which may be the result of management policy or actions. Finally, the auditor must formulate realistic, practical solutions to these problems. This is where the auditor's experience in working with numerous other departments and/or organizations is valuable. A good rule for the auditor to follow is not to recommend any course of corrective action that he or she could not assist in implementing.

2. *Locating opportunities for eliminating waste and inefficiency; that is, cost reduction.* Keep in mind that each dollar of cost reduction (without sacrificing efficiency or effectiveness) contributes dollar-for-dollar to the bottom line. Cost reduction is a significant element in operational audits. However, be wary of short-term cost reductions causing long-term problems (for instance, downsizing of operations and/or personnel when business falls off). It is the role of the operational auditor to assist management in operating at the lowest possible cost in all situations, in relationship to adequate plans. Costs should always be at the correct level, and when costs need to be cut, proper decisions are made so as not to adversely impact operations. This is in contrast to typical cost cutting across the board, which not only constricts all operations, but also fails to provide for the necessary resources for those operations that actually need increased funds.

3. *Locating opportunities to increase revenues; that is, income improvement.* Increasing revenues also has an effect on the bottom line, yet only to the extent of profit margins for this additional amount of revenue. Increasing revenues may, in fact, be detrimental in terms of profits and operating efficiencies (both short-term and long-term). Often revenues or sales are increased to present a more favorable sales picture in the short term or to fill plant or service capacity, rather than on the basis of sound planning. Please note that in most organizations a greater amount of resources and emphasis is devoted to revenue improvement than to cost economies, even though effective cost cutting offers greater rewards.

4. *Identifying undefined organizational goals, objectives, policies, and procedures.* It would be nice to think that all organizations are doing effective long-term and short-term planning. However, in reality this is usually more the exception than the rule. This means that the auditor will have to assist management in recognizing undefined goals, objectives, and detailed

plans and to assist in developing such plans prior to starting an operational audit. For without defined plans, there are no yardsticks or milestones against which to measure the organization's effectiveness.

5. *Identifying criteria for measuring the achievement of organizational goals and objectives.* As mentioned in item 4, there is great likelihood that plans and related goals and objectives are not in existence. Even when they do exist, there may not be appropriate criteria for measuring their achievement, thus requiring the auditor to assist management in the development of such criteria.

6. *Recommending improvement in policies, procedures, and organizational structure.* The auditor may find instances in which the cause of the problem lies with existing policies or procedures. Policies should be set by senior management and relate to the rules by which the organization conducts its business (e.g., service to the customer). However, many times either such policies get in the way of operations personnel performing their functions (e.g., excessive controls and paperwork to process a customer credit) or insufficient authority is delegated to allow them to be most effective (e.g., sending a service representative to the customer to investigate a complaint). In these instances, the policies may be wrong and in need of correction.

Procedures are the ways in which functions are performed based on stated policies. As such procedures refer to operations, it might seem that operations personnel would be involved in establishing and implementing them. However, in most instances, procedures are set by management, causing operations personnel to resist them (and many times sabotage them) and work against their success.

Organization structure tends to evolve over a period of time, with minimal regard to economy, efficiency, or effectiveness. In most organizations there are built-in incentives to increase organizational levels, such as budget systems that reward the growth of organizations and encourage politicking to build empires. It is the auditor's role to identify such organizational inefficiencies and to recommend improvements. However, when auditors do this, they do not put themselves in the position of recommending specific individual cuts. Assuming that the organization's personnel are all good employees (and that hiring, orientation, training, and promotion policies and procedures are adequate), the auditor may recommend achieving desired results with fewer overall personnel. However, it is then management's responsibility to decide what to do with extraneous personnel, possibly effecting departmental transfers, retraining, lateral moves, etc. It is usually more desirable to use existing good personnel elsewhere in the organization than to terminate them. It is interesting to note that in most

1.11 BENEFITS

organizations that have a policy of termination, their personnel departments are hiring at the same time—often for similar positions.

7. *Providing checks on performance by individuals and by organizational units.* Assuming that proper results have been defined for individuals and work units, it is the auditor's responsibility to ensure that adequate checks or measurement criteria have been established to monitor progress toward their achievement.

8. *Reviewing compliance with legal requirements and organizational goals, objectives, policies, and procedures.* The auditor makes sure that the organization complies with the laws and internal rules under which it performs its functions. If there is a lack of compliance, the auditor defines the consequences.

9. *Testing for existence of unauthorized, fraudulent, or otherwise irregular acts.* Such testing is a requirement for private and public sector financial audits and normally for operational audits as well—particularly where such acts have an adverse effect on operations.

10. *Assessing management information and control systems.* The auditor will address a number of concerns in this area: Are such reporting systems adequate to provide management and operations personnel the information necessary to effectively operate all aspects of the organization? Is the level of detail commensurate to the level of operations (that is, more detail at lower levels; less detail at higher levels)? Is there information lacking that should be present? Are all key indicators being considered (e.g., units shipped as well as items rejected and returned)?

11. *Identifying possible trouble spots in future operations.* Many times the auditor senses a future problem based on troubles in the past. For instance, problems with past computer conversions may indicate future troubles with an extensive computer processing upgrade.

12. *Providing an additional channel of communication between operating levels and top management.* In many organizations there is a clear (or unclear) separation between management and operations; that is, management makes the decisions and operations personnel carry them out. One of the most important benefits of an operational audit is the auditor's ability to convey operational concerns to management in those instances where such concerns are not being communicated on an ongoing basis.

13. *Providing an independent, objective evaluation of operations.* Both management and operations personnel are often too close to what is going on within their own operations to effectively evaluate their results. The independent operational auditor can do this objectively, pointing out those areas in need of improvement as well as those that are being performed well.

1.12 PHASES

Operational auditing consists basically of gathering information, making evaluations, and developing recommendations where appropriate. An operational audit is essentially the evaluation of an activity for potential improvement. Management has the primary responsibility for proper planning, conduct, and control of activities. Thus, review and evaluation of the way management itself plans, conducts, and controls the activities become a major consideration and focal point in the conduct of the audit. In addition, the audit includes reviewing results and being alert to problems. These also provide insights into the effectiveness of management and the potential for improvements.

The phases through which an operational audit progresses are as follows:

1. Planning
2. Audit programs
3. Field work
4. Development of findings and recommendations
5. Reporting

The operational auditor may perform two types of operational audits: *preliminary* and *in-depth*. Both types will have all five phases. The difference between the two is the degree of emphasis, the specific techniques chosen, and the objectives of a particular phase.

In a preliminary audit, for example, field work might consist of limited transaction testing and interviewing, and the report may be a briefing to management. In an in-depth audit, field work might consist of detailed examination using techniques such as work measurement, workload analysis, cost-benefit analysis, etc., and the report may be formally written, with wider distribution. The type and objectives of the audit to be performed will determine the nature of the work to be done. The operational audit phases can be described as follows:

(a) Planning

The auditor obtains general information about the kinds of activities performed, the general nature of those activities and their relative importance, and other general information to help plan the early portions of the audit.

(b) Audit Programs

The auditor prepares the operational audit program and work plan for the preliminary review of those activities selected for review in the planning phase. Well-constructed audit programs are essential for conducting operational audits in an efficient and effective manner. Such programs must be individualized for each situation, and each work step must state clearly the work to be done and why.

(c) Field Work

The auditor analyzes operations to determine the effectiveness of management and related controls. Such functions and controls are tested in actual operation, with particular emphasis on areas difficult to control and having high potential for weakness. The purpose of this phase is to determine whether a situation needs improvement, whether it is significant, and what should be done about it.

(d) Development of Audit Findings and Recommendations

Based on the significant areas identified during the field work phase, specific findings are developed according to the following attributes:

- Condition: What did you find?
- Criteria: What should it be?
- Effect: What is the impact on operations?
- Cause: Why did it happen?
- Recommendation: What needs to be done to correct the situation?

(e) Reporting

The auditor prepares the report relative to the results of the audit. The purpose of the report is to bring these results to the attention of those having an interest in or responsibility for the findings. In reality, the majority of audit findings, if not all, should have been reported to management, with remedial action already being taken or completed, prior to the auditor's formal report. The report becomes a summary of the results of the operational audit.

1.13 WHAT FUNCTIONS TO AUDIT

The most critical question to answer for an organization is what function or functions to include in the operational audit. Where shall we audit? Do we perform the operational audit for all functions of the organization or for only selected areas? A good starting point is to list the organization's major functions, to check off those where operational auditing would be most helpful, and then to prioritize each function as to its criticalness and/ or the desired order of auditing. Figure 1.3 is a sample checklist.

One way to decide which functions to audit is to determine how critical each function is to the overall organizational operation. For instance, for a manufacturing business, the most critical area might be the inventory or production control functions. For a service-oriented concern, where personnel costs approximate 70 percent of total expenditures, the personnel function would be more critical. Normally, auditors work with a limited budget in terms of hours allocated to the operational audit, so they are greatly concerned with spending these hours on functional areas that offer the greatest potential for operational improvements in return for their effort. Criteria for determining a company's critical areas include the following:

1. Areas with large numbers in relation to other functions; such as revenues, costs, percentage of total assets, number of sales, units of production, and personnel.

2. Areas where controls are weak; e.g., there may be a lack of an effective manufacturing control system, management reporting system, or organizational planning and control system.

3. Areas subject to abuse or laxity; e.g., there may be inventory and production controls that allow transactions to go unreported and undetected, uncontrollable time and expense reporting, and ineffective personnel evaluation procedures.

4. Areas that are difficult to control; e.g., there may be ineffective storeroom, shipping, or time-recording procedures.

5. Areas where functions are not performed efficiently or economically; e.g., there may be ineffective procedures, duplication of efforts, unnecessary work steps, inefficient use of resources such as data processing equipment, overstaffing, and excess purchases.

6. Areas indicated by ratio, change, or trend analysis; such as characterized by wide swings up or down when compared over a number of

1.13 WHAT FUNCTIONS TO AUDIT

FIGURE 1.3. Checklist of major organizational functions.

Board of Directors

Management
Organizational
Departmental
Reporting and
  control

Planning Systems
Organizational
Departmental
Detail planning

Personnel
Hiring procedures
Evaluation
  procedures
Staffing levels
Payroll procedures

Accounting
Assets
Liabilities
Budget
  procedures
Payroll
Accounts payable
Accounts
  receivable
Billing and
  collections
Financial
  reporting
Cost-accounting procedures
Borrowing and debt outstanding
General ledger and journal entry system

Electronic Data Processing
Systems design and analysis
Programming and software
  development
Equipment
Operating procedures
Data control
Reporting

Operations
Purchasing
Personnel administration
Plant operations
Manufacturing controls
Production control
Inventory control
Marketing
Sales
Engineering
Equipment
Fixed assets
Insurance

periods. Examples include sales changes by product line, costs by major category, number of personnel, inventory levels, and so forth.

7. Areas where management has identified specific weaknesses or needs for improvement; such as personnel functions, manufacturing procedures, data processing operations, and management reporting.

Another factor to consider when choosing the critical operational area to audit is the willingness of the personnel in the area to cooperate in the performance of the audit. First, those in operational management should want to have their operations reviewed and be willing to work with the auditor in the improvement of their operations. Without such top management commitment, the operational audit is not likely to succeed. Second, staff and operating personnel must be willing to work with the auditors both in performing the operational audit and in the subsequent implementation of operational improvements. Cooperation at all levels of the organization is essential to a successful operational audit.

The auditor must enlist the cooperation of all personnel: members of management to ensure top commitment to the audit, and operations personnel to help in identifying areas to audit and in implementing proposed improvements. Normally, in most operations, the staff or operating personnel know precisely what is going on day by day, and with firsthand knowledge of operations, can help you to identify the most critical areas to audit.

1.14 THE BUDGET

In addressing the number and extent of critical areas to be covered in the operational audit, it is important to understand the relationship between budgeted audit time and the scope of operational audit work desired to be accomplished. In many situations, the audit budget hours are established first and then the scope of the operational audit is made to fit within the budget. While this procedure may work from an internal standpoint in regard to budget and staffing, it does not fully take into account the aspect of such auditing that requires flexibility and expandability of formulated operational audit work programs.

In addition, it is extremely important for both the auditor and management to consider the cost against the expected benefits of the specific operational audit. This is a significant concept in helping to determine how much audit time to allocate to the operational audit.

Remember: When performing a financial audit, the audit group is budgeting staff time and related costs. In effect, the financial audit becomes a cost center. In an operational audit, on the other hand, operational benefits and dollar savings should greatly surpass the cost of the audit (savings should be at least three times its cost). In effect, the operational audit becomes a profit center. Theoretically, the more operational auditing is done, the greater the savings realized by the organization. In reality, however, some guidelines are needed to establish the extent of an operational audit in a given functional area, once the critical areas for review have been identified.

There are a number of factors to consider in establishing the operational audit budget:

1. *The scope of the operational audit.* For example, are all significant operational areas to be reviewed, or only the major ones identified?

2. *The frequency of the operational audit.* Is the operational audit to be done on a one-time basis, which requires more up-front planning and research; or is it to be performed for an area that is reviewed on a regular basis and requires minimal up-front efforts?

3. *The nature of the business operations.* For example, a service business dealing primarily with selling staff time, such as a medical, legal, or CPA practice, would normally require less time for an operational audit than a manufacturing business that produces, ships, sells, and services a fairly wide product line.

4. *The degree of management effectiveness.* Functional areas that are ineffectively managed will normally require more operational audit time to review than those that are more effectively managed.

5. *The expectation of benefits.* Those areas that afford the greatest expected benefits, in terms of the number of potential recommendations or savings, should be the areas audited first. However, these areas will take more time to review than those with lesser expectations.

Operational audits, as compared with financial audits, require a large amount of preplanning, fact gathering, and research. This can make the costs of conducting an operational audit considerable. However, when compared with the potential benefits and savings, costs become less significant. That is why, when determining how much time to spend on the operational audit, it is best to use a cost-versus-benefit approach—tempered, of course, with the reality of available staff and audit hours. In effect, an effort should be made to cover competently as many of the major critical areas as possible within the limited staffing constraints.

1.15 THE INITIAL SURVEY

To achieve the greatest results from limited operational audit resources, the auditor identifies those areas of major importance and those offering the greatest potential savings or benefits. The identification of these areas is done as part of an initial survey, either prior to or as part of the planning phase of the operational audit. If performed before the planning phase, either because the client requests it, because of the relatively small audit scope or budget, or for some other reason, the survey usually consists of some type of management and operational questionnaire. The purpose of the questionnaire is to determine what functions are performed, who performs each function, why each is performed, and how each is performed.

Answers to these questions should provide insight into the organization's objectives, activities, work performance, systems and procedures, limits of authority and so on. The auditor uses the questionnaire as a guideline and does not rely solely on yes or no responses. This is a quick audit tool to help identify critical areas for further review where it is not feasible to implement the more desirable, but time consuming, full planning phase. However, a survey of this kind should not be used in lieu of the planning phase, as it is still the auditor's responsibility to substantiate, with adequate evidence, the identification of critical operational areas to be reviewed.

Figure 1.4 is a sample operational audit initial survey form. The purpose of the initial survey is to identify areas of major importance in the total organization or specific operations to be reviewed. Improper identification results in spending unnecessary effort on less significant activities and insufficient effort in more important areas. The survey should provide for more detailed answers, rather than simple yes or no responses. The same questions are reviewed with various personnel, such as departmental management, functional supervision, and operations and support personnel. The auditor thus isolates patterns of agreement and disagreement, as well as various interpretations and perceptions that lead to the correct conclusions. Where necessary, each question is supported by available documentation. This form could also be used as part of the more formal planning phase, but should be more specific to a departmental or functional area.

1.16 ENGAGEMENT DEVELOPMENT

An operational audit could be conducted by an external CPA firm, an internal audit group, an independent in-house unit, departmental personnel, or a combination of staff from these entities. Whichever audit organization has primary responsibility for conducting the operational audit, the major steps in its development and performance should be similar. These steps are summarized in Figure 1.5.

(a) Recognize and Define the Problem

The first step is to recognize and define the problem. Normally, it is management's prerogative to identify the major problem area or areas to be addressed in an operational audit. However, if requested by management, the auditor can assist in such problem definition as described previously—or the auditor may perform a preliminary survey to identify significant operational areas to be reviewed.

1.16 ENGAGEMENT DEVELOPMENT

FIGURE 1.4. Sample operational audit initial survey form.

Planning and Budgeting
1. How does the organization plan? Describe the system of planning.
2. Does a long-range plan exist? Attach copy.
3. Do current plans exist? Attach copy.
4. What are plans for expansion or improvement?
5. What are plans for physical plant development?
6. What are plans for future financing?
7. What are personnel plans?
8. How does the organization budget? Describe the budgeting system.
9. Does a current budget exist? Obtain or prepare copy.
10. Do budget versus actual statistics exist for the last five years? Obtain or prepare copy.

Personnel and Staffing
1. Does an organizational chart exist? Obtain or prepare copy.
2. Do functional job descriptions exist for each block on the organization chart? Obtain or prepare copy.
3. Do staffing statistics by functional area exist? Obtain or prepare copy.
4. Is there a system of employee evaluations? Obtain or prepare copy.
5. How are employees recruited, hired, evaluated, and fired? Describe procedures.
6. What are promotional policies? Describe.
7. How are new employees oriented? Describe.
8. How are raises and promotions determined? Describe.
9. Is there a grievance mechanism? Describe.
10. What type of personnel records are maintained? Obtain copies.

Management
1. Does a board of directors exist? Attach list of names and credentials.
2. Who is considered "top" management? Attach list of names and credentials.
3. Who is considered "middle" management? Attach list of names and credentials.
4. Who is considered "lower" management? Attach list of names and credentials.
5. How adequate are existing reports in furnishing information for making management decisions? Describe.
6. Are there tools for internal downward communication to the staff? Attach copies.

Policies and Procedures
1. Do written policies exist? Obtain copy.
2. Are written policies current?
3. Are systems and procedures documented? Obtain or prepare copy.

FIGURE 1.4. *(Continued)*

Accounting System
1. What is the chart of accounts used? Obtain or prepare copy.
2. Is the accounting system mechanized? Obtain documentation.
3. What financial reports are produced? Obtain documentation.
4. Is there an internal audit function? By and to whom?
5. Are internal operating reports produced? Obtain copies and determine uses.

Revenues
1. What are the sources of revenue for the last five years? Obtain or prepare statistics.
2. Have there been any substantial changes during this period? Document any that have been made.
3. Are actual versus budgeted data available? Obtain or prepare copy.

Expenses
1. What are the major expense accounts used? Obtain or prepare copy.
2. What are actual expenses for these accounts for the last five years? Obtain or prepare copy.
3. Have there been any substantial changes during this period? Document any that have been made.
4. Are actual versus budgeted data available? Obtain or prepare copy.

Electronic Data Processing (EDP)
1. Where is data processing presently located in the organization? Obtain or prepare copy of EDP organization.
2. What EDP equipment is used? Obtain or prepare copy of equipment list.
3. What is total cost of equipment rental or purchase price if owned?
4. What is physical location(s) of EDP department?
5. What are the major applications computerized? Obtain or prepare copy of list of applications, with general systems narratives.

Purchasing
1. What is purchasing authority? Obtain or prepare copy of policy relative to purchasing authority.
2. Is purchasing centralized or decentralized? Describe operations.
3. How are purchase requisitions initiated? Describe general procedure.
4. Who determines quality and quantity desired?
5. Are purchase orders used? Describe procedure.
6. Are competitive bidding procedures used? Describe procedure.

Production Control
1. Is a manufacturing control system being used? Is it computerized? Obtain or prepare copy of general procedures.
2. What types of manufacturing processes are being used? Describe.
3. What is location(s) of manufacturing facilities? Document.

1.16 ENGAGEMENT DEVELOPMENT

FIGURE 1.4. *(Continued)*

4. Are production cost centers used to control the routing of manufacturing orders? Obtain or prepare copy of cost centers.
5. Is a manufacturing cost system used? Obtain or prepare copy of cost-accounting procedures.
6. Are operational and management reports provided to control manufacturing operations? Obtain copies.

Inventory Control
1. Is an inventory control system being used? Is it computerized? Obtain or prepare copy of general procedures.
2. What types of inventory control procedures are being used? Describe.
3. Where are inventory storeroom locations? Obtain or prepare copy of locations and describe storeroom procedures.
4. How are inventory records maintained? Describe procedures.
5. Is perpetual inventory maintained? Describe procedures.
6. Are inventory statistics and data maintained? Obtain data as to items in inventory, dollar value, usage, on-hand balances, etc.
7. What is basis for reordering inventory items, and how are reorder quantities determined? Describe procedures.

(b) Gather Appropriate Data

The second step is to gather the appropriate supporting data, and is usually accomplished by the operational auditor. The purpose of this data gathering is to provide background information relative to the problem areas defined in step 1, so as to substantiate the problem situation.

(c) Evaluate the Situation

The next step is to evaluate the situation within the organization to determine such things as the organizational structure and resources available. These are the factors on which the auditor bases the proposal to management for conducting the operational audit.

(d) Proposal Letter

The auditor has gathered sufficient background data on the operational problem areas identified for review and has decided on the plan for con-

FIGURE 1.5. Operational audit engagement development.

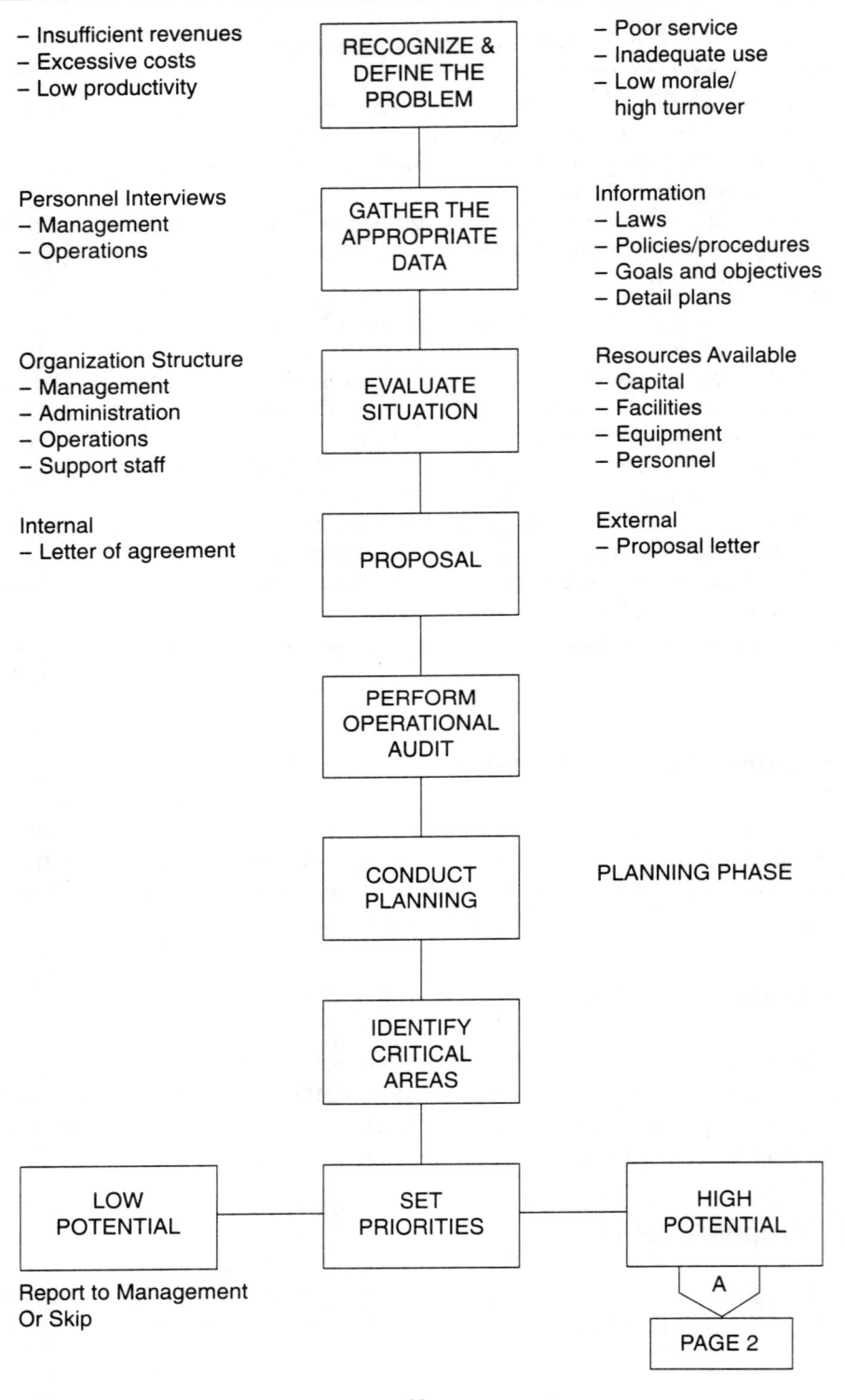

1.16 ENGAGEMENT DEVELOPMENT

FIGURE 1.5. *(Continued)*

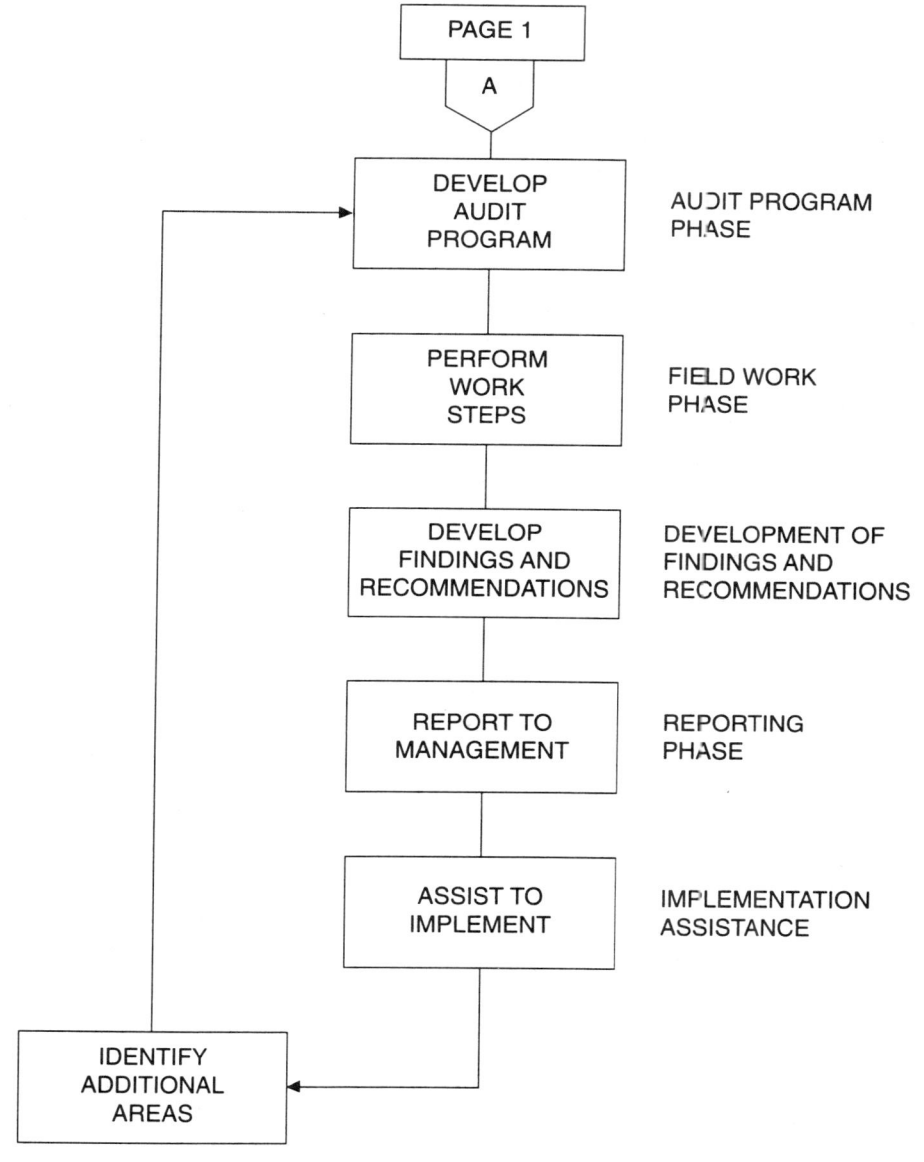

ducting the operational audit. Now the auditor needs to submit a written proposal or engagement letter to clarify for management such considerations as these:

- Background of the situation describing the need for the operational audit.
- Operational audit engagement objectives.
- Scope of the operational audit engagement or which operational areas are to be included.
- The auditor's approach to conducting the operational audit.
- Proposed general work steps to be included in the conduct of the operational audit.
- Operational audit staff and client personnel who are expected to participate in the operational audit, including each one's responsibilities and expectations as well as time commitments.
- Reporting requirements to management, such as progress meetings and final reporting, including a description of all deliverable output.
- Benefits to be provided to the organization as a result of conducting the operational audit.
- Estimates of time and cost.

Although it is usually the external CPA firm that submits the proposal letter to management, it is also good practice for the internal audit group to submit a similar proposal prior to the start of the operational audit engagement. The major purpose of such an internal proposal letter is to ensure clear communication, as to the purpose and scope of the operational audit, between the audit group and management. In this context, the internal proposal becomes a letter of understanding between the internal audit group and management. The contents of the proposal letter would differ somewhat from an external proposal, and would include only those areas necessary to the situation.

Figure 1.6 provides an example of an operational audit proposal, or engagement letter, for the Example Company, as well as sample time and cost budget estimates for the planning and field work phases. These cost estimates are for the auditor's use in determining the cost of the engagement and are not given to operations management. Note that an external CPA firm proposing to perform an operational audit for a client may have to estimate time and costs before starting the engagement. To do this requires sufficient initial survey work and adequate prior experience on similar

1.16 ENGAGEMENT DEVELOPMENT

FIGURE 1.6. Sample operational audit proposal letter: The Example Company.

Dear Mr. Worthington:

It was a pleasure meeting with you on January 23, 19XX to discuss how Reider Associates might assist the Example Company in the review and analysis of Purchasing Department operations. This proposal letter summarizes our understanding of your situation, the assistance to be provided by us, our approach to providing such assistance, and an estimate of our time and fees.

Background
You have expressed some concern relative to the quality of present systems and methods that your Purchasing Department personnel are currently using. In addition, you are concerned about implementing more sophisticated operating and data processing techniques, so that Purchasing Department personnel can better manage their operations and provide the necessary services in an economical and efficient manner.

In response to these and other situations, you have recognized the need to provide system review and analysis assistance addressing these concerns. Accordingly, you have requested that Reider Associates submit this proposal relative to how we might assist your efforts in designing and implementing such an operational improvement to meet your needs.

Objectives
The objectives of the operational review of Purchasing Department operations would be to:

1. Determine which systems and procedures would be best to improve Purchasing Department effectiveness.
2. Design operating systems and data processing procedures to enable Purchasing Department functions to operate more efficiently and economically.
3. Identify opportunities for operational improvements within the Purchasing Department.
4. Review and analyze present data processing procedures to determine their effectiveness and to recommend improvements, for greater efficiency of operations.

Scope of the Engagement
This engagement is to be confined to those Purchasing Department areas reporting to the vice-president of operations, located at your central headquarters. Therefore, the engagement will exclude all non-Purchasing Department operating areas reporting to the vice-president of operations located at central headquarters, as well as Purchasing Department functions at other sites.

FIGURE 1.6. *(Continued)*

As we discussed, we would plan to review operating systems and procedures, as well as interview selected management/supervisory and operating personnel in the following Purchasing Department work units:

- Purchasing
- Purchasing Supervisor
- Buyers I & II
- Clerk Supervisor
- Clerical Supervisor
- Clerk Typist
- Standard Specifications Unit
- Standard Specifications Unit Supervisor
- Procurement Technician
- Management Trainee
- Clerk Stenographer
- Clerk

Our Approach

We propose to assist you in the review and analysis of present Purchasing Department operating procedures and methods, which will encompass techniques and procedures needed presently, as well as provide for flexibility for growth and adaptation to changed circumstances. Accordingly, we plan to provide our assistance in the following steps:

1. General review of existing operational methods and procedures to provide us with a clear understanding of your Purchasing Department functions so that we can provide effective consulting assistance in developing and implementing improved procedures. This would include a review of management/administrative practices and procedures, as well as related operating systems and methods.

2. Interview a number of Purchasing Department management/supervisory and operating personnel so that we can assess individual needs and concerns as well as incorporate such concerns into overall considerations.
   We will, of course, discuss the findings of our general review and interviews with you so that we can jointly agree as to the major issues for change to be included in our detailed review and analysis.

3. Detailed operational review and analysis of those critical areas identified in our general review. We will perform sufficient analytical work to fully determine the present condition of each area, what it should be, the effect on operations, the cause of the condition, and recommendations for improvement.

1.16 ENGAGEMENT DEVELOPMENT

FIGURE 1.6. *(Continued)*

4. Develop detailed findings and recommendations for improvement, which will be developed in a manner that will optimize each Purchasing Department function's achievement of its individual goals and objectives, as well as deal with issues identified by us in our general operational review and participant interviews.

    These findings and recommendations will be documented for your review in both an oral and a written report.

5. Provide assistance to you and your staff in the implementation of recommendations which can be accomplished during the course of this consulting assistance. Other longer-term recommendations will be reviewed with you at the oral presentation at the conclusion of our field work and subsequently documented in the final report summarizing the results of the consulting engagement.

Our Participation
Mrs. Betty White, manager in our MAS department, will be personally responsible for the technical conduct and successful completion of this operational improvement program. She has provided similar assistance to numerous clients.

We plan to assign Mr. Bill Brown, supervisor, and Mr. Joe Super, senior, of our MAS staff to this engagement. Both of these people are uniquely qualified to perform the tasks required in this engagement. They will be responsible for the performance of the worksteps, as described in the section "Our Approach." We will assign other personnel as necessary, with your approval. We also plan to utilize the services of Mike Clark, an independent consultant, in the areas of his expertise, which are systems and procedures, flow charting, facilities layout and work flow, and data processing.

We are attaching to this proposal resumes for each of these people.

Client Participation
Based on our experience, we consider client participation to be essential for such an operational improvement program to be effective and successful. Accordingly, we recommend that a management member be assigned as part of a task force to work along with us in formulating the details of the operational improvement program. We would expect this person to participate in the engagement as necessary, to be available to attend progress meetings as scheduled, and to provide us with necessary input (particularly related to his or her functional area) as required. We would recommend Mr. Cliff Chambers, purchasing supervisor, to assume the overall client management responsibility.

In addition, we would suggest assigning an operations staff member from both the Purchasing and Standards Specifications work units to this engage-

FIGURE 1.6. *(Continued)*

ment to work along with us. We would not expect either one of them to be assigned duties that would consume more than two days per week during the course of the engagement.

Progress Meetings
Progress meetings will be held at least every three weeks, at which time we will discuss such things as (1) progress to date, (2) specific findings and recommendations, (3) decisions to be made, (4) implementation efforts, and (5) ongoing plans. We will, of course, document these progress meetings in brief written reports.

Reporting
At the conclusion of this engagement, we will submit our findings and recommendations to you at an oral presentation, which will provide you with an opportunity to review and discuss these findings and recommendations. As a follow-up to the oral presentation, we will subsequently document our findings and recommendations in a formal, written report.

Benefits to Be Provided
The benefits to be derived from the conducting of an operational audit for your Purchasing Department are many and varied. However, you should expect at least the following:

- Identification of operational problem areas, related causes, and alternatives for improvement.
- Effective reduction of unnecessary costs through the identification of opportunities for eliminating waste and inefficiency.
- Identification of undefined organizational goals, objectives, policies, and procedures.
- Assessment of the existing management information and control system.
- Identification of possible trouble spots in future operations.
- An independent, objective evaluation of operations.

We believe the assistance to be provided by us will also ensure a positive and effective method of implementing improved operating techniques, which will enable all levels of Purchasing Department personnel to:

- Understand their basic roles and functions so that all individuals can implement such operational techniques, and principles within their own areas,
- Develop meaningful operating procedures that will enable them to better control, monitor, and evaluate the results of their operations,
- Perform their current job responsibilities more effectively with a greater level of competency, a better understanding of operational procedures, and a greater ability to apply their knowledge in their particular situations, and

1.16 ENGAGEMENT DEVELOPMENT

FIGURE 1.6. *(Continued)*

- Develop a greater sense of teamwork and working together, which should make operations more effective and efficient.

Time and Cost
We recommend that the operational audit be conducted in two phases to be most effective and to optimize the benefits to be derived by your organization, as follows:

Phase I: Planning
The planning phase would consist of a general review of your purchasing operations to provide us with a working knowledge of your operations, as well as to identify those significant areas offering the greatest payout in operational improvements that we believe should be analyzed in greater depth during the Phase II field work. We would, of course, bring to your attention all operational improvements and related recommendations identified by us during Phase I so that you will be able to implement immediate or short-term positive changes.

Phase II: Field Work
As a result of the Planning Phase, we will identify those critical operational areas where we believe further review and analysis will result in substantial improvements which will far outweigh the costs of conducting the operational audit. Based on our mutual agreement, we would then develop an operational audit work program directed toward further review and analysis of each of these critical areas, resulting in the development of findings which would include the reporting of specific recommendations for improvement.

Our fees are based on the amount of time expended on the engagement, extended by our standard billing rates. Based on our experience in similar engagements, our initial survey of your operations, and discussions with you, we estimate our time participation and related costs to be as follows:

Phase I: Planning
Three weeks of elapsed time, at an estimated cost of $10,000 to $12,000

Phase II: Field Work
From 10 to 12 weeks of elapsed time, at an estimated cost of $28,000 to $32,000.

Our estimated costs for the Field Work phase are based on our present knowledge of your situation and what we believe is necessary at this time. However, should the situation change, based on what we find out in the planning phase, we will inform you immediately as to the need to change our time and cost estimates either upward or downward.

In addition, we are to be reimbursed for out-of-pocket expenses incurred for travel, lodging, subsistence, and the like. We will, of course, attempt to

OVERVIEW

FIGURE 1.6. *(Continued)*

minimize both fee and expenses and will bill you only for actual time and expenses incurred.

It is our practice to submit progress billings at two-week intervals.

We are ready to begin this engagement within one week of your acceptance of this proposal. However, to meet your desired timetable, we suggest starting no later than March 1, 19XX.

* * * * * * * * * *

We appreciate the opportunity to submit this proposal and look forward to working with you on this important and challenging project. If the arrangements described above meet with your approval, you may indicate your acceptance by signing and returning the enclosed copy.

Very truly yours,

Harry Reider
Reider Associates

Approved by_____
George Worthington, Vice-President Operations

Date _____

1.16 ENGAGEMENT DEVELOPMENT

FIGURE 1.6. *(Continued)*

Work Program and Operational Audit Engagement
Budget Estimate (in hours)

Client Name: The Example Company Date: February 2, 19XX
Phase I: Planning

Engagement Work Program

	Mgr.	Supv.	Staff	Out. Cons.	Cli. Time	Total
1. Goals & Objectives						
a. Review legislative/internal materials					6	6
b. Planning systems & procedures		26				26
2. Budgets		11				11
3. Organization Chart and Procedures Manual	14					14
4. Flowcharts				28		28
5. Reports					18	18
6. Personnel			21		12	33
7. Facilities			4	12		16
8. Review Planning Phase Results	10					10
Total Audit Time	24	37	25	40	36	162
Other:						
9. Prepare Audit Program	12				12	24
10. Audit management	24				16	40
Total Other Time	36				28	64
Grand Total Time	60	37	25	40	64	226
Standard Billing Rates	$80	$60	$30	$75	—	
Total Estimated Fees	$4,800	$2,220	$750	$3,000	—	$10,770
Contingency: 10%						1,230
Grand Total						$12,000
Proposed Fee Quoted						$10,000 to $12,000

FIGURE 1.6. *(Continued)*

Work Program and Operational Audit Engagement
Budget Estimate (in hours)

Client Name: The Example Company   Date: February 2, 19XX
Phase II: Field Work

Engagement Work Program

	Mgr.	Supv.	Staff Sr/Jr	Out. Cons.	Cli. Time	Total
1. Company Policy & Organization						
a. Organization Status of Purchasing		50				50
b. Responsibility for Purchasing		20				20
c. Authority for Purchasing			10			10
d. Decentralized Purchasing			20			20
2. Purchasing Department Operations						
a. Proceedings flowcharts				50		50
b. Department Forms					20	20
c. Physical Facilities					12	12
d. Value Analysis Prog.					8	8
e. Collateral Operation			16			16
3. Review of Purchase Transactions						
a. Selected Transactions		8	12			20
b. Examination of Purchasing Transactions		12	18			30
4. Records & Reports			34			34

1.16 ENGAGEMENT DEVELOPMENT

FIGURE 1.6. *(Continued)*

	Mgr.	Supv.	Staff Sr/Jr	Out. Cons.	Cli. Time	Total
5. Review Field Work Results	24	24			12	60
6. Development of Findings	8	18	22		32	80
7. Oral Reporting	10				10	20
8. Written Report	12	20			8	40
Total Audit Time	54	132	40	112	50	102	490
Other						
9. Prepare Audit Program	12	8	4	6	2	8	40
10. Audit management	80				20	100
Total Other	92	8	4	6	2	28	140
Grand Total	146	140	44	118	52	130	630
Standard Billing Rates	$80	$60	$40	$30	$75	—
Total Estimated Fees	$11,680	8,400	1,760	3,540	3,900		$29,280
Contingency: 10%							2,720
Grand Total							$32,000
Proposed Fee Quoted							$28,000 to $32,000

engagements to enable the auditor to estimate accurately. While it is obviously advantageous to estimate the amount of field work required after completion of the planning phase, the client normally wants to know these amounts up front. The samples provided are for a relatively sizable operational audit. In a situation where potential operational audit engagements may be smaller in scope, the two phases may be combined and the numbers scaled down.

(e) Perform the Operational Audit

The proposal letter has been submitted and accepted by management. Now what? Now begins the actual operational audit, using the proposed phase approach of planning, audit program, field work, development of findings and recommendations, and reporting. Should management request it, the auditor might also help to implement the recommended operational improvements. Or client personnel may feel confident that they can implement the agreed-upon recommendations on their own.

As part of the reporting process, it is also important to identify other significant operational areas where the operational audit approach could offer specific improvements and quantifiable benefits. This could lead to a follow-up operational audit engagement for the external CPA firm, particularly if it has proven its worth in the current operational audit. For the internal audit team, it could result in management's asking for additional operational audits. Not only is such an approach productive in selling the entire operational audit concept, but it reinforces the concept of the internal audit group existing as a "profit center" in the conducting of operational audits. The "profit center" concept is based on convincing management that the benefits to be derived from operational auditing far exceed the costs involved. This is where the quantification of findings is extremely important.

Another aspect to consider is that if the operational audit is performed properly with the help of departmental personnel, the department retains the residual ability to perform operational audit procedures in other areas. As the operational audit team cannot normally cover every operational area that could be improved within the scope of the original operational audit, the team should identify those additional areas for further review and, possibly, for audit by the department. Management then decides whether to pursue these areas on their own or with the operational auditor's help.

One of the goals in acquainting an organization with the operational audit approach is to multiply the effectiveness of operational auditors. In other words, while performing the operational audit, auditors are also training client personnel. In this way, operational audit procedures and results are quickly multiplied throughout the organization, and the auditors can then spend their time on the most significant areas and tasks.

This concludes Chapter 1, "Overview," which discussed operational auditing principles and concepts. In succeeding chapters, each of the operational audit phases are discussed, as well as how the auditor performs each phase. Before continuing on to Chapter 2, "Planning Phase," review the operational audit situation in Figure 1.7.

1.16 ENGAGEMENT DEVELOPMENT

FIGURE 1.7. Leasing insurance costs.

During the course of your operational audit procedures, you found that the auditee was paying for liability and property damage insurance as part of their lease agreement on 14 tractors and 19 trailers being leased. The cost of the insurance was hidden in the fixed weekly/mileage rates billed by the lessor.

The auditee's policy is to self-insure or assume certain risks (such as auto collision and certain other property losses, and the front end of unknown claims such as liability claims) and to purchase protection for other risks under a blanket policy.

Questions and Solutions for Consideration
1. What steps would you take to follow through on this finding?
   a. Compare annual hidden insurance costs paid to the lessor as part of fixed weekly/mileage rates, with what insurance would cost under auditee's self-insurance and blanket insurance for major losses.
   b. Request insurance charges from lessor for preceding year.
   c. Determine insurance costs under auditee's blanket policy.
   d. Based on amount of savings (if any), decide what to recommend:
      - If substantial savings, recommend insurance provided by the lessor to be dropped, and insurance to be purchased under auditee's blanket insurance policy.
      - If no savings or if savings are not substantial, recommend continuing present practice of lessor providing insurance. (May also look into lessor reducing coverage and/or insurance premiums presently being carried).
      - If practice of obtaining insurance as part of the lease agreement is more economical than the policy of self-insurance, consider changing the self-insurance policy.
      - If the policy of self-insurance is the most economical route, review operations to determine to what extent the policy is being ignored and resultant cost.

Note: In a "real life" version of this particular situation, it was found that lessor insurance costs totaled $39,000 for the year, and that the costs under the auditee's self-insurance policy would have been $6,000. Accordingly, an annual savings of $33,000 was realized by reverting back to the self-insurance policy.

FIGURE 1.7. *(Continued)*

2. What components (financial, compliance, economy and efficiency, and effectiveness) of operational auditing relate to this situation? How?
   a. Financial: Proper accounting and reporting procedures. Insurance costs show as leasing costs.
   b. Compliance: With policy of self-insurance and blanket coverage.
   c. Economy and Efficiency: Is this the most economical method for providing such insurance? In this case, no.
   d. Effectiveness: Is present practice achieving intended purpose? As the purpose of insurance is to protect the organization against unnecessary and large risks, the practice of obtaining insurance as part of the lease agreement is most likely more effective in providing ultimate protection than a self-insurance fund, which might not be sufficient to cover extremely large insurance claims.

CHAPTER TWO

The Planning Phase

2.1 INTRODUCTION

This chapter discusses the planning phase of an operational audit. The planning phase is where the auditor first learns about the organization's operations through various techniques such as interviewing, gathering and analyzing information, physical inspection of facilities and work procedures, and so forth. Through the performance of these work steps, the auditor identifies possible critical operational problem areas to be analyzed in more depth in the field work phase, through the development of an operational audit program. In addition, the proper steps to be taken in the planning phase to ensure successful results from an operational audit are fully discussed in this chapter.

This chapter will:

1. Increase understanding of the purpose of the planning phase in an operational audit.

2. Introduce information that must be obtained during the planning phase and related sources of information.

3. Increase knowledge of how to use planning phase information in the identification of critical operational areas.

4. Increase understanding of financial audit expansion into operational areas and related principles of good operational controls.

5. Introduce a sample planning phase audit program.

THE PLANNING PHASE

The starting point for the operational audit is management's decision as to which operational area or areas are to be audited or reviewed, and whether the operational audit is to be preliminary or in-depth. Based on management's decision, the operational auditor then starts the planning phase of the operational audit. The primary purposes of the planning phase are to

1. Gather information about the operational area,
2. Identify possible operational problem areas, and
3. Start to develop the basis for the operational audit program.

In the planning phase, general working information on all important aspects of the organization's operations is obtained in a relatively short time. This is usually accomplished on site at the company's facilities. However, if this is a new area of review, the auditor may need to do some additional on-site research and learning.

It is important to get this information quickly. The information gathering need not be a long, drawn-out process, involving laborious readings of manuals and other materials. Time-consuming efforts to show the existence of significant deficiencies should not be undertaken. However, if any indications of serious deficiencies are found, the auditor should document them so that they will be considered in deciding on areas for additional work. This procedure provides for an orderly approach to the planning phase and directs operational audit effort to those areas with the greatest payout in terms of significant improvement.

Remember the 80/20 rule. Its application in this case states that 20 percent of the problems cause 80 percent of the critical impact and 80 percent of the problems cause only 20 percent of the impact. So the auditor is advised to chase the elephants, the 20 percent, and not the mice, the 80 percent.

At the end of the planning phase, the auditor should have adequate working knowledge of the objectives and controls of the audited area. The auditor should be familiar with the organization: its objectives, its problems, its physical layout, and the relative significance of the various responsibilities it has been assigned or has assumed. This enables the auditor to determine at the outset how much time is required to perform the remaining phases of the audit.

2.2 INFORMATION TO BE OBTAINED

All of the documents gathered during the planning phase are used to start the permanent audit files for the operational audit. The planning phase can be performed efficiently and systematically if the auditor has a clear idea of what is needed. The records and information that could be required may include the following:

Laws and regulations that apply to the activities being reviewed

Material on the organization

Financial information

Operating methods and procedures

Management information and reports

Problem areas

(a) Laws and Regulations That Apply to the Activities Being Reviewed

An understanding of the basic legal authorities governing the area and its activities is necessary. The satisfactory performance of an operational audit requires that the auditor ascertain the purpose, scope, and objectives of the activities being reviewed, the way those objectives are to be achieved, and the extent of authority and responsibility conferred.

In addition to the basic legislation relating to the area. the auditor needs to obtain information on all important laws that specifically apply to the area or activity, including related regulations and legal decisions. As to each law, the auditor should find out:

- Its history and background,
- The objectives sought,
- The authority vested to achieve the objectives,
- The responsibilities imposed,
- The nature of any restrictions imposed, and
- Any other significant requirements.

THE PLANNING PHASE

In operational audits in which related legislation is a major consideration, the auditor should be aware of the following factors:

1. Management may justify certain activities on the basis of general authority contained in basic laws. Whenever general authority is relied on for conducting an activity, the auditor obtains complete and clear explanations as to such reliance. The auditor determines and reports on the extent to which such general authority has been used, and makes full disclosure of unused authority, if significant.

2. Legislation may impose various restrictions on an organization in carrying out an activity. Compliance with these restrictions is a basic responsibility of management. The auditor should be familiar with the nature of these restrictions and determine specifically how management provides for ensuring compliance.

(b) Material on the Organization

The second area in which the auditor needs to gather information involves the organization and its activities. Primary emphasis should be on the activities that are within the scope of the operational audit. This information should include the following:

- Division of duties and responsibilities;
- Principal delegations of authority;
- Nature, size, and location of each operational entity (that is, any field offices);
- Number of employees by organization segment and location; and
- Nature and location of physical assets and accounting records.

Among the auditor's primary concerns is to determine how the company is organized to carry out its functions and how duties and responsibilities are assigned. In addition, the auditor must determine where the area being reviewed fits into the organizational pattern of the whole company and its relationship to other areas. This knowledge is necessary for a full understanding of the organization's operations.

(c) Financial Information

The third area of interest to the auditor is all pertinent financial information, such as:

- Cost of operations by periods,
- Year-by-year record of income from revenue-producing operations,
- Budget versus actual data for the present and past periods,
- Cash-flow analysis, and
- Cost-accounting data.

(d) Operating Methods and Procedures

Normally, the auditor is more concerned with operating data than with the data typical in a financial statement. A fourth area is investigated to obtain a general description of the organization's operating methods and procedures. The auditor analyzes and documents the operating methods and procedures by which activities being reviewed are performed. In the planning phase, the auditor should obtain information as to the general methods and procedures top management prescribes for operating in the area under consideration. In this phase, the review of methods and procedures should not extend below the management level. If it is necessary to get accurate information on which to base a conclusion of how certain systems and procedures actually work, the auditor may want to talk with a limited number of operations personnel. However, the information obtained may be generalized and may require further development later in the audit to determine the precise methods and procedures at the operating level.

(e) Management Information and Reports

A fifth category of interest is management information and reports. The auditor should identify all available management information as well as the nature, content, and timing of all reporting. The auditor should also look for management information that should be present, but is not. It is extremely important to identify the key operating indicators that management has singled out for reporting purposes and those items subject to exception reporting.

(f) Problem Areas

Finally, the auditor gathers information regarding any problem areas. The auditor identifies and documents all important problem areas relative to the activities to be reviewed. Areas of major deficiency and those that lend themselves to the greatest improvements are to be emphasized. Remember, these are the items to be pursued in the audit program and field work phases. To spend audit time most efficiently, it is important to analyze those operational areas with the largest potential payout in terms of improvements. Again, the organization's "elephants" should be identified in terms of present problem areas, and the "mice" considered only for in-house correction.

2.3 SOURCES OF INFORMATION

What are the sources of the information to be gathered in the planning phase? Such information could come from various sources; however, the following are the most usual sources:

Effective interviewing

Organizational data

Financial data

Policies and procedures

Operating and management reports

Physical inspection

(a) Effective Interviewing

One of the major sources of information about an organization's activities, procedures, systems, and so on, is an effective interview. The purpose of the interview is to find out what is going on and why. Interviews in the planning phase should normally be limited to management, to obtain an overview of the operations without becoming involved in the time-consuming details of interviewing the technical personnel more directly engaged in the operation. In practive, however, limited interviews with operations personnel are usually conducted to ensure that a full and accurate picture is obtained.

(b) Organizational Data

Organizational data may include such things as copies of organization charts, functional job descriptions, and position charts. The auditor should

2.3 SOURCES OF INFORMATION

be sure to ascertain actual duties, responsibilities, and levels of authority for each individual; written job descriptions should not be automatically accepted at face value. This could entail talking to selected management and operations personnel and/or having them prepare a description of their perceived job duties and responsibilities.

(c) Financial Data

Another source of planning phase information is financial data, such as financial statements over a number of years, budget versus actual reports (present and past), cost of operations by period, revenues year-by-year by source, cash-flow analysis, cost-accounting data, and ratio, change, and trend analysis.

(d) Policies and Procedures

Existing policies and procedures, which should be documented in procedures manuals, policy pronouncements, directives, and regulations, are yet another source of information. For many small organizations such materials will probably not exist, except in the heads of management personnel. In this case, the auditor would then interview these persons to determine what they believe to be existing policies and procedures, and then test them to determine whether they are actually being followed.

(e) Operating and Management Reports

A further source of information are operations and management reports submitted either internally or externally, prior and related audit reports and workpapers, and, if available, internal audit and review reports. The auditor would also determine whether management has responded to any findings identified in these reports and whether any action has been taken.

(f) Physical Inspection

Finally, the auditor makes a physical inspection of the operation, including a tour of all pertinent operational areas and the observation of significant activities being performed. A physical review of the operations area, whenever appropriate, should be made relative to the nature of the activities to be examined. The purpose of this physical review is to improve under-

THE PLANNING PHASE

standing of the activity in physical terms, and to provide support for information about the activity obtained during interviews.

2.4 IDENTIFICATION OF CRITICAL PROBLEM AREAS

Now that needed information has been obtained, how should it be used? The planning data gathered provide the background and general working information for the operational audit staff. It should also be used to help decide which specific areas of activity to examine in the field work phase. In most operational audits, the audit staff decides which specific areas to review. The general objective is to direct attention to those matters that most urgently need it. Identifying these critical areas is an important component of each operational audit.

Techniques for preliminary identification of critical areas vary with the type of engagement. They require an auditor's ingenuity and judgment. Such techniques include the following:

Identification of key activities

Use of management reports

Examination of audit reports

Physical inspection of the activities

Discussions with responsible personnel

(a) Identification of Key Activities

The information obtained may disclose key activities or aspects of an activity which appear to be difficult to control or susceptible to abuse or laxity. For instance, in a purchasing operation, the key critical areas might well be:

- Determinations of quantities and qualities to be purchased,
- Methods used in obtaining the most advantageous price, and
- Methods of determining whether the correct quantities and qualities are actually received.

2.4 IDENTIFICATION OF CRITICAL PROBLEM AREAS

(b) Use of Management Reports

Examining the reports management uses to assure itself that work is progressing within established time and cost goals should provide valuable information in selecting areas of inquiry. Examples of such reporting are operational exception reporting and actual-versus-plan reporting, which would compare actual results with goals and objectives. The auditor should look closely at those items management has selected as critical for exception reporting, such as inventory levels, productivity measures, sales analysis, and so on. Indications of critical areas to look at will surface if major deviances are found between the plan and actual results. Keep in mind that the plan could be satisfactory and the operational results critical, or vice versa.

Where such reports are not being used effectively, the auditor should inquire as to the methods by which control is exercised. This inquiry may point up a lack of effective control with related administrative weakness. Or it may disclose other less formal control procedures, which may, in turn, disclose operational weaknesses. Similar considerations would apply if proper performance yardsticks have not been established.

(c) Examination of Audit Reports

Audit reports (internal and external) may be a valuable source of information in determining direction of effort. There should be an examination not only of reports prepared by the internal or external audit groups, but also of those of other internal review organizations, as well as supervisory groups, where applicable, such as bank examiners. The auditor should determine whether management agrees with specific audit findings, particularly if mentioned by more than one audit group, and whether any action has been taken to correct the situation.

(d) Physical Inspection of the Activities

A physical inspection of activities requires alertness for signs of ineffectiveness or inefficiency such as bottlenecks, excess accumulations of equipment or material, and idleness of personnel. Such inspections may disclose serious weaknesses warranting inquiry, or they may depict a pattern prevalent throughout the organization.

THE PLANNING PHASE

(e) Discussions with Responsible Personnel

Finally, discussions with responsible officials and personnel directly concerned with the activity may assist in the identification of critical areas. Sometimes valuable leads can be obtained through discussions with responsible officials and others directly concerned with the activities performed. These individuals can often identify troublesome areas or request that the auditor look into specific matters that they are concerned about, but for which they lack information regarding the actual conditions.

2.5 SAS 55: CONSIDERATION OF THE INTERNAL CONTROL STRUCTURE

Note that the extension of the scope of the traditional financial audit toward a review of administrative or operating controls is consistent with the AICPA's current definition of internal control. In April 1988, the AICPA issued SAS 55, "Consideration of the Internal Control Structure in a Financial Statement Audit," which refers to three elements of an entity's internal control structure: the control environment, the accounting system, and control procedures. "This statement provides guidance for the independent auditor's consideration of an entity's internal control structure in an audit of financial statements in accordance with generally accepted auditing standards. It describes the elements of an internal control structure and explains how an auditor should consider the internal control structure in planning and performing an audit."[1]

For purposes of a financial statement audit, internal control structure consists of the following three elements[2] (SAS 55, page 5):

Control environment

Accounting system

Control procedures

(a) Control Environment

The control environment represents the collective effect of various factors on establishing, enhancing, or mitigating the effectiveness of specific poli-

---

[1] AICPA, *Statement on Auditing Standards No. 55*, "Consideration of the Internal Control Structure in a Financial Statement Audit, 1988, p. 1.
[2] IBID, p. 5, 6.

cies and procedures. Such factors include:

- Management's philosophy and operating style.
- The entity's organizational structure.
- The functioning of the board of directors and its committees, particularly the audit committee.
- Methods of assigning authority and responsibility.
- Management's control methods for monitoring and following up on performance, including internal auditing.
- Personnel policies and practices.
- Various external influences that affect an entity's operations and practices, such as examinations by bank regulatory agencies.

(b) Accounting System

The accounting system consists of the methods and records established to identify, assemble, analyze, classify, record, and report an entity's transactions and to maintain accountability for the related assets and liabilities. An effective accounting system gives appropriate consideration to establishing methods and records that will:

- Identify and record all valid transactions.
- Describe on a timely basis the transactions in sufficient detail to permit proper classification of transactions for financial reporting.
- Measure the value of transactions in a manner that permits recording their proper monetary value in the financial statements.
- Determine the time period in which transactions occurred to permit recording of transactions in the proper accounting period.
- Present properly the transactions and related disclosures in the financial statements.

(c) Control Procedures

Control procedures are those policies and procedures instituted in addition to the control environment and accounting system that management has established to provide reasonable assurance that specific entity objectives will be achieved. Control procedures have various objectives and are applied at various organizational and data processing levels. They may also be integrated into specific components of the control environment and the accounting system. Generally, they may be categorized as procedures that pertain to the following:

- Proper authorization of transactions and activities,
- Segregation of duties, which reduces opportunities to allow any person to be in a position to both perpetrate and conceal errors or irregularities in the normal course of his or her duties—assigning different people the responsibilities of authorizing transactions, recording transactions, and maintaining custody of assets,
- Design and use of adequate documents and records to help ensure the proper recording of transactions and events, such as monitoring the use of prenumbered shipping documents,
- Adequate safeguards regarding access to and use of assets and records, such as secured facilities and authorization for access to computer programs and data files, and
- Independent checks on performance and proper valuation of recorded amounts, such as clerical checks, reconciliations, comparison of assets with recorded accountability, computer-programmed controls, management review of reports that summarize the detail of account balances (for example, an aged trial balance of accounts receivable), and user review of computer-generated reports.

2.6 REVIEW OF ADMINISTRATIVE AND OPERATIONAL CONTROLS

Certain key areas are part of the operational auditor's review of internal administrative and operational controls in the planning phase:

Organization

Policies and procedures

Accounting and other records

Performance standards

Information systems and internal reports

2.6 ADMINISTRATIVE AND OPERATIONAL CONTROLS

(a) Organization

Adequate organizational control requires that each employee know clearly what his or her role and function is in the organization, and exactly what authority and responsibility have been assigned. It also requires proper separation of duties so that the same individual is not charged with the responsibility for recording and reporting on how a particular task has been accomplished.

(b) Policies and Procedures

Policy sets forth the organization's operating guidelines and specifies what is required, and procedures outline how the policies will be carried out.

(c) Accounting and Other Records

The results of business operations must be recorded promptly, accurately, completely, and in conformity with both operating responsibilities and generally accepted accounting principles. Accounting and other records must accurately reflect the financial condition of the organization and provide the means for making future business decisions, based on past results.

(d) Performance Standards

Performance standards are used to measure results and highlight conditions or trends for management's actions. The auditor will determine the existence and appropriateness of any performance standards established and what actions have been taken.

(e) Information Systems and Internal Reports

Major tools in the management control process are information systems and internal reports. They must be economically viable, timely, accurate, concise, and complete and must provide adequate control over the organization's resources, revenues, and expenditures. That is why the appraisal of the effectiveness of internal reports and communications is so important. The task of appraising the effectiveness of such reports involves the determination of three factors:

1. The purpose of the report or the primary communication function management intends the report to perform (the intended function),

2. The way in which the report affects supervisees (the actual function); and

3. The correlation or degree of correspondence between the report's intended effect and the actual effect on the function.

The auditor's task is to determine that the intended function and the actual function (how the report's recipient perceives his or her function) are the same. If they are not the same, there is a lack of effective communication. If, on the other hand, such reports are not used, inquiry can be made as to the methods by which control is exercised—which may point to a lack of effective control, with related laxity and administrative weakness.

A form for recording violations of good principles of administrative control is shown in Figure 2.1. This form can be used by the auditor as a checklist, or by management and staff as a feedback mechanism in identifying agreed-upon critical areas or patterns of perceived problem areas.

2.7 PLANNING PHASE AUDIT PROGRAM

After the gathering of operational data and information and the preliminary identification of critical operational problem areas, a planning phase audit program can now be constructed. This audit program provides guidance and direction as to which additional audit steps must be performed to finalize the areas to be included in the in-depth operational audit. A sample of such an audit program is shown in Figure 2.2. Note that the items included in this audit program are based on the initial review previously described.

2.8 FINANCIAL STATEMENT ANALYSIS

The planning phase principles will be illustrated with a case study of the fictional Example Company, also used to illustrate various concepts throughout this book. The Example Company materials may apply to a relatively large organization but the same principles apply, regardless of the organization's size.

Because an operational auditor may also be a financial auditor, a good place to start in determining critical operational areas is to analyze the organization's financial statements. Keep in mind that financial statements, produced from a financial accounting standpoint, are essentially historical

2.8 FINANCIAL STATEMENT ANALYSIS

FIGURE 2.1. Violations of good principles of administrative control.

A. *Planning*

1. Not setting or updating standards or goals.
2. Not training or instructing subordinates.
3. Not prescribing a system of review and approval.
4. Not establishing a central control (charts, logs, registers, work orders).
5. Not providing for the receipt or submission of new and relevant information.

B. *Organizing*

1. Not assigning sufficient personnel.
2. Not providing adequate resources, facilities, or equipment.

C. *Scheduling*

1. Not providing schedules and budgets for each job.
2. Not highlighting oldest, off-schedule, or overbudget jobs.
3. Not setting priorities for incoming work.
4. Not requiring special approval for nonscheduled or nonbudgeted work.

D. *Coordinating*

1. Not providing for coordination of plans, objectives, policies, and procedures of the unit with those of the company and interfacing units.
2. Not periodically reviewing the needs of services units.
3. Not informing subordinates about policies and procedures of interfacing organizations.
4. Not providing information on breakdowns in cooperation.
5. Not coordinating or interchanging reports on activities of interfacing organizations.

(continued)

THE PLANNING PHASE

FIGURE 2.1. *(Continued)*

E. Directing

1. Not making sure that employees read and understand instructions.
2. Not providing for review of work and evidence of that review.
3. Not fixing responsibility for deviations from instructions.
4. Not providing for approvals commensurate with the importance of the work.
5. Not periodically reviewing work load and priorities.
6. Not providing for documenting completed work and for having it checked, initialled, and referenced.
7. Not providing for a system of follow-up work in process.
8. Not maintaining current information on the work of all employees.

F. Obtaining Feedback

1. Not providing feedback on the quality and acceptability of the work produced.
2. Not comparing results with expectations and investigating variances.
3. Not returning to the originator work that does not meet standards.
4. Not spot-checking ongoing processes and obtaining reports of status at strategic points in the system.
5. Not acting on complaints or reporting to management on customer contacts.

G. Achieving Improvement

1. Not replacing ineffective standards, procedures, or systems.
2. Not establishing a program of improvement.
3. Not reviewing operations so as to keep costs consistent with results.
4. Not reinstating personnel when existing practices do not work.
5. Not encouraging employees to upgrade capabilities.
6. Not correcting reported deviations promptly.
7. Not reporting variances to those responsible for correcting them.

2.8 FINANCIAL STATEMENT ANALYSIS

FIGURE 2.2. Planning phase audit program.

1. *Goals and Objectives*
    a. Review legislative and internal materials that define the general goals and objectives of the area.
    Find out if auditee has elaborated on legislative goals and objectives. Does the area have a formal procedure for doing this?
    b. Planning Systems and Procedures
        - Document the planning procedure either with a narrative or with a flowchart plus narrative.
            Relate to copies of forms and reports.
            Note: Planning must be a coordinated effort between upper- and lower-level management—lower management levels incorporating broader objectives of upper management, as well as defining their own specific objectives.
        - Determine the extent of planning: use of short-term (current year) and long-term planning (five years forward).
            Do objectives and goals coordinate with those of other related and unrelated functions?
            Is there a formal procedure for identifying needs for operating improvements?
            Do planning procedures include a formal statement of justification and a statement of impact?
        - Review present plans and related goals and objectives.
            Substantiate definition of needs incorporated in the planning process through a review of documentation, such as minutes of meetings and correspondence files.
            Describe how priorities of needs are established.
            Review statement of goals and objectives and evaluate relationship to the needs.
            Note: Goals and objectives should be:
                clearly stated.
                communicated to various management levels.
        - Review detail plans of action and procedures involved in administering the plan.
            Are the steps clearly outlined?
            Are the program responsibilities assigned?
            Are progress review dates established and slippages in schedules promptly reported and corrected?
            Are budget (plan) versus actual dollars controlled?
            Sometimes there are alternate courses to achieve program objectives. Have alternatives been analyzed in terms of effectiveness and cost?

THE PLANNING PHASE

FIGURE 2.2. *(Continued)*

2. *Budgets*
   a. Review budget process as related to planning procedures.
      - Are budget procedures integrated with the planning process?
      - Are budgets justified in terms of plan?
   b. Budget Justification Procedures
      - Review justification for all budget levels and measure these against actual conditions. Evaluate soundness of budget allocations.
      - Review justification and evaluate soundness for new and increased funding, and measure against actual conditions.
      - Relate one aspect of budget to another aspect. Some may be realized, others may not.
         Example: An expanded program requires:
            additional personnel.
            more equipment.
            more furniture.
            more supplies.
      The employees are not hired, but the department, meanwhile, has gone ahead and purchased the equipment, the furniture, and the supplies.
         Examples of other areas where correlation is helpful:
            higher postage expenses with increased correspondence (e.g., billings).
            more equipment with increased supplies or paper.
            increased activities in one department matched by an increase in another department.
            request for fixed assets, if not for an expanded area, should alert the auditor to ask about asset retirement, scrap or surplus sales.
   c. Analyze budget reporting procedures and their effectiveness:
      - Budget versus actual reporting.
      - Use of flexible budgeting (relating budget to actual conditions).
      - Effective monitoring and control.
3. *Organization Chart and Procedures Manuals*
   a. Obtain copy or prepare organization chart, and analyze as to possible inefficiencies, such as:
      - One-on-one administration or supervision.
      - Span of administration much too wide for one person. This should be evaluated by competence of the administrator, capability of supervisees, complexity of functions performed.
      - Overlapping, so that personnel report to more than one person.
      - Apparent illogical placement of units within the organization.
      - Administrative positions that do not appear to be commensurate either with extent of responsibilities or with numbers supervised.

2.8 FINANCIAL STATEMENT ANALYSIS

FIGURE 2.2. *(Continued)*

   b. Obtain copies of procedures manuals and review for:
- Absence of definitions of jobs and responsibilities.
- Existing but outdated or inadequate procedures.

4. *Flow Charts*
   a. Prepare for flowcharting by becoming familiar with the department and its operations.
   - Review the budget detail.
   - Review the procedures manual.
   - Review the organizational charts.
   - Review all reports.
   - Review analysis of expenditures and revenues.
   - Obtain copies of all forms used.
   - Discuss operations in a general way with auditee personnel.

   b. Prepare general systems flowcharts of major systems and procedures.
   c. Analyze flowcharts to identify such things as:
   - Weaknesses in internal control.
   - Work-flow bottlenecks or uneven distribution of work.
   - Unnecessary handling of documents.
   - Inefficient routing of documents.
   - Unnecessary document copies or records or unused information.
   - Duplication of efforts.
   - Insufficient use of equipment.

5. *Reports*
   a. Obtain copies of management and operating reports.
   b. Discuss reports with appropriate personnel and prepare written description of contents and purpose of each report.
   - Do reports provide usable information based on the auditor's understanding of the operation?
   - Are users really using the reports? If not, discuss and document reasons.
   - Prepare list of distribution of reports and frequency of their issuance.

   c. Review and analyze reports and related discussions with users to determine whether:
   - There is adequate existing decision-making and performance information.
   - There is adequate operating information to enable the department's activities and responsibilities to be performed efficiently.
   - The information is timely. Are reports issued or prepared within acceptable schedules?
   - Exception reporting is used. Has management defined levels of acceptance, with exceptions automatically brought to their attention?
   - The information increases in detail as it is disseminated to each lower level of management and operations.

FIGURE 2.2. *(Continued)*

- The information build-up at each level of management and operation is well integrated horizontally as well as vertically, or whether the various subunits function independently.
- The reports are accurate and reliable.

6. *Personnel*
   a. Obtain and review current job descriptions for the various positions within the department. Compare these with the current procedures manual.
   b. Review personnel folders and compare backgrounds with job descriptions.
   c. Analyze personnel functions within the department as to:
      - Determination of the experience and training requirements for each personnel position.
      - Subsequent review to determine that personnel levels are adequate.
      - Determination as to the number of personnel requested in its budget.
      - Existence of formal or informal staff training and how successful it is.
      - Employee evaluation procedures and their effectiveness.
   d. Prepare a summary of positions, the number of employees in those positions, and the salary range for each position.
      Compare this with:
      - Organization charts.
      - Budget requests.
      - Job descriptions.
   e. Observe employees at work; apply simple work-sampling techniques:
      - Start late?
      - Quit early?
      - Long lunches?
      - Long time away from desk?
      - Lengthy conversations?

      Minimum—one week's observations, daily for about one hour per day. Time all observations in order to arrive eventually at a cumulative time.
   f. Review employee statistics such as:
      - Employee turnover rates.
      - Use and patterns of sick leave.
      - Lateness: beginning of day, breaks, and lunchtime.
      - Employee overtime rates.

7. *Facilities*
   a. Observe and analyze work layout and working conditions. Do they provide for:
      - Easy work flow?
      - Unencumbered access ways?

2.8 FINANCIAL STATEMENT ANALYSIS

FIGURE 2.2. *(Continued)*

- Sufficient space without extravagance?
- Sufficient light?
  b. Prepare and analyze preliminary layout flow diagram.
    - A good technique is to obtain or prepare a sketch of various work areas in the department. Identify functions in each area and the number of personnel. Integrate this information with the general systems flowcharts and identify bottlenecks, uneven work distribution, etc.
    - Observe working conditions in each area. They reveal information about work attitudes, work loads, employee performance, work layout, and work space. Look for such things as:
      - Papers stored on tops of desks.
      - Computer reports stacked on tops of tables.
      - Lack of filing space.
  c. Review use of equipment. Look for equipment:
    - Not being used.
    - Not being used effectively.
    - Too sophisticated for needs.
    - Too costly for purposes.
    - Too primitive for purposes.

    Quantify exceptions on the basis of the amount of time used, and the salary levels of personnel using them.
  d. Analyze the department's general operating procedures. Are they:
    - Manual when automated would be better?
    - Automated when manual would be better?
    - Automated, but not fully utilized?
  e. Review fixed assets used in operations and related records. Some idea of the care the department lavishes or does not lavish on its fixed assets can be gleaned from these results.

---

documents which present the organization's assets, liabilities, and equity in a balance sheet, and its revenues and expenses in an income statement. These financial statements tell what has happened within the organization during a particular period or series of periods.

The same financial statements can be used from an operational audit standpoint to help identify present and future critical areas for audit. The use of certain analytical tools (see Figure 2.3) can effectively help to analyze the financial statements, determine how the organization is doing, and zero in on critical areas that need attention and improvement. These tools are summarized as:

THE PLANNING PHASE

Comparisons

Trend percentages

Common-size statements

Financial ratios

(a) Comparisons

Financial statements are primarily static historical documents showing data related only to a specific period of time. Operational auditors are concerned with the period being reported, and what the trend of events has been and will be over longer periods of time. Accordingly, comparing financial statement data with the results of other periods, or of other organizations, provides a better understanding of trends and helps in making proper decisions as to their relative significance. Comparisons can be made with the historical performance of the company, a competitor's performance, performance of other organizations within the same general industry, and organizational goals, objectives, and detail plans.

In making such comparisons, it is important to be reasonably sure that the data are comparable; that is, that they are calculated on a consistent basis between or among years, companies, and so on. If not, incorrect or misleading conclusions may be drawn, resulting in the expenditure of a substantial amount of operational audit time on the wrong functional area.

An initial analytical procedure in financial statement analysis is to format the company's statements comparatively. This may entail comparing this year with last year or comparing a number of years' data, arriving at numerical and/or percentage differences. Preparing statements in such comparative form can disclose valuable information as to present conditions and what to expect about future financial and operating performance.

Comparison of two or more years' data is known as "horizontal analysis," which identifies changes over time by displaying data changes from year to year in both dollars and percentages. Dollar changes help to identify key factors having an impact on future operations, financial position, or profitability. The Example Company's comparative financial statements for the last three years are shown in Figures 2.4 through 2.6. These statements should be reviewed and then the possible critical areas of the Example Company's operations to be considered for operational audit should be listed. A list of such critical areas is shown in Figure 2.7.

2.8 FINANCIAL STATEMENT ANALYSIS

FIGURE 2.3. Financial statement analysis: Summary of analytical tools.

1. *Comparisons*
   a. Historical performance of the company itself.
   b. Competitors' performance.
   c. General industry performance, or performance of other organizations within the same industry.
   d. Organizational goals, objectives, and detail plans.
2. *Trend Percentages*
   a. Used to state a number of years' financial data in terms of a base year.
   b. Three data points need to be examined before a trend can be identified.
   c. Use percentages as well as differences in real numbers to show proper perspective.
   d. Example:

	19X9		19X8		19X7	
	$	%	$	%	$	%
Sales	$12,500	119%	$11,000	105%	$10,500	100%
Net Income	$ 1,200	133%	$ 900	100%	$ 900	100%

3. *Common-size Statistics*
   a. Show financial statement line items as percentages in addition to absolute dollars.
   b. Each line item on financial statement shown as a percentage of a total—such as assets or sales.
   c. Preparation and presentation of common-size statements is known as "vertical analysis."
4. *Financial Ratios*
   a. Provide for the measurement and evaluation of the organization's progress toward accomplishment of its goals and objectives.
   b. Organization's financial position usually involves two considerations:
      - Its chances for survival, measured by its short-term liquidity or its ability to meet short-term financial obligations, and
      - Its performance toward meeting financial and operational goals, as measured by its asset management and profitability results.

Ratios, which represent a mathematical relationship between two conditions, are the primary method used for such financial analysis. Ratios, when measured over a period of time, can also be used to depict changes or trends in the organization's operations.

FIGURE 2.4. Comparative balance sheets as of December 31, 19XX: The Example Company.

	19x9	19x8	19x7	19x6
	($$ in 000s)			
	$	$	$	$
Assets				
Cash	100	450	400	400
Marketable securities	-0-	500	300	200
Accounts receivable	1,900	1,600	1,700	1,500
Inventory	2,000	1,500	1,500	1,300
Prepaid expenses	200	150	100	100
Current Assets	4,200	4,200	4,000	3,500
Property, plant, & equipment	7,700	3,500	3,000	2,800
Less accumulated depreciation	(1,800)	(1,000)	(800)	(700)
Net Property, Plant, & Equipment	5,900	2,500	2,200	2,100
Intangibles & miscellaneous	600	600	600	500
Total Assets	10,700	7,300	6,800	6,100
Liabilities & Stockholders' Equity				
Notes payable	100	100	100	100
Accounts payable	700	300	250	350
Accrued expenses	550	500	400	350
Income taxes payable	400	350	500	200
Current maturity, long-term debt	250	150	150	150
Current Liabilities	2,000	1,400	1,400	1,150
Long-term debt	3,000	950	1,100	1,250
Total Liabilities	5,000	2,350	2,500	2,400
Preferred stock	100	100	100	100
Common stock (1 million shares)	1,000	1,000	1,000	1,000
Additional paid-in capital	1,100	1,100	1,100	1,100
Retained earnings	3,500	2,750	2,100	1,500
Total Stockholders' Equity	5,700	4,950	4,300	3,700
Total Liability & Stockholders' Equity	10,700	7,300	6,800	6,100

2.8 FINANCIAL STATEMENT ANALYSIS

FIGURE 2.5. Comparative income statements for years ended December 31, 19XX: The Example Company.

	19x9	19x8	19x7
	($$ in 000s)		
	$	$	$
Net Sales	12,500	11,000	10,500
Cost of Goods Sold			
Material	3,500	2,400	1,600
Labor	2,200	2,700	3,200
Manufacturing expenses	2,400	2,200	2,000
Total Cost of Goods Sold	8,100	7,300	6,800
Manufacturing Profit	4,400	3,700	3,700
Selling expenses	1,100	900	900
General & administration expenses	1,200	1,300	1,200
Total Operating Expenses	2,300	2,200	2,100
Operating Profit	2,100	1,500	1,600
Other (income) expenses			
Interest, net	150	140	160
Other	(50)	10	40
Total Other	100	150	200
Profit Before Income Taxes	2,000	1,350	1,400
Provision for income taxes	800	450	500
Net Income	1,200	900	900

FIGURE 2.6. Statement of cash flow for years ended December 31, 19XX: The Example Company.

	19x9	19x8	19x7
	($$ in 000s)		
	$	$	$
Operating Activities			
Net income	1,200	900	900
Depreciation	800	200	100
Changes in assets and liabilities			
Accounts receivable	(300)	100	(200)
Inventory	(500)	0	(200)
Prepaid expenses	(50)	(50)	0
Other assets	0	0	(100)
Accounts payable	400	50	(100)
Accrued expenses	50	100	50
Income taxes payable	50	(150)	300
Total Cash Provided by Operating Activities	1,650	1,150	750
Investing Activities			
Plant and equipment	(4,200)	(500)	(200)
Financing Activities			
New borrowing	2,200	0	0
Repayment of debt	(150)	(150)	(150)
Increase in short-term debt	100	0	0
Preferred stock dividends	(10)	(10)	(10)
Common stock dividends	(440)	(240)	(290)
Total Cash Provided (Used) by Financing Activities	1,700	(400)	(450)
Increase (decrease) in cash	(850)	250	100
Beginning Cash Balance	950	700	600
Ending Cash and Marketable Securities Balance	100	950	700

FIGURE 2.7. Financial statement analysis, comparative statements: Suggested list of critical areas.

BALANCE SHEET

Assets

Cash Management: Decrease in cash (from $400 to $450 to $100) with corresponding sell-off of marketable securities.

Accounts receivable: Increase of 18% from $1,600 to $1,900. Also, could be large in relation to sales ($12,500/$1,900 = 6.58%). Could also indicate ineffective billing and collection procedures.

Inventory: Increase of 33% from $1,500 to $2,000. Could indicate weaknesses in inventory control and related purchasing procedures.

Property, plant, and equipment: Large increase of 120% from $3,500 to $7,700 indicates large recent expansion which may have been unnecessary, controlled ineffectively, or used improperly.

Liabilities

Accounts payable: Increase of 133% from $300 to $700, which could indicate unnecessary purchasing, overextension or expenditures, and weakened ability to pay.

Long-term debt: Large increase of 226% from $950 to $3,000, which indicates substantial changes in the organization resulting in increased property, plant, and equipment with corresponding decrease in the company's cash position.

Stockholder's Equity

Retained earnings: Increase of $650 and $750 for the two years, which indicates that the company has increased its net income as the result of changes noted above. However, is this significant expected change and should the company have been able to do even better?

INCOME STATEMENT

Sales: Sales have increased from $10,500 to $11,000 to $12,500 over the past few years. Analysis by product line should be made to determine the causes for such an increase in sales.

Cost of goods sold: Cost has increased in total from $6,800 to $7,300 to $8,100. However, material costs are the major contributor to this increase—indicating a possible major critical operational area. In addition, labor costs have greatly decreased over the last three years (from $3,200 to $2,200). This indicates a possible shift in manufacturing and products produced, which could also be a major area for consideration. It appears that the company is becoming less labor intensive.

Looking at changes in percentage between years also assists in providing proper perspective as to changes. For example, a different conclusion is reached when sales increase by $2 million over a previous year's sales of $4 million (a significant increase of 50 percent), than when the previous year's sales were $100 million (an increase of only 2 percent). In the Example Company's Comparative Balance Sheets there are other examples where the combination of dollar and percentage changes provide a more complete analysis and help to determine a future trouble spot. For instance, an Accounts Receivable increase from $1,600 in 19X8 to $1,900 in 19X9 does not appear too critical; however, expressed as an 18 percent increase (and as 7 percent of sales of $12,500), it takes on greater significance. As seen in the Example Company's Comparative Income Statements, sales increased by $500,000 from 19X7 to 19X8; however cost of goods sold also increased by $500,000—exactly offsetting the change in sales and adding nothing to profitability.

(b) Trend Percentages

Financial statement analysis can also be accomplished through the use of trend percentages, which are used to state a number of years' financial data in terms of a base year. The rule in using trend percentages is that at least three data points need to be examined before a trend can be identified.

Consider the Example Company:

	19X9	19X8	19X7
Sales	$12,500	$11,000	$10,500
Net Income	$ 1,200	$ 900	$ 900

Analyzing the dollar data alone, it could be concluded that both sales and net income have increased over the three-year period. However, it cannot readily be concluded how fast sales have increased and whether the increases in net income have kept pace with sales increases. Using dollar data alone may make it difficult to conclude adequately. Now assume that the base year 19X7 is equal to 100 percent; the other years can be stated as a percentage of the base year:

	19X9		19X8		19X7	
	Dollars	*%*	*Dollars*	*%*	*Dollars*	*%*
Sales	$12,500	119%	$11,000	105%	$10,500	100%
Net Income	$ 1,200	133%	$ 900	100%	$ 900	100%

By using these trend percentages as well as the differences in real dollars (or numbers), the increase in sales and net income can be put into proper

2.8 FINANCIAL STATEMENT ANALYSIS

perspective. It can now be clearly seen that the relative growth in sales has been surpassed by the growth in net income; sales in 19X9 are 19 percent greater than the base year, but net income is 33 percent greater. Note also that sales growth was better than net income growth in 19X8, and that the growth in sales in 19X9 over 19X8 was considerably below the growth in net income for the same year. Such an analysis could indicate major operational areas for review, such as sales analysis, cost of goods sold analysis, selling price procedures, and cost analysis.

(c) Common-Size Statements

A common-size financial statement shows the line items as percentages in addition to absolute dollars. Each line item on the financial statement is shown as a percentage of some total, such as assets or sales. The preparation and presentation of common-size statements is known as "vertical analysis"—revealing changes in the relative significance of each line item. Common-size balance sheets and income statements for the Example Company for the past three years are shown in Figures 2.8 and 2.9. An analysis of these statements could disclose such areas as shown in the following:

	% of Total Assets		
BALANCE SHEET	19x7	19x9	Change
Current assets	58.8%	39.3%	−19.5%
Property, plant, & equipment	32.4	55.1	+22.7
Intangibles	8.8	5.6	−3.2
Current liabilities	20.6	18.7	−1.9
Long-term debt	16.2	28.0	+11.8
Stockholders' equity	63.2	53.3	−9.9

Comments: There has been a major shift into property, plant, and equipment, financed by reduction of current assets and additional long-term debt. The reason for this major investment needs to be investigated.

INCOME STATEMENT	19x7	19X9	Change
Material	15.2%	28.0%	+12.8%
Labor	30.5	17.6	−12.9
Manufacturing expenses	19.1	19.2	+0.1
Cost of Goods Sold	64.8	64.8	-0-
Selling expenses	8.6	8.8	+0.2
G & A expenses	11.4	9.6	−1.8
Operating Expenses	20.0	18.4	−1.6
OPERATING PROFIT	15.2	16.8	+1.6

FIGURE 2.8. Common-size balance sheets as of December 31, 19XX: The Example Company.

	19x9		19x8		19x7		19x6	
	($$ in 000s)							
Assets	$	%	$	%	$	%	$	%
Cash	100	0.9	450	6.2	400	5.9	400	6.6
Marketable securities	-0-	0.0	500	6.9	300	4.4	200	3.3
Accounts receivable	1,900	17.8	1,600	21.9	1,700	25.0	1,500	24.6
Inventory	2,000	18.7	1,500	20.5	1,500	22.0	1,300	21.3
Prepaid expenses	200	1.9	150	2.0	100	1.5	100	1.6
Current Assets	4,200	39.3	4,200	57.5	4,000	58.8	3,500	57.4
Property, plant & equipment	7,700	71.9	3,500	48.0	3,000	44.1	2,800	45.9
Less accumulated depreciation	(1,800)	(16.8)	(1,000)	(13.7)	(800)	(11.7)	(700)	(11.5)
Net Property, Plant, Equity	5,900	55.1	2,500	34.3	2,200	32.4	2,100	34.4
Intangibles & miscellaneous	600	5.6	600	8.2	600	8.8	500	8.2
TOTAL ASSETS	10,700	100.0	7,300	100.0	6,800	100.0	6,100	100.0
Liabilities & Stockholders' Equity								
Notes payable	100	0.9	100	1.4	100	1.5	100	1.6
Accounts payable	700	6.6	300	4.1	250	3.7	350	5.7
Accrued expenses	550	5.2	500	6.9	400	5.9	350	5.7
Income taxes payable	400	3.7	350	4.8	500	7.3	200	3.3
Current maturity long-term	250	2.3	150	2.0	150	2.2	150	2.5
Current Liabilities	2,000	18.7	1,400	19.2	1,400	20.6	1,150	18.8
Long-term debt	3,000	28.0	950	13.0	1,100	16.2	1,250	20.5
Total Liabilities	5,000	46.7	2,350	32.2	2,500	36.8	2,400	39.3
Preferred stock	100	0.9	100	1.4	100	1.5	100	1.6
Common stock (1 million shares)	1,000	9.4	1,000	13.7	1,000	14.7	1,000	16.4
Additional paid-in capital	1,100	10.3	1,100	15.0	1,100	16.2	1,100	18.1
Retained earnings	3,500	32.7	2,750	37.7	2,100	30.8	1,500	24.6
Total Stockholders' Equity	5,700	53.3	4,950	67.8	4,300	63.2	3,700	60.7
TOTAL LIABILITY & STOCKHOLDERS' EQUITY	10,700	100.0	7,300	100.0	6,800	100.0	6,100	100.0

2.8 FINANCIAL STATEMENT ANALYSIS

FIGURE 2.9. Common-size income statements for years ended December 31, 19XX: The Example Company.

	19x9		19x8		19x7	
	($$ in 000s)					
	$	%	$	%	$	%
Net Sales	12,500	100.0	11,000	100.0	10,500	100.0
Cost of Goods Sold						
Material	3,500	28.0	2,400	21.8	1,600	15.2
Labor	2,200	17.6	2,700	24.6	3,200	30.5
Manufacturing expenses	2,400	19.2	2,200	20.0	2,000	19.1
Total Cost of Goods Sold	8,100	64.8	7,300	66.4	6,800	64.8
MANUFACTURING PROFIT	4,400	35.2	3,700	33.6	3,700	35.2
Selling expenses	1,100	8.8	900	8.2	900	8.6
General & administrative expenses	1,200	9.6	1,300	11.8	1,200	11.4
Total Operating Expenses	2,300	18.4	2,200	20.0	2,100	20.0
OPERATING PROFIT	2,100	16.8	1,500	13.6	1,600	15.2
Other (income) expenses						
Interest, net	150	1.2	140	1.2	160	1.5
Other	(50)	(0.4)	10	0.1	40	0.4
Total Other	100	0.8	150	1.3	200	1.9
PROFIT BEFORE INCOME TAXES	2,000	16.0	1,350	12.3	1,400	13.3
Provision for income taxes	800	6.4	450	4.1	500	4.7
NET INCOME	1,200	9.6	900	8.2	900	8.6

Comments: The switch between labor and material indicates a major change from in-house manufacturing to outside sourcing of parts, or some other significant change in product. The drop in G&A expenses is also significant, but may be the result of increasing volume. Other changes are not material. The change away from in-house manufacturing when related to the investment in property, plant, and equipment raises a disturbing conflict which needs to be explained.

(d) Financial Ratios

Proper financial analysis of an organization's results provides for the measurement and evaluation of its progress toward accomplishment of financial goals and objectives, for example, earning an adequate return on investment or maintenance of a satisfactory financial position. The organization's financial position usually involves two fundamental considerations:

- Potential for Survival: measured by short-term liquidity (ability to meet short-term financial obligations) and long-term solvency (ability to meet long-term financial obligations).
- Performance: (toward meeting financial and operational goals) measured by asset management and profitability results.

Financial ratios, which represent a mathematical relationship between two quantitative conditions, are the primary means used for such financial analysis. Measured over a period of time, these ratios can be used to identify changes or trends in operations. They can also be used to provide information for identifying operational trouble spots. By analyzing changes and trends using ratios, and comparisons between time periods of various accounts (such as inventory, sales, expenses, and so on), they can also provide advice and insight into the client's operations as well as indicate where the most critical problems might lie. Presented on the following pages are some specific financial ratios derived from the data on the Example Company financial statements. Specific examples are provided which indicate the possible risks and conditions to the Example Company. These ratios should be analyzed in combination, as well as related to specific operations.

(i) SURVIVAL RATIOS These address the prospective ability of the company to continue as an economically viable entity.

2.8 FINANCIAL STATEMENT ANALYSIS

Liquidity Ratios Liquidity measures the organization's ability to meet current obligations in the short term (one year or less), or the ability to convert noncash assets into cash or otherwise to obtain cash to meet current liabilities. These ratios are of particular interest to short-term creditors of the company—banks, vendors, and other suppliers of goods and services.

Working Capital is determined by subtracting current liabilities from current assets. It provides a safety cushion for the company and creditors. Relatively higher levels of working capital may be desirable if the firm has difficulty obtaining short-term borrowed funds. In the following illustration from the Example Company, the decrease in working capital is a negative sign, as the organization has reduced its capacity for meeting its short-term obligations by more than 20 percent.

	Current Assets −	Current Liabilities =	Working Capital
19X9	$4,200	$2,000	$2,200
19X8	4,200	1,400	2,800
	Decrease in Working Capital		$ 600

Current Ratio is calculated by dividing current assets by current liabilities. It measures the organization's ability to pay off current liabilities by use of its current assets. Within reason, the higher the current ratio, the more safety and security the company's balance sheet demonstrates for short-term purposes. However, the ratio may be misleading if, for example, an organization has merely improved its cash position by selling off fixed assets, resulting in an improved current ratio but possibly adverse long-range effects. Moreover, a too high current ratio indicates that the company may not be employing its resources to maximum advantage. The Example Company's current ratios follow:

	19X9	19X8	19X7
Current Assets	4,200	4,200	4,000
Current Liabilities	2,000	1,400	1,400
= Current Ratio	2.10:1	3.00:1	2.86:1

Quick (Acid-Test) Ratio is calculated by dividing cash plus marketable securities plus accounts receivable by current liabilities. This is a more rigorous test of liquidity in that it eliminates inventory and prepaid expenses from the analysis. This ratio represents a comparison of the most liquid assets (cash, marketable securities, and receivables) to current liabilities. The quick ratios for the Example Company are as follows:

	19X9	19X8	19X7
Quick Assets	2,000	2,550	2,400
Current Liabilities	2,000	1,400	1,400
= Quick Ratio	1.00:1	1.82:1	1.71:1

An analysis of the Example Company liquidity ratios shows that the organization appears to be in a deteriorating liquidity position. Possible areas for improvement could be cash management, better collection procedures, or tighter control over expenditures. A current ratio of at least 2.0 and a quick ratio of 1.0 or better are considered acceptable as rough rules of thumb. However, every situation must be evaluated on its merits before any definitive conclusions are drawn, because each industry may have entirely different standards of acceptability for its liquidity status, and the rules of thumb may be totally inapplicable for the specific company being evaluated.

Leverage Ratios (long-term solvency) These ratios measure the long-term solvency of the organization—its ability to meet long-term obligations as they come due. Long-term lenders and creditors may have a particular interest in these ratios.

Debt to Equity Ratio is calculated by dividing total liabilities by total equity, and measures the amount of long-term debt in relation to the amount of shareholder equity the company has in its capital base. Too much debt may cause difficulty for an organization in meeting current interest charges and principal payments as they come due and may cause lending institutions to be wary of lending additional money. The following data are from the Example Company:

	19X9	19X8	19X7
Total Liabilities	5,000	2,350	2,500
Stockholders' Equity	5,700	4,950	4,300
= Debt to Equity Ratio	0.88:1	0.47:1	0.58:1

This means, for every dollar of equity capital outsiders have supplied, respectively, 88, 47, and 58 cents of financing for the three years. Here the organization seems to be fairly well balanced in its capital structure, although 19X9 shows a substantial jump in external financing, which may

2.8 FINANCIAL STATEMENT ANALYSIS

be some cause for concern. As a general rule of thumb, the company's debt to equity ratio is likely to fall within the range of 0.50 to 1.00. Below that range, the company is not making adequate use of the leverage available to it through use of borrowed funds; yet a company's being above that range may cause lending institutions to feel there is too much leverage and thereby too much risk. Each industry, however, will have different ranges of acceptable ratios, which will be much more useful measures of what is acceptable or not.

Debt to Assets Ratio is calculated by dividing total liabilities by total assets. It is a variation of the debt to equity ratio and measures similar characteristics of the company's financial position—namely, how much of the company's total financing needs is being supplied by lenders and creditors. The range of ratios is likely to fall between 0.33 and 0.50, with variations again depending on the nature of the particular industry in which the company operates. The Example Company results follow:

	19X9	19X8	19X7
Total Liabilities	5,000	2,350	2,500
Total Assets	10,700	7,300	6,800
= Debt to Assets Ratio	0.47:1	0.32:1	0.37:1

The increase in 19X9 indicates that the Example Company has increased its borrowing at a faster rate than its equity. This conclusion can be verified by examining the underlying dollar amounts in the balance sheet or by reviewing the debt to equity ratio.

Interest Coverage Ratio is determined by dividing earnings before interest and taxes (EBIT) by interest expense, and it shows the number of times pre-tax earnings cover the interest expense. It provides a safety margin indicator as it shows how much of an earnings decline can be absorbed before the company is unable to meet interest expenses out of current earnings. For the Example Company:

	19X9	19X8	19X7
EBIT	2,150	1,490	1,560
Interest Expense	150	140	160
= Interest Coverage Ratio	14.3 ×	10.6 ×	9.8 ×

While the increase in the ratios seems a positive indicator since more earnings are available to meet interest expenses, and existence of substantially more debt on the balance sheet warns of a possible future decline in this ratio.

(ii) PERFORMANCE RATIOS These measure how well the organization performed in terms of resource management and profits.

Acitivity Ratios These ratios, also referred to as turnover ratios, measure the organization's use of assets to generate revenue and income. Generally, the higher the turnover, the more efficiently the organization is managing its assets, although too high a turnover may cause problems in that the operating needs of the business may not be met.

Accounts Receivable Collection There are two accounts receivable ratios that should be examined:

- **Accounts Receivable Turnover,** which provides the number of times accounts receivable are collected in the year. Turnover is calculated by dividing total sales by the average accounts receivable (beginning balance plus ending balance divided by 2). The higher the accounts receivable turnover, the better the organization is at collecting more quickly from customers. The funds are thus available for use in the company's operations. However, if the turnover is too high, it can be a signal that the company is overstrict in its credit policies and may thereby be losing valuable business. The Example Company results show:

	19X9	19X8	19X7
Credit Sales	12,500	11,000	10,500
Avg. Accts Receivable	1,750	1,650	1,600
= Accts. Receivable Turnover	7.14 ×	6.67 ×	6.56 ×

The increase in the accounts receivable turnover ratio is not enough to be significant, but a turnover ratio in the range of seven times per year may be too low, as will be more clearly explained in the next ratio calculation.

- **Accounts Receivable Collection Period,** which measures the number of days it takes the company to collect its receivables. The calculation is made by dividing the average daily sales (credit sales divided by 365

2.8 FINANCIAL STATEMENT ANALYSIS

days) into the accounts receivable balance. The Example Company calculations indicate the following:

	19X9	19X8	19X7
Accounts Receivable	1,900	1,600	1,700
Average Daily Sales	12,500/365	11,000/365	10,500/365
= Days Collection	55.5 days	53.1 days	59.1 days

This means that it is taking over 55 days for a sale to be converted to cash by the company in 19X9, which seems to be a rather long time unless the industry standard is this long or the company's credit terms allow more than 50 days to pay. The increase from the prior year is another cause for concern, raising the possibility that the company's collection effort is not being pursued vigorously enough, or that the credit policy is too loose and too many sales are being made to marginal customers. The latter raises the possibility of future collectibility problems for the company.

Inventory Turnover The inventory turnover ratio is a measure of how efficiently the company is using its inventory resources. It is frequently calculated by dividing the inventory balance into the sales to generate an annual turnover amount, but a more useful measure is to divide the cost of goods sold for the year by the inventory balance, since this relates two comparably calculated numbers. Inventory turnover for the Example Company can be shown as follows:

	19X9	19X8	19X7
Cost of Goods Sold	8,100	7,300	6,800
Average Inventory	1,750	1,500	1,400
= Inventory Turnover	4.63 ×	4.87 ×	4.86 ×

The average age of the inventory can be calculated by dividing the turnover rate into 365 (days in the year).

	19X9	19X8	19X7
Days/Turnover	365/4.63	365/4.87	365/4.86
= Average Age	78.8 days	74.9 days	75.1 days

An inventory turnover rate of just under five times per year indicates an organization with possibly slow-moving inventory. When examining the

THE PLANNING PHASE

change in this figure over time—in this instance a reduction from 4.86 to 4.63—the analyst may conclude that the company is stocking more inventory or that the inventory is becoming less sellable. It is also possible that slow-moving or obsolete inventory is building up. Under these circumstances management may wish to consider doing a product-mix analysis or implementing more effective inventory control procedures. The longer the inventory needs to be held, the more expensive it is for the company, since carrying costs and risk of loss, obsolescence, or deterioration become higher. On the other hand, it is also possible that in comparison with other similar companies the inventory turnover is within reasonable limits.

Asset Turnover This is the ratio of sales divided by total assets. It measures the level of capital investment relative to sales volume and provides an indication of how well the company is managing its assets and how efficiently those assets are being utilized to generate sales and profit. Once again, consider the Example Company:

	19X9	19X8	19X7
Sales	12,500	11,000	10,500
Average Assets	9,000	7,050	6,450
= Asset Turnover	1.39 ×	1.56 ×	1.63 ×

The decrease in asset turnover may indicate too heavy an investment in fixed assets or too low a utilization of the investments the company has made. The absolute number is meaningful only in relation to other companies in the same line of business—some capital-intensive businesses such as steel making work on very low asset turnover ratios, while other types of businesses, such as supermarkets, have extremely high asset turnover rates.

Profitability Ratios These ratios measure an organization's ability to earn a satisfactory profit and return on investment. They can be extremely important, as investors may avoid companies with poor earnings potential and creditors may be wary of insufficient profitability because of the increased risk of loss.

Net Profit Margin is probably the most commonly used measure of performance, though it may not be the most useful. It measures how much of each dollar of sales is retained as profit. If compared with that of other similar companies or with the company's past performance, this ratio pro-

2.8 FINANCIAL STATEMENT ANALYSIS

vides an effective measure of performance, but results can vary significantly from industry to industry. The Example Company results show:

	19X9	19X8	19X7
Net Income	1,200	900	900
Net Sales	12,500	11,000	10,500
= Net Profit Margin	9.6%	8.2%	8.6%

In this instance the net profit margin has increased favorably over the three-year period, indicating that the company is improving its profitability relative to sales volume.

Gross Profit Margin is a related profitability measure which calculates gross profit as a percentage of sales to determine the profitability of a company's manufacturing or processing activity. The Example Company results are as follows:

	19X9	19X8	19X7
Gross (Mfg.) Profit	4,400	3,700	3,700
Net Sales	12,500	11,000	10,500
= Gross Profit Margin	35.2%	33.6%	35.2%

Here again the increase in the return, even though small, from 19X8 to 19X9 indicates the company's ability to maintain the profitability of its principal activities. A negative trend in either the gross or net profit margin percentages or a significant drop from one year to the next may indicate to management the need for a cost study or for an intensive look at productivity.

Return on Investment (ROI) is an exceedingly important measure to review, in that it indicates how effectively the company has utilized its invested funds. "Return on Investment" is a generic term inasmuch as there are numerous ways in which it can be calculated, and it is necessary for the reviewer to be fully aware of the particular ROI calculation being utilized before any evaluations can be made. There are two basic measures that are commonly used:

THE PLANNING PHASE

- **Return on Assets (ROA)** measures the profit-generating *efficiency* of the total assets of the company. For instance, the Example Company ROA can be calculated as follows:

	19X9	19X8	19X7
Operating Profit	2,100	1,500	1,600
Average Total Assets	9,000	7,050	6,450
= Return on Assets	23.3%	21.3%	24.8%

- **Return on Equity (ROE)** measures the *effectiveness* of the investment made by stockholders in the company. It is a measure of the overall return to the shareholders, which they can use to compare with alternative investment opportunities. ROE for the Example Company:

	19X9	19X8	19X7
Net Income	1,200	900	900
Average Equity	5,325	4,625	4,000
= Return on Equity	22.5%	19.5%	22.5%

Considering alternative rates of return available in financial and capital markets, both ROA and ROE seem to be rather attractive. The subjective factor that needs to be taken into account is the element of risk and how much extra return is appropriate to compensate for that risk. There is no single answer to that question, since risk is a factor that must be evaluated by each analyst personally. Needless to say, however, a higher return would be more appropriate for a business than for an investment in a government Treasury bill, because the possibility for loss is certainly greater in the former than in the latter, and there should be appropriate compensation for that greater risk.

2.9 USE OF GRAPHICS

With the availability of microcomputers and easy-to-use graphics capabilities, visual presentation of financial information is quite feasible. The advantages of graphics and pictorials are well known, and these tools have been used for a long time—even before the use of microcomputers.

Graphics appeal to the reader who is confused by or unable to readily comprehend information presented in standard tabular form or who wants a quick, overall sense of what is going on without having to be concerned

2.9 USE OF GRAPHICS

FIGURE 2.10. Pie charts (a) 19X9 and (b) 19X7.

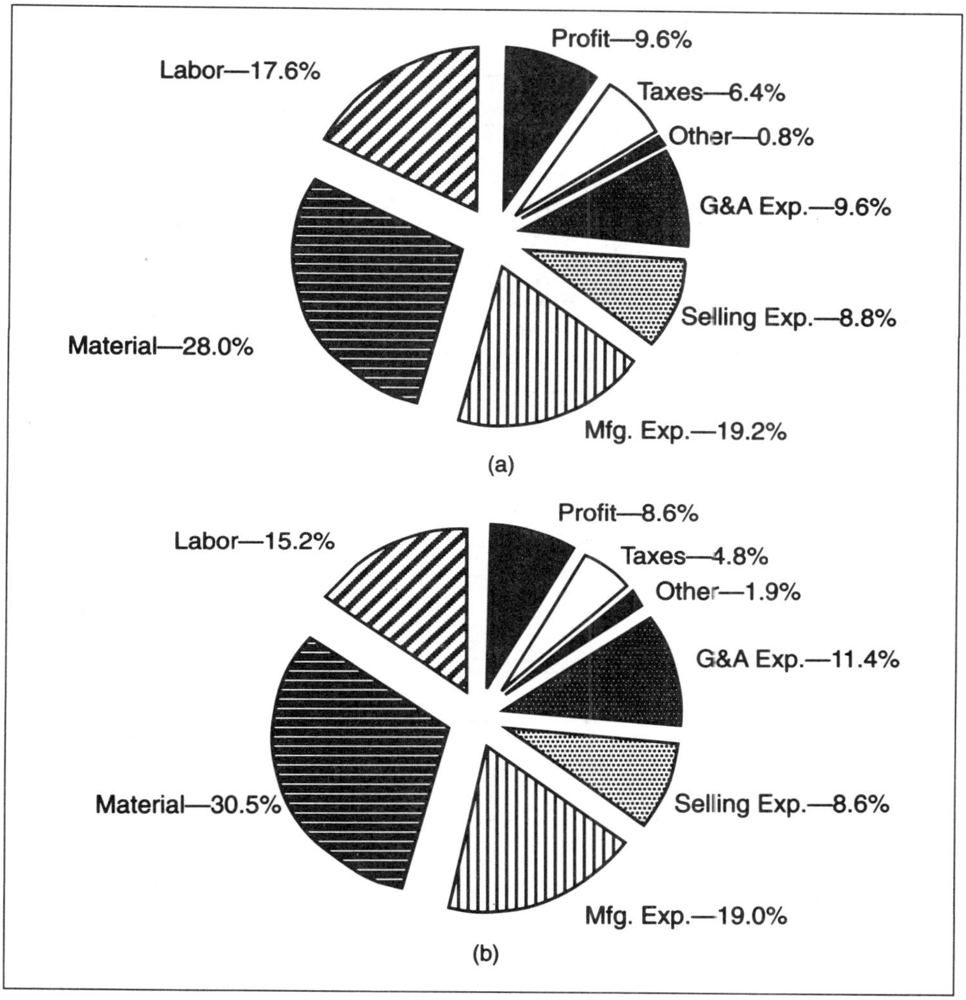

about the supporting detail. One of the purposes of financial reporting is to present information in readily understandable form so as to minimize the amount of time that the reader must spend in comprehending the message. Graphics, properly used, can achieve this goal.

Graphics can be used to assist in analyzing the company's needs for operational auditing. Examples of such graphic capabilities are shown in Figures 2.10 and 2.11—pie charts, bar charts, and line charts. These examples are representative and not intended to show complete capabilities, as each software package differs.

FIGURE 2.11. (a) Bar chart and (b) line chart.

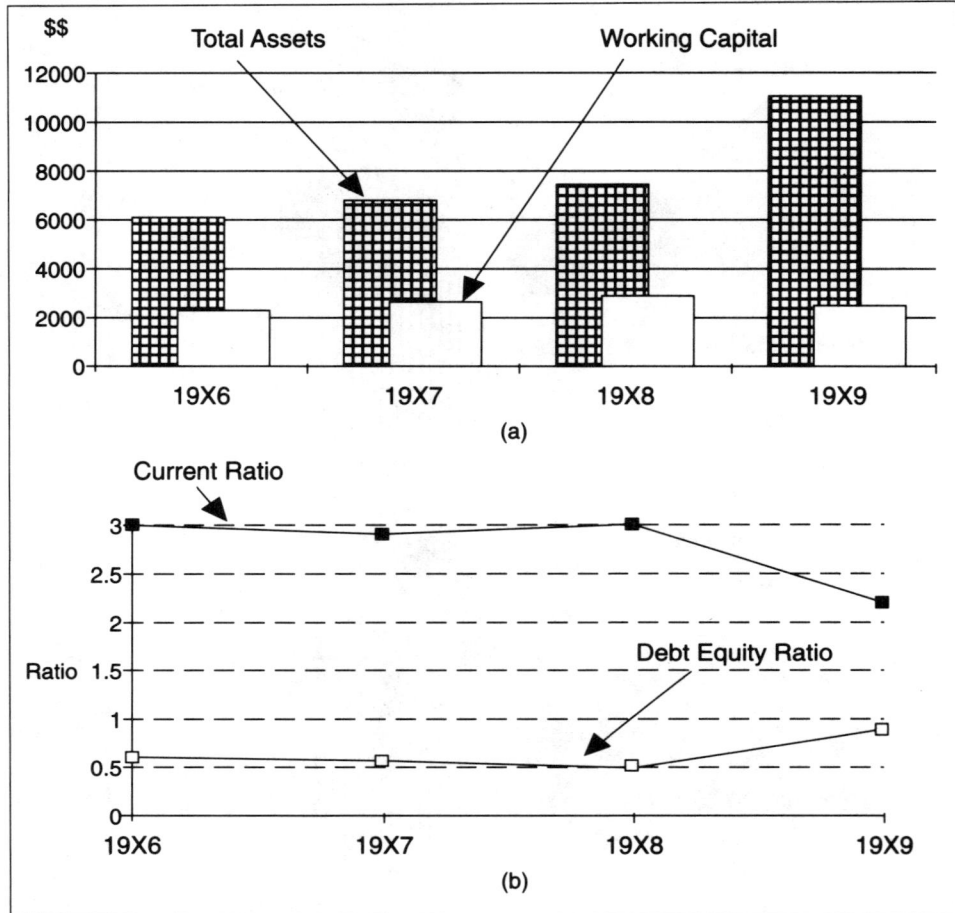

More advanced graphics capabilities can enhance the process by providing increasingly sophisticated graphs, color presentations, and the ability to review data in different graphic formats. Presentation of accounting and financial information in graphic form is one way to dramatically and effectively make the numbers work for clients.

2.10 IDENTIFYING CRITICAL AREAS

As a result of the initial survey and analysis of financial statement data of the Example Company, the operational auditor should be able to help management identify its critical operational areas where operational audit procedures would provide the most benefits. This step is not always required, as quite often management has already decided which areas would provide the biggest payout through operational audit procedures. However, based on the auditor's analysis of the Example Company financial statements, a list of potential areas for operational audit is shown in Figure 2.12.

Although all of the operational areas recommended for operational audit should produce beneficial results and adequate payout, the Example Company's management has decided to review the purchasing function first. Their rationale is that purchasing is responsible for the economy of operations related to additions to inventory; manufacturing material costs; additions to property, plant, and equipment; expediting on-time vendor deliveries; and overall vendor relations. Because the Example Company has become increasingly material-dependent in its manufacturing operations, with resultant increases in inventory, this does appear to be a good place to start. In addition, the initial survey disclosed that Purchasing Department systems and procedures were antiquated and quite ineffective.

2.11 PLANNING PHASE: EXAMPLE COMPANY

Now consider the Example Company and how the planning phase might work for the purchasing function. The major objective of the planning phase of an operational audit is to gather information about the area to be audited, to analyze the information, and to determine which parts of the operations contain possible inefficiencies and lend themselves to positive changes and improvements.

FIGURE 2.12. List of potential areas for operational audit: The Example Company.

1. Cash management
2. Billing and collections
3. Inventory control procedures
4. Purchasing
5. Capital expenditures (property, plant, and equipment)
6. Financing/borrowing
7. Sales and pricing analysis
8. Manufacturing and production control procedures
9. Cost accounting
10. Marketing
11. Storeroom operations
12. Electronic data processing (EDP)

THE PLANNING PHASE

If the operational auditor is the organization's ongoing internal or external auditor, management usually expects the auditor and associated staff to be familiar with the company's operations, particularly the area subject to the operational audit. In this example, the purchasing function is under consideration. This may not, however, always be the case; the auditor may be engaged solely to perform a particular operational audit.

(a) Information to Be Gathered

In either situation described in the preceding paragraph, to assist in successfully planning for the operational audit, the auditor must become fully familiar with the organization and its products or services, goals, objectives, detail plans, policies, procedures, practices, systems and methods, organizational atmosphere, and so on. To ensure full familiarity with these areas, the auditor should either have collected previously or request from management information related to the organization's operations, such as:

- Long-range and short-term plans, including organizational and departmental goals, objectives, and detail plans.
- Organizational data: structure, reporting relationships, divisions, departments, work units, and so on.
- Functional responsibilities and corresponding authority relationships of each functional area.
- Personnel data: job positions and number of employees in each job classification.
- Personnel relations: hiring, orientation, training, evaluation, promotion, and firing procedures.
- Personnel statistics: turnover rates, sick leave, lateness, firings, disciplinary actions, and grievances.
- Work statistics: production data, work levels, and work backlogs.
- Facilities: locations, type, purpose, use, and so on.
- Policies, procedures, systems, methods, and practices, particularly for the operational areas to be reviewed.

(b) Organizational Philosophy

The auditor should also try to understand fully why the organization is in existence. Although in the private sector top management may honestly

2.11 PLANNING PHASE: EXAMPLE COMPANY

tell you that the company is in existence to make money or profits through providing a product or service, and in the case of a governmental or social service entity, to provide services, the organization also exists to satisfy its customers, clients, and/or the general public. In addition, the auditor should also make an effort to determine the organization's philosophy. Is it to provide the best quality product or service to meet customer desires at the least possible cost? Is it to sell products or services at the highest possible prices to maximize profits? Or is just to survive and provide jobs and ensure employment for management?

(c) Operational Audit Objectives

Once the auditor is fully familiar with the organization and the operations to be included in the operational audit, he or she can then begin to plan the actual operational audit. As part of the planning process, the auditor and management should agree as to the objectives of the operational audit, for example:

- To assess performance as compared with appropriate measurement criteria,

- To identify operations for improvement from an economy, efficiency, and effectiveness standpoint,

- To develop recommendations for improvement or further action, or

- A combination of these objectives.

(d) Scope of Operational Audit

Another aspect to consider is the scope or type of operational audit to be performed. For example, management might want an organizational review, which could encompass a study or review of the entire organizational structure and how it functions. Managers might want just a functional review or study of a specific department or work unit such as purchasing, inventory control, or personnel. They might request a systems review or a study of an operating system, such as purchasing, from purchase requisition to payment of vendor invoices, including both manual and computerized procedures. Finally, they could request a program or project review consisting of a one-time review or study of a singular project or activity such as capital improvement or construction, special marketing or sales, or a research and development project.

(e) Illustration: The Example Company

The Example Company's Purchasing Department can be used to illustrate how these types of reviews help to determine the full audit scope of the specific operational audit. First, the audit scope includes an organizational review of the organizational structure of the Purchasing Department and where it fits in the rest of the organization; then, a more detailed analysis of each work unit within the purchasing function, that is, what each employee does and why. Second, a functional review is conducted for each specific operating work unit within the Purchasing Department, such as Buyers, Standard Specifications Unit, and so on. Third, a systems review would be performed of the full purchasing cycle from requisition through vendor payment. Finally, a program or project review is performed within the purchasing function, such as a value analysis program.

(i) Selecting Functions to Audit An operational auditor should concentrate on those areas or functions on which management spends most of its efforts, that is, the highest payback areas. This does not mean that areas of lesser importance are to be disregarded, but rather, that they should be treated in their proper perspective. Management often ignores areas of significance through misunderstanding or negligence. Those areas should be emphasized as well, whether management has recognized them or not. Tasks to accomplish during the planning phase include:

- Determining the department's functions,
- Reviewing the methods the department uses to carry out these functions,
- Reviewing the organizational structure, including reporting relationships, hierarchy, personnel, and interrelationships,
- Reviewing policies and procedures through which the department operates and performs its functions,
- Analyzing financial and budget data, and
- Reviewing management reporting.

By performing these tasks and others that may be required, the auditor is able to identify those areas of the department's operations that have the greatest likelihood of inefficiency or are susceptible to abuse or laxity. As mentioned earlier, the major objective is to direct attention to those areas that will pay off most in terms of increased efficiency or economy.

2.11 PLANNING PHASE: EXAMPLE COMPANY

(ii) Understanding the Function One of the first criteria for ensuring operational audit success is a full understanding of the specific function under review, as well as of desirable operating systems and procedures. This could entail some research into the particular function in general, including which practices are considered good or bad and how other organizations perform the same function. This work step might require reading available up-to-date literature on the subject, as well as visiting facilities at a similar business. For the Example Company's Purchasing Department, some suggested areas with which the auditor might become familiar during this initial step of the planning phase include:

- The purchasing cycle (see Figure 2.13),
- The purchasing information system (see Figure 2.14),
- Desirable operating systems (see Figure 2.15), and
- Purchasing control and risk areas (see Figure 2.16).

(iii) Purchasing Function Initial Survey Similar to the initial survey of the entire organization discussed in Chapter 1, an initial survey of the purchasing function should also be made in the planning phase. If such an initial survey of the purchasing function has not been made as part of the survey to determine organization wide critical operational areas to review, then it needs to be done as part of the planning phase. A sample initial survey form for the purchasing function is shown in Figure 2.17. The items included on the survey form should be supplemented according to the specific situation and the objectives of the operational audit.

(iv) Organization Chart Review As part of the planning-phase documentation requested from management, the auditor obtained a list of the Example Company's Purchasing Department personnel, which is included as Figure 2.18. Through interviews with Purchasing Department management and operations personnel, the auditor was able to identify reporting relationships within the department and prepare an organization chart (see Figure 2.19) for the department as it relates to the entire organization. Based on the review of the organizational chart, the auditor's suggested areas for study are documented in Figure 2.20.

(v) Significant Data During the planning phase of the operational audit, the auditor normally discovers an immense amount of data, from which must be derived what is significant. As a result of the planning phase of

PLANNING PHASE

FIGURE 2.13. Understanding of the purchasing cycle.

1. *Forecasting commodity and service needs*
   How are necessary purchases determined?
   Are planned purchases supported by a sales and production forecast?
   Does a planning system exist which ties budgeted purchases into planned results?
2. *Establishing and maintaining a vendor list*
   Are vendors accepted based on objective evaluative criteria?
   Is the vendor list updated through periodic vendor analysis for additions and deletions to the list?
3. *Review and approval of purchasing specifications*
   Are purchases made based on approved written purchasing specifications?
   Is a work unit independent of any requisitioning department responsible for purchase specifications development?
   Are purchase specifications reviewed and updated in an effective and efficient manner?
4. *The purchase process*
   Are purchases made according to acceptable systems and procedures?
   Do these systems and procedures include such practices as:
   - Purchase approval based on preapproved plans and budgets.
   - Purchase requisition procedures.
   - Purchase order processing and control.
   - Vendor negotiations, including applicable competitive bidding.
   - Effective purchase follow-up.
5. *The expediting function*
   Are purchases followed-up to ensure timely deliveries?
   Does a system exist which allows for effective expediting?
6. *Control over receipts*
   Are purchased items accurately identified at the time of receipt so that the receipt can be accurately recorded against open purchase orders?
   Are controls adequate to ensure against receiving items that have not been purchased?
7. *Vendor performance*
   Are vendors effectively evaluated relative to their performance as to quality, quantity, and timeliness?
   Does a reporting and recording system exist to analyze vendor performance?
   Are vendors dropped, based on poor performance?
8. *Purchasing information*
   Does an adequate purchasing information-reporting system exist, which includes elements such as those shown in the purchasing information system in Figure 2.14?

2.11 PLANNING PHASE: EXAMPLE COMPANY

FIGURE 2.14. Purchasing information system.

1. *Parts/items catalog*
   - Part number coding system.
   - Standards for items.
   - Specifications of items.
   - Item descriptions.
2. *Vendor lists and data*
   - Demographic data: name, address, locations, contacts, etc.
   - Commodities supplied.
   - Pricing data.
3. *Stock status reporting*
   - Material requirements plan.
   - Reorder point exception reporting.
   - Number of items available.
   - Items on order.
   - Item usage information.
4. *Open purchase order file*
   - Open purchase order control.
   - Expediting report: what to follow up based on due date.
   - Partial shipment control.
5. *Vendor performance*
   - Vendor master file.
   - Delivery data.
   - Quality data.
   - Price history.
6. *Statistical reporting*
   - Lead time analysis.
   - Cost of processing a purchase order.
   - Average usage over a period of time.
   - Obsolete and slow-moving material.
   - Department performance reporting.
   - Scrap and salvage reporting.
   - On-time and not-on-time delivery reporting.
   - Quality of receipts/receiving reject reporting.
   - Competitive bidding reports.
   - Vendor analysis.

THE PLANNING PHASE

FIGURE 2.15. Desirable operating systems and procedures.

- Well-documented organization structure with defined responsibilities and authority.
- Well-defined objectives and program.
- Adequate position descriptions.
- Hiring of employees with appropriate experience and training.
- Employee orientation and training.
- Purchasing manual describing policies and operating procedures.
- Basic operating and information system.
- Use of efficient purchasing techniques:
  - Traveling requisitions: use of standardized purchase requisitions for repetitive purchases of common items, rather than preparation of individual requisitions.
  - Blanket purchase orders: for ordering large quantities at one time at favorable prices and then requesting delivery as needed. This method is used so that the vendor warehouses purchases until they are needed.
- Industry comparisons.
- Integrated mechanized information processing.
- Quantitative performance measurements.
- Work measurement.
- Efficient work flow.
- Proper physical layout.

FIGURE 2.16. Control and risk areas.

- Shortages of materials/supplies.
- Emergency purchases.
- Excess investment in inventories.
- Build-up of slow-moving and obsolete items.
- Inventory valuations or pricing policies.
- Overall steady increase in inventories.
- Pilferage and spoilage.
- Segregation and numerical identification of items.
- Breakdown in specification changes.
- Vendor performance.
- Lack of controls in document flow.
- Accurate physical inventories (write downs).
- Legal aspects of purchasing and contracts.
- Circumvention of normal purchasing system and approvals.
- Bidding process, where applicable.
- Reputation and financial condition of the vendors.

FIGURE 2.17. Purchasing function: Sample initial survey form.

I. *Purchasing Department Organizational Status*
   A. To whom does the head of the Purchasing Department report?
   B. What control is exercised over purchasing policy through:
      1. Company executives outside of purchasing organizational lines of authority?
      2. Administrative or other committees?
      3. Board of directors?
   C. Does a Purchasing Department organization chart exist? Obtain or prepare copy.
   D. What are the duties and responsibilities of each employee in the Purchasing Department?
   E. Is there a division of purchasing responsibility among buyers? Document such responsibilities.
II. *Purchasing Department Responsibility*
   A. Is the responsibility of the Purchasing Department clearly defined and understood by:
      1. Purchasing Department employees?
      2. Other departmental personnel?
   B. Does the Purchasing Department have knowledge of conflicting purchasing responsibility assumed by other departments? Document any conflicting responsibilities.
   C. Is company policy on purchasing covered by a written manual? Obtain or prepare copy of policy relative to purchasing authority.
   D. Are there purchasing activities for which the Purchasing Department has no responsibility or limited responsibility? Document those areas.
   E. Do other departments have any relations with vendors? Is there a policy regarding such vendor relations? Document any such relations.
   F. Does the Purchasing Department work with operating departments on such matters as:
      1. Favorable purchasing opportunities?
      2. Economical ordering quantities?
      3. Purchase specification changes?
III. *Purchasing Authorization*
   A. What is the general policy for approval of purchases by departments requiring materials? Obtain copy or document policy.
   B. Are approval limits covered in written instructions? Obtain copy.
   C. Are approval limits definite as to amount and classification of expenditures? Obtain or prepare copy.
   D. What are policies regarding special approvals, such as:
      1. Capital expenditures?
      2. Budget limitations prior to purchase commitment? Obtain or prepare copy of policies.
   E. What is the approval policy where the final cost of an order exceeds the amount originally estimated on the purchase order?

FIGURE 2.17. Purchasing function: Sample initial survey form.

---

        1. Where limit of approval of original signer is not exceeded by final cost?
        2. Where limit of approval of original signer is exceeded?
    F. What is the approval policy where changes are made in the quantity or specifications of the original purchase requisition? Document.

IV. *Physical Facilities*
    A. Are the layout and general facilities of the Purchasing Department conducive to effective operations? Obtain or prepare copy of physical layout.
    B. Are purchasing functions physically set up as appropriate?
        1. Buyers.
        2. Expediters.
        3. Purchasing specifications unit.
        4. Reception area.
        5. Salespeople interviews.
        6. Purchase order preparation.
        7. Support functions.

V. *Decentralized Purchasing*
    A. Is there a policy on purchases made by decentralized operating units, such as petty cash funds, sales offices, etc.?
        1. Limits of authority.
        2. Reporting responsibility.
        3. Review or control by central Purchasing Department.

VI. *Purchasing Department Procedures*
    A. Are Purchasing Department procedures oral or written? Obtain or prepare copy.
    B. What are procedures regarding:
        1. Handling of purchase requisitions?
        2. Placing of purchase orders?
        3. Flow of forms?
        Obtain copy or document.
    C. Are there procedures related to bidding by vendors? Document.
    D. What specialized forms are used by the Purchasing Department? Obtain copies of each form. These should be reviewed so that the purpose and usage is thoroughly understood.
    E. Are there policies and procedures relative to:
        1. Purchasing locally where possible?
        2. Purchasing from users of company products?
    F. Does the Purchasing Department maintain or participate in a "value analysis" program?
        Note: In a value analysis program, the Purchasing Department will work with vendors and with affected company departments (such as engineering and production) in the analysis of specifications, consumption, and requirements. Through such analysis and cooperative effort, it is possible to make savings through redesign, change in specifications, purchase in more economical quantities, or manufacture by the company itself.

2.11 PLANNING PHASE: EXAMPLE COMPANY

FIGURE 2.18. Purchasing Department personnel, Reporting to vice president, Operations: The Example Company.

	Number of Personnel
1. *Purchasing*	
Purchasing Supervisor	1
Buyer II	7
Buyer I	4
Clerk-Stenographer	1
Clerical Supervisor	1
Clerk-Typist	2
2. *Standard Specifications*	
Standard Specifications Supervisor	1
Procurement Technician	2
Management Trainee	2
Clerk-Stenographer	1
Clerk	1
3. *Inspections*	
Chief Inspector	1
Inspectors	3
Clerk-Typist	1
4. *Inventory Control*	
Inventory Supervisor	1
Inventory Control Supervisors	2
Inventory Control Clerks	4
Clerical Supervisor	1
Clerk-Typist	2
5. *Warehouse*	
Warehouse Manager	1
Stores Manager	2
Stores Supervisor	2
Equipment Operator	3
Storesman	2
Stock Handler	1
Semiskilled Labor	2
6. *Staff Services*	
Market Analyst	1
Administrative Analyst	1
Clerk-Stenographer	1
Clerk-Stenographer I	1

THE PLANNING PHASE

FIGURE 2.19. Organization chart: The Example Company.

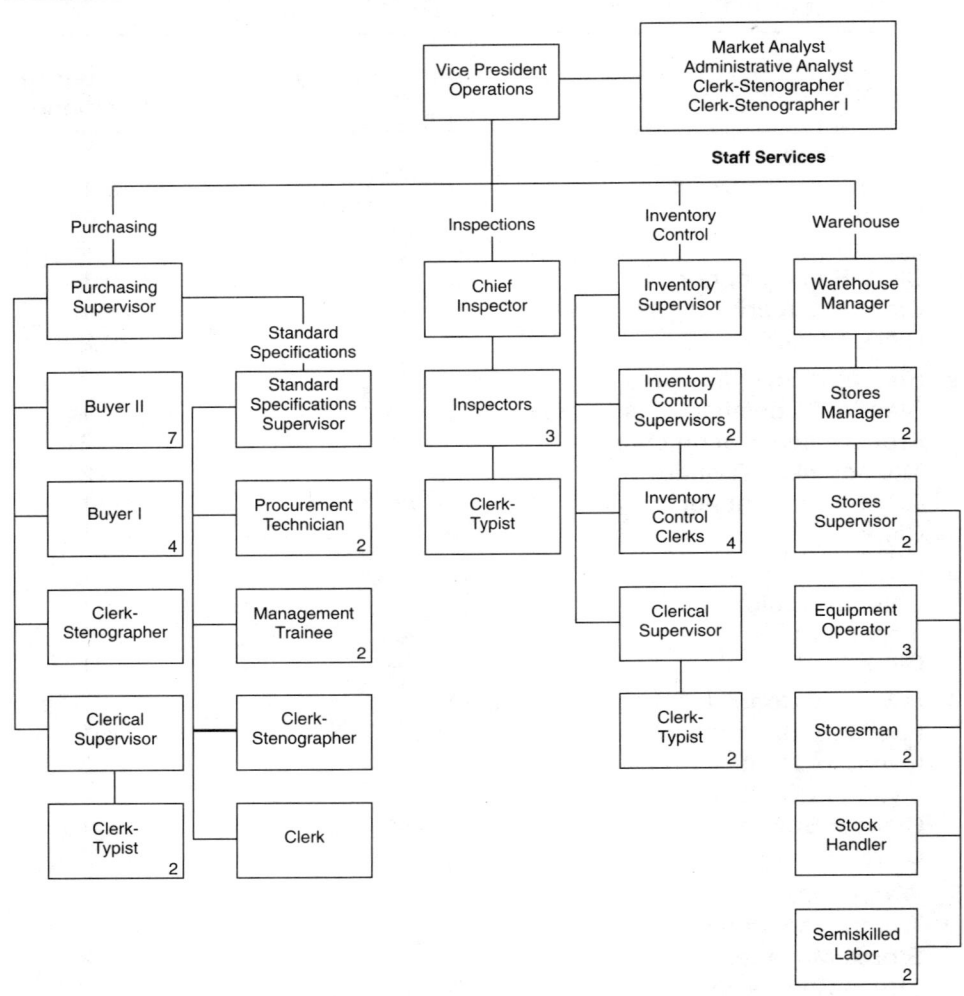

2.11 PLANNING PHASE: EXAMPLE COMPANY

FIGURE 2.20. Organization chart analysis, suggested areas for review: The Example Company.

1. Why does the Purchasing Department report to the vice president of Operations?
2. What are the functions, responsibilities, and authority of staff functions such as:
   a. Market analyst?
   b. Administrative analyst?
3. Why are two clerk-stenographers reporting directly to the vice president, Operations?
4. What is the function and authority of the purchasing supervisor?
5. What are buyers' functions, and how are they used within the Purchasing Department?
6. What is the difference between a Buyer II and a Buyer I?
7. Are all buyers necessary based on respective work load of each buyer?
8. What is the function of the clerk-stenographer, and how does it differ from those of the clerical supervisor and clerk-typists?
9. What does the clerical supervisor do, and is supervision of the two clerk-typists necessary?
10. What are the functions of the two clerk-typists, and is the work load appropriate?
11. What is the function of the Standard Specifications unit?
12. Is the personnel complement within the Standard Specifications unit appropriate to the present work required?
13. What are the specific functions of the Standard Specifications unit personnel, and are they necessary?
    a. Standard Specifications supervisor.
    b. Procurement technicians.
    c. Management trainees.
    d. Clerk-stenographer.
    e. Clerk.
14. Should other units such as Inspection, Inventory Control, and Warehouse be reporting to the same individual (vice president, Operations) as the Purchasing Department?

the operational audit of the Example Company's Purchasing Department, the following annual statistics were disclosed:

- Number of regular POs   18,100
- Number of "emergency" purchases   666
- Number of direct purchases   2,315
- Total dollar value of regular purchases $4,815,861
- Average dollar value of a regular purchase $266

(vi) Selecting Areas for Further Review Based on this information, the auditor documents those areas to review during the audit program phase. Normally, all operational areas targeted for further study that were identified during the planning phase are considered. Then, through a process of analysis and evaluation, using the best professional judgment, the auditor identifies the most critical areas, offering the best possibility for significant improvements in terms of economies, efficiencies, or effectiveness. Those areas identified for possible further review for the Example Company's purchasing function during the planning phase are listed in Figure 2.21.

In reviewing the areas identified in Figure 2.21, it is usually found that the areas identified to review further in the audit program and field work phases would require far more audit time than allowed by the operational audit budget. Accordingly, these areas must be evaluated and prioritized as to which afford the greatest opportunity for payback through additional operational audit effort. Based on such an analysis, the areas that were determined for further review have been indicated by asterisks in Figure 2.21. Those areas will be used as examples in the Example Company's case study for the audit program, field work, and reporting phases.

(vii) Areas Not Selected for Review The other operational areas for which it is determined that additional operational audit work will not be performed at this time are not to be merely put aside. They should all be mentioned to organizational and departmental management in an oral and/or written report, recommending further action, such as:

1. Immediate action. For example, facility changes can be made so that buyers have privacy when talking with vendors, and a set schedule established for vendor appointments.
2. Further analysis and review by organizational and departmental management. For example, management might consider changing the Purchasing Department reporting to the vice-president of operations, as well as inspections, inventory control, and warehouse.
3. Future operational review by the operational audit team or internal departmental personnel. For example, the review of special approval procedures such as capital expenditures, over-budget limitations, and special projects.

2.11 PLANNING PHASE: EXAMPLE COMPANY

FIGURE 2.21. Possible areas for further review.

1. *Organization*
   * a. Function and authority of Purchasing Department and related personnel.
   * b. Function and necessity of specific job classifications:
      - Purchasing supervisor.
      - Buyers I and II.
      - Clerk supervisor.
      - Clerical supervisor.
      - Clerk-typist.
      - Standard Specifications Unit:
         - Standard specifications supervisor.
         - Procurement technician.
         - Management trainee.
         - Clerk-stenographer.
         - Clerk.
   c. Organizational position:
      - Reporting to vice president, Operations.
      - Vice president—Operations staff functions:
         - Market analyst.
         - Administrative analyst.
         - Clerk-stenographer.
         - Clerk-stenographer I.
      - Other units also reporting to vice president, Operations:
         - Inspections.
         - Inventory Control.
         - Warehouse.
2. *Purchasing Department Responsibility*
   * a. Processing of regular purchase orders:
      - Central purchasing policies (all purchases over $50).
      - Systems and procedures.
      - Present cost of processing a purchase order.
      - Analysis of purchase orders: by source and dollar value.
   b. Purchasing outside central Purchasing Department:
      - Emergency purchases.
      - Direct purchases.
      - Petty cash purchases.
   c. Special approvals:
      - Capital expenditures.
      - Budget constraints.
      - Special projects.
      - Final cost exceeding purchase order amount.

PLANNING PHASE

FIGURE 2.21. *(Continued)*

---

3. *Purchase Order Processing Procedures*
* a. Purchase requisitions.
* b. Purchase order processing.
* c. Open purchase order control.
  d. Relations with vendors.
  e. Coordination with user departments:
     - Favorable purchasing opportunities.
     - Specification changes.
     - Value analysis.
     - Order quantities.
* f. Work flow.
  g. Competitive bidding.
  h. Other areas:
     - Local purchases.
     - Purchases from customers.
4. *Physical Facilities*
   a. Layout of Purchasing Department.
   b. Facilities: work space, equipment, etc.
   c. Physical setup.
5. *Purchase Order Costs*
* a. Calculation of cost to process a purchase order.
* b. Relationship to amount of actual purchases (average purchase order amount: $226).
     - Under $50 (present policy states Purchasing Department processes all purchase orders over $50).
     - $50 to $100.
     - $100 to $200, etc.
* c. Annual cost to process small purchases.

* Areas determined for further review.

2.12 CONCLUSION

As a result of the work steps conducted in the planning phase as described above, a properly indexed and organized planning-phase workpaper file should have been developed for all the materials gathered and work steps performed. The workpaper file is then used as a resource in developing the in-depth audit program and the corresponding field work. These materials can be compared to permanent audit file data in a financial audit.

A number of critical operating areas should also have been developed where more in-depth audit procedures need to be performed in the audit program phase leading toward development of a significant operational audit finding. For example, the following areas may have been identified for more in-depth analysis from the planning phase audit program in Figure 2.2:

- Inadequate planning procedures, resulting in no identification of auditee goals, objectives, and detail plans,

- Sales trends on a downward spiral in certain product lines,

- Overall expenditures increasing, particularly:
    Cost of goods sold, including production, labor, and materials
    Production support functions such as inventory and quality control
    General and administrative personnel
    Material and supplies
    Repairs and maintenance

- Increased inventories, with an increase in obsolete inventory,

- Increase in the number of administrative positions,

- Increase in employee turnover,

- Inefficient use of data processing equipment, and

- Crowded working conditions, in both production and office.

The in-depth operational audit program should also have been started. Based on the identification of possible critical operational areas, each auditor on the audit staff should have begun thinking about and have documented suggested audit work steps to be incorporated into the in-depth audit program. This is the starting point for developing the operational audit program. The steps required for its finalization are discussed in Chapter 3. Before continuing, review the operational audit situation in Figure 2.22.

FIGURE 2.22. Purchase order quantity tolerances.

During the planning phase of an operational audit, the auditor found in reviewing the Purchasing Department's methods and procedures that vendors could be allowed to ship the ordered quantity plus or minus 10 percent. However, this practice was approved only for certain commodities such as nuts, bolts, wire, and rope.

During physical inspection of the Purchasing Department and discussions with the manager of the Purchasing Department as part of the planning phase of the operational audit, the auditor found that:

1. The 10 percent quantity tolerance was being used for items that did not require a tolerance, such as office supplies, maintenance items, cleaning supplies, etc.
2. Most vendors took advantage of the tolerance terms and shipped the ordered quantity plus 10 percent.
3. Although procedures existed relative to such purchase order tolerances, each buyer was deciding what was appropriate, based on personal knowledge of industry practice.

Questions and Solutions for Consideration
Q. What additional steps might the auditor want to perform in the planning phase relative to this situation?
A. Time-consuming efforts to show the existence of significant deficiencies should not be undertaken. Accordingly, this situation should only be documented at this point, for consideration when deciding on areas for additional work.
Q. What could the auditor suggest, if anything, to the Purchasing Department to correct the situation at this point?
A. Written instructions should be prepared for each buyer stating the specific items that require tolerance and the level of tolerance to be used.

Note that the institution of such written instructions, and the control and exercise of granting such purchase tolerances only to those items requiring it, resulted in a net annual savings of approximately $320,000 for the Example Company.

CHAPTER THREE

Audit Program Phase

3.1 INTRODUCTION

The operational audit program is written for the review of selected activities as determined in the planning phase. It becomes the bridge between the planning phase and the field work phase. The operational audit program is a plan of action for conducting the operational audit. The operational auditing team considers each significant area identified in the planning phase for further review and develops specific audit work steps that they believe will most clearly demonstrate the extent and cause of the operational deficiency and lead to recommendations for improvement. The audit program is as important to the operational auditor as a map is to a navigator.

This chapter discusses the audit program phase of the operational audit. It is in the audit program phase that the operational auditor focuses on the significant operational areas identified in the planning phase and develops specific audit work steps for further review and analysis. Through the performance of these work steps, in the field work phase, the auditor determines the extent of any operational deficiencies and begins to develop operational audit findings. In effect, as stated earlier, the audit program phase is the bridge between the planning phase and the field work phase. The operational audit program is, therefore, the plan of action for conducting the operational audit. However, it is initially written for the preliminary review of those selected activities as determined in the planning phase. Accordingly, it is subject to change based on actual findings during the field work phase.

The following points will be discussed in this chapter:

AUDIT PROGRAM PHASE

1. Purpose of the audit program phase in an operational audit.
2. Benefits of the operational audit program.
3. Standards by which operational audit programs are developed.

In addition, a sample operational audit program and related work steps will be presented. By the end of this chapter, via the use of case study materials, an increased understanding of the development of an operational audit program for areas identified in the planning phase will have been obtained.

3.2 BENEFITS OF THE OPERATIONAL AUDIT PROGRAM

A well-constructed operational audit program is essential to conducting the operational audit in an efficient and effective manner. Operational audit programs are the key to successful operational audits as they provide benefits such as:

1. A systematic plan for the work to be performed in the operational audit, which can be communicated to all operational audit staff.
2. A systematic basis for assigning work to audit staff members, according to their specialized skills, technical competencies, and type of task.
3. A means by which audit supervisors and other reviewers can compare performance with approved plans, audit standards, and requirements.
4. Assistance in training inexperienced staff members and acquainting them with the scope, objectives, and work steps of the operational audit.
5. The basis for a summary record of work actually performed in the operational audit.
6. Aid in familiarizing successive audit groups with the nature of the work performed in this operational audit.

While these written audit work programs are essential to efficient and effective management of an operational audit assignment, they should never be used simply as a checklist of work steps to perform in a way that stifles individual auditor initiative, imagination, and resourcefulness in achieving the desired objectives. Remember that the operational audit program is written for the preliminary review of selected activities as determined in the planning phase, but is subject to change based on what is actually found in the field work phase of the audit.

3.3 OPERATIONAL AUDIT PROGRAM STANDARDS

The operational audit program is really a plan for the audit work steps that the auditor believes will achieve the best results. Once the actual results are determined, the auditor may want to change the plan. For instance, in conducting an audit work step it may be determined that the perceived deficiency is not really significant. In this case, the auditor would curtail this work step and any others associated with it. On the other hand, if it is determined that a particular area is really more significant than expected, then the audit program should be increased by additional work steps.

The operational audit program is developed for the specific circumstances of the organization or department under review. Therefore, each operational audit program is a unique entity. This being the case, the operational audit program is normally developed for one-time use. Unlike financial audits, operational audits have no last year's workpapers to refer to. Although there may be previous operational audits available for reference, keep in mind that each situation is unique and the use of "borrowed" work steps should be minimized and used only in those cases where they are appropriate.

In preparing the operational audit program, the auditor should consider certain standards, such as the following:

1. The operational audit program should be tailor-made to fit the specific operational audit assignment as to type of organization, personnel involved, systems and procedures in effect, degree of sophistication, and so on.
2. Each audit program work step should clearly set forth the work to be done and the reason for doing it. Including a clear explanation of the reasons for each audit step is helpful because:
   a. The staff member carrying out the work must know why the audit step is being done. With this information, the auditor can be expected to do a much better job than if he or she is asked to perform an audit step without sufficient background.
   b. It minimizes the inclusion of unnecessary work steps. Sometimes the inability to cite a good reason for doing something leads the audit program writer to the conclusion that the work step is not really needed.

     c. It makes possible a more intelligent review of the audit program for advance approval and postaudit review of work performed.
3. The audit program should be flexible and permit application of initiative in deviating from prescribed procedures. As the audit program is really a plan based on the audit work steps that the operational audit team believes will achieve the best results, once the actual results are determined, the auditors may want to change the plan.
4. The audit program should specifically provide for the development of individual findings. In this respect, it should help to:
     a. Determine why the results and conditions found are as they are, not just how they are. In effect, performance is analyzed, not simply reported.
     b. Direct attention to evidential matter in support of conclusions.
     c. Evaluate performance and evidence in comparison with relevant standards and norms of performance. Note that relevance is a judgment factor dependent on the experience, imagination, and common sense of the operational auditor.

3.4 WHO DEVELOPS THE AUDIT PROGRAM?

There is no good reason that the audit manager needs to be solely responsible for the development of the audit program. In fact, the more input into audit program development, the better the finished product. As a general rule, all members of the operational audit team should be involved in developing the audit program, particularly those staff members who were involved in the planning phase. In addition, others might be considered to provide input into the audit program development process, such as:

- Audit staff members who have some expertise in the area under review or who have participated in a similar audit in the past,
- Client personnel who work in the area being reviewed, who have some special input to provide (take care that such client personnel maintain their objectivity),
- Outside consultants or experts who have special expertise in the area being reviewed or in the operational audit process, and
- Personnel from similar organizations or functions who may be able to offer another perspective.

    The same personnel can also be used in the field work, development of audit findings and recommendations, and reporting phases of the operational audit. In fact, normally, the greater the mix of personnel involved in the operational audit, the greater the potential for positive results. Involving client personnel to the extent possible usually ensures a greater likelihood of the acceptance of recommendations. Often, the use of outside assistance enhances the quality of the operational audit, while allowing for the use of operational audit personnel in areas where they are most familiar. However, be aware that outside consultants can be costly—so use them judiciously.

Although the use of the team approach is recommended for the optimum development of the operational audit program, it can be more costly and time-consuming than having one or two operational audit team members develop the program. Moreover, it is not always cost-effective to use the team approach—particularly when there are a number of different areas or locations involved. Many times, the approach to be taken depends on the size of the audit and the total of budgeted operational auditing hours.

3.5 AUDIT PROGRAM WORK STEPS

After deciding on the makeup of the operational auditing program team, the next step is to develop the audit steps to be performed for each area identified as significant in the planning phase. Although, as previously mentioned, each operational auditing program is unique, this does not prevent the auditors from using specific audit work steps from previously completed operational audits—but they must be careful to use them only if they meet the requirements of the present operational audit. Otherwise, entirely new audit work steps need to be developed. To help in developing these work steps, the auditor needs to be aware of some of the more common techniques that can be used in the performance of the operational audit in the field work phase, such as the following:

1. Review of existing documentation, such as policy and procedures manuals.

2. Preparation of organization charts and related functional job descriptions.

3. Analysis of personnel policies and procedures related to hiring, orientation, training, evaluation, promotion, and firing.

4. Analysis of organizational policies and related systems and procedures, both administrative and operational.

5. Interviews with management and operations personnel.

6. Flowchart preparation:
   - Systems flowcharts, showing the processes of a functional area, and
   - Layout flow diagrams, showing the physical layout of a work area and its related work flow.
7. Ratio, change, and trend analysis.
8. Questionnaires, for use by the auditor or client's personnel.
9. Surveys, by phone or in written form, for customers, vendors, and so on to respond to.
10. Questions within the audit program.
11. Review of transactions, in which the different types of normal and abnormal transactions are considered.
12. Review of operations by techniques such as observation, work measurement, time studies, work performance forms or logs, and so on.
13. Forms analysis.
14. Analysis of results.
15. Review and analysis of management information system and related reports.
16. Compliance reviews, as to compliance with laws, regulations, policies, procedures, goals, objectives, and so forth.
17. Use of data processing, using computer-auditing "through the computer" techniques or review and analysis of computer-produced information.

These field work techniques should be used, of course, only where they are appropriate. Relative to the determination of which techniques to use in operational auditing is this rule: Whatever audit step works best in the situation, use it. There is no reason an auditor cannot use specific audit techniques that he or she or others used on different operational audits in the past. In fact, this should be encouraged, as it is usually easier and ensures a greater degree of success to use tried and true techniques rather than untried innovative approaches. However, this is not meant to discourage creative and innovative approaches to operational auditing work steps, as quite often such approaches are necessary to fit a specific situation and yield the greatest results in improved operations. To reemphasize: in establishing which operational auditing work steps to use, the goal is to identify those specific audit techniques that most closely fit the situation and have the best possibility of providing operational benefits.

3.6 AUDIT PROGRAM DEVELOPMENT PROCEDURES

In the development of the operational audit program, the audit team needs to keep in mind the following procedural steps:

1. Identification of the critical operational areas and their related control and risk areas. These risk areas usually relate to the inability to achieve the operational areas' goals and objectives. Objectives of such risk areas were presented in Chapter 2 for the purchasing function.

2. Development of key questions and work steps to validate and quantify the perceived risk areas. For instance, for the purchasing function, the auditor might question procedures relative to purchase specification changes, price changes, competitive bidding, and vendor relations and analysis.

3. Identification of the work steps needed to provide answers to the perceived risk areas and key questions. This entails the matching of the field work tasks mentioned above and others appropriate to the risk area in question. Work steps could include observations, flowcharts, interviews, and so on.

4. Development of audit work plans for each area to be reviewed; including personnel assignments, time schedules, and audit budgets.

As an example of using these steps to develop the audit program, consider the purchase requisitioning procedure. The identified control and risk areas include the possibility of not ordering needed materials and services, ordering materials or services that should not be ordered, or ordering more materials than are needed. The objective of the audit steps might then be to ascertain that only those materials or services that are needed are properly and timely ordered. The audit work steps that could help the auditor meet the audit objective might include the following:

1. Selecting a number of operating departments or units where the auditors would interview and review with department management and operations personnel the way their purchase requisitions are controlled and processed;

2. Identifying the need for selected materials, equipment, or services for approved purposes, plans, or programs;

3. Determining authority for purchase requisition approvals, including purpose and budgetary requirements within the operating department;
4. Analyzing the establishment of purchase lead times and their integration with departmental plans and activities;
5. Flowcharting the purchase requisition process to determine that there are adequate controls and processing procedures to ensure the accurate recording of all purchase requisitions and the subsequent processing by the purchasing function; and
6. Reviewing and analyzing purchase specification and quality control procedures to ensure that the right items are being ordered at the most economical prices.

3.7 SAMPLE AUDIT PROGRAM

A more complete sample operational audit program for the purchasing function that provides examples of many of these audit work step techniques is shown in Figure 3.1. Note that the sections of the work program and the corresponding areas within each section should relate back to the areas for further review as identified in the planning phase. For demonstration purposes, a number of different areas are presented for review, each of which could have been identified as significant in the planning phase. However, in the conduct of a typical operational audit, the number of areas to be reviewed would be based on the establishment of priorities as related to their significance and criticalness to overall operations and the amount of audit budget time allocated to this particular operational audit. In the audit program example in Figure 3.1, the following operational areas were selected for review:

1. Company policy and organization, including organizational status of the Purchasing Department, responsibility for purchasing, authorization for purchasing, and decentralized purchasing.
2. Purchasing Department operations, including department procedures, department forms, physical facilities, value analysis program, and collateral operations.
3. Review of purchase transactions, including selection of transactions to include various types of transactions that the auditor has identified as possible areas of deficiency, and examination of purchase transactions selected.
4. Records and reports—management information and controls being reported, as well as those that should be, but are not being reported.

3.7 SAMPLE AUDIT PROGRAM

FIGURE 3.1. Operational audit program: Purchasing function.

I. *COMPANY POLICY AND ORGANIZATION*
  A. *Organizational Status of Purchasing Department*
    1. Secure or prepare an organization chart of the Purchasing Department with descriptions of each work unit's specific functions. Determine to whom the head of the Purchasing Department reports. Perform analytical work to determine whether such reporting is proper or whether it results in operational concerns and problems. Analyze each work unit's functions to determine whether they are appropriate and proper Purchasing Department functions.
    2. Document the duties and responsibilities of each Purchasing Department employee. Obtain copies of existing job descriptions, and validate through interviewing each employee and related supervisor. Observe actual work being performed. Determine necessity of all duties and responsibilities.
  B. *Responsibility for Purchasing*
    1. Obtain or prepare company policy on purchasing functions and activities. Determine that the responsibility of the Purchasing Department is clearly defined and understood by Purchasing Department personnel and other nonpurchasing employees. Ascertain whether the Purchasing Department staff has knowledge of conflicting purchasing responsibility assumed by other departments. Document any principal procurement activities for which the Purchasing Department has no responsibility or limited responsibility.
    2. Obtain or prepare policy covering other departments' relations with vendors as to contacts or discussions with sales personnel or correspondence. Analyze such activities within selected operating departments to determine the extent of such vendor relations. Select a number of heavily used and critical vendors to survey as to their relations with the Purchasing Department and other departmental personnel. Use both telephone survey and written response survey techniques.
  C. *Authorization for Purchasing*
    1. Obtain copy of document policies as to:
        - Approval of purchases by departments requiring material.
        - Approval limits as to types of purchases and amounts.
        - Capital expenditures.
        - Budget approval prior to commitment.
    2. Analyze procedures through the review of selected transactions where the final cost of an order exceeds the amount originally estimated on the purchase order:
        - Where limit of approval of original signer is not exceeded by final cost.
        - Where limit of approval of original signer is exceeded.

AUDIT PROGRAM PHASE

FIGURE 3.1. *(Continued)*

   3. Analyze procedures through the review of selected transactions where changes are made in the quantity or specifications of the original purchase requisition.
   D. *Decentralized Purchasing*
      1. Determine company policies and procedures on purchases made by decentralized operating units, through petty cash, etc., as to:
         - Limits of authority.
         - Reporting responsibility.
         - Review or control by central Purchasing Department.
      2. Select a number of such decentralized operating units for review. Analyze their operations as to compliance with existing company policies related to decentralized purchasing.

      Note: The purpose of this portion of the audit is to learn of the policies and general conditions under which the Purchasing Department operates. The sources of information will usually be the head of the Purchasing Department, other Purchasing Department staff, and company manuals.

      Where policies are lacking or indefinite, there may be weakness in control, duplicating fields of responsibility, or other deficiency that will be evidenced in the course of the audit. Also evidenced will be variations between policy and actual operations.

II. *PURCHASING DEPARTMENT OPERATIONS*
   A. *Department Procedures*
      1. Obtain or prepare a copy of the Purchasing Department operating procedures.
      2. Prepare flowcharts of the major purchasing operations, such as the handling of requisitions, processing of purchase orders, control over open purchases, receipt of merchandise, and vendor payment procedures.
      3. Review procedures related to bidding by vendors:
         - Dollar amounts of orders on which bidding is required.
         - Requests for bids.
         - Forms of bids (sealed, oral, etc.).
         - Summarization of bids and selection of vendors.
   B. *Department Forms*

   Obtain a copy of each specialized form used by the Purchasing Department. These should be studied so that the purpose and usage is thoroughly understood. Areas to be considered include:
   - Purchase order form clear and complete, so that the vendor understands all terms and conditions.
   - Protection of blank purchase order forms.
   - Routing of copies of purchase order forms.
   - Necessity of each copy of the form.

3.7 SAMPLE AUDIT PROGRAM

FIGURE 3.1. *(Continued)*

- Forms designed for efficient and simple completion.
- Use of specialized forms to eliminate repetitive processing such as:
- Traveling requisitions: for repetitive orders of the same item.
- Blanket purchase orders: for repetitive purchases from the same vendor.

Note: It is common to find overelaborate routines relating to the preparation of purchasing forms, particularly the purchase order. The result is the unnecessary duplication of files in various departments.

C. *Physical Facilities*

Prepare a layout flow diagram of the Purchasing Department showing its layout and general facilities, with particular attention to:
- Work flow efficiencies and inefficiencies.
- Arrangements for reception of and interviews with salespeople.
- Office layout for effective/ineffective operations.

D. *Value Analysis Program*
1. Review the Purchasing Department's "value analysis" program, including:
   - Determination that price revisions covering changes in materials and methods are negotiated with vendors.
   - Review of market trends, particularly on long-term contracts and contracts containing escalation clauses.

   Note: In a value analysis program, the Purchasing Department works with vendors and with affected company departments (such as engineering and production) in the analysis of specifications, consumption, and requirements. Through such analysis and cooperative effort, it is possible to make savings through redesign, change in specifications, purchase in more economical quantities, or manufacture by the company itself.

E. *Collateral Operations*
1. Determine and describe all operations performed in the Purchasing Department that are not directly concerned with placing orders and follow-up for delivery. For example, the Purchasing Department may be assigned responsibility for such operations as:
   - Reporting on quantity, quality, and timeliness of received materials.
   - Authorization of payments to vendors.
   - Sale of scrap.
   - Purchases for employees.

   In the audit of the collateral operations of the Purchasing Department, the auditor will have a twofold concern: first, the effect that the inclusion of these operations under the responsibility of the Purchasing Department will have, as far as internal control is concerned; second, the audit of the assigned collateral operations.

FIGURE 3.1. *(Continued)*

Because of the many variables, it is not possible to specify any definite program for the audit of specific collateral responsibilities of the Purchasing Department. The auditor must shape his or her study to cover each situation, and it may develop that a supplementary interdepartmental survey of a particular field should be made.

III. *REVIEW OF PURCHASE TRANSACTIONS*
  A. *Selection of Transactions*
  Examine files covering all purchase orders placed over a period of XX months. From these, select, for detailed examination, orders that include some of each of the following:
  - Purchases made by each buyer.
  - Requisitions by each major operating department.
  - A number of "Rush" and "Confirming Delivery" orders.
  - Single orders divided among several suppliers.
  - Orders in which purchase is not made from lowest bidder.
  - Orders in which final specifications or quantities are revised from the original requisition.
  - Orders in which freight is allowed.
  - Orders for capital equipment.
  - Orders in which price is not specified, or that include some variable pricing arrangement.
  - Orders providing for trade-in allowances.
  - Orders in which substantial overshipment is made and accepted.
  - Blanket or continuing orders, in which a number of deliveries are made over a period.
  - Orders in which specification of item, quantity, or price is not definite.
  - Orders placed under long-term purchase contracts.

  Note: The selection of an adequate sample of orders is of utmost importance. The objective is to set aside for detailed examination a group of purchase orders that will adequately represent both the "normal" and the "abnormal." There must be enough of the "normal" for the auditor to verify general policies and procedures and reveal situations that may call for more extensive examination.

  B. *Examination of Purchase Transactions Selected*
  The examination of each type of purchase transaction selected should be completed in enough detail, through examination of all supporting records, to enable the auditor to acquire sufficient knowledge as to how each of the operations—from origination and approval of requisition to the completion of the order—was handled. The auditor must be constantly concerned with what was done and why, to achieve satisfaction that each order was placed and handled in the best interests of the company.

3.7 SAMPLE AUDIT PROGRAM

FIGURE 3.1. *(Continued)*

It is through this examination that the auditor may become aware of situations, in the Purchasing Department or in other departments of the company, that require further study. The objectives are (1) through verification, to provide the basis for appraisal of current policies and procedures and (2) to give a basis for constructive recommendation. The following list is intended only as a sample of questions that will occupy the auditor's attention and may be the subject for further inquiry:

- Where an order was divided among several vendors, what was the reason?
- On "Confirming Orders," did an operating department really assume the purchasing function?
- If orders are placed for such items as memberships, just what is gained by clearing these through purchasing routines?
- Are there any indications of favoritism to vendors?
- Where changes are made from original specifications in a requisition or order, are these adequately approved and brought to the attention of those who should be concerned?
- How are allowances and adjustments handled and approved?
- Are transportation allowances verified?
- If price is omitted from an order, why?
- If an order calls for services or materials on a "cost plus" or other basis indefinite as to exact amount, how are final charges verified?
- Does the employee approving a requisition appear to have adequate information to enable intelligent approval?
- How are trade-in arrangements determined and approved? (It is often possible to secure more for replaced equipment by outside sale than by trade-in.)
- How completely do possible sources of supply seem to be covered?
- Are F.O.B. points and routings shown and followed?
- Does it appear that effort is made to ship by most economical methods? Is the traffic department consulted regarding routes and methods?
- How were long-term contracts negotiated?
- What consideration is given to the tax status of materials—sales and use taxes, excise taxes, etc.?

IV. *RECORDS AND REPORTS*

The various records that are used in current operations will have been reviewed and appraised in the study of departmental procedures. This will include such records as those showing sources of supply and numerical listings of purchase orders placed.

Beyond these will be a variety of records and reports that are not required in the normal flow of work but are maintained to provide informa-

FIGURE 3.1. *(Continued)*

tion considered valuable for administrative response. Examples of this type of record or report are:
- Records of orders placed with each vendor.
- Records of orders placed by each buyer, showing number of orders and total value.
- Reports of future commitments.
- Reports of departmental operations to management.
- Reports of commodity price trends to operating departments.
- Reports that have been rendered to management covering special savings or other accomplishments.

The examination and appraisal of records and reports has two objectives:

A. First should come verification of the accuracy of the records or statements that are maintained or reported. This should be done on a test basis. For example, if a saving was claimed, there should be a test to be sure that the claimed saving was actually realized.

B. After verification of the general accuracy, the second step is appraisal of the value to the department or executive using or receiving the record or report. In this appraisal, the auditor should ascertain the answers to such questions as:
- Is each record really used?
- Does each report serve a useful purpose?
- Does each report give a complete and accurate picture?
- Are reports incomplete, so that important factors are not brought to management's attention?

The answers to these and other questions that arise will require discussions with those who prepare the records and reports and with those who receive and use them.

3.8 OPERATIONAL AUDIT ENGAGEMENT BUDGET

At this point, the operational auditing team has finalized the initial audit program. This was accomplished by identifying the specific audit work steps and techniques to use for the significant operational areas selected for review. Now the amount of time necessary to complete each work step must be determined to arrive at an overall engagement budget. For those audit work steps and techniques that have been used on previous operational audits, there is some experience upon which to base budget estimates. However, for new work steps or techniques best professional judgment will have to be used in arriving at budgeted hours.

Keep in mind that an operational audit budget needs to be flexible and is subject to change, unlike a financial audit budget, which is more static. Such flexibility in budgeting is necessary because of the greater possibilities of budget changes. These changes result from activities performed in the field work phase—either requiring additional time for areas warranting more attention or less time for areas found to be less critical than expected.

For instance, additional field work may be needed when the area under review requires more analysis to identify findings and recommendations for operational improvements; or additional significant operational deficiencies may be identified that were not included in the initial audit program scope, which require additional budget hours or reallocation of existing budget hours. It can also happen that an area under review may not yield significant operational audit findings to the extent originally expected. If that happens, the auditor should stop operational audit efforts as soon as this situation is determined and reallocate any hours remaining in the budget for these planned work steps to other work steps.

Sample operational audit budgets for the Figure 3.1 audit work program are shown for the Planning Phase in Figure 3.2 and for the Field Work and Reporting Phases in Figure 3.3. Note that these budgets are prepared prior to the actual work and are best estimates, subject to change.

The operational audit budgets presented in Figures 3.2 and 3.3 are for a relatively large audit of a purchasing function. They are presented as examples of audit programs for both the planning phase and the field work and reporting phases. The scope, extent, and number of hours needed to perform a specific operational audit in a given situation would, of course, need to be scaled downward or upward as appropriate.

The estimated budget hours shown in the audit program examples are intended only as representations. They are not meant to imply or relate to actual hours required. Note that the planning phase normally takes a substantial amount of audit time as compared with the field work phase—in the example, 226 hours as compared with 630 hours, or approximately one-third.

AUDIT PROGRAM PHASE

FIGURE 3.2. Operational audit budget: Purchasing function, planning phase.

PLANNING PHASE

	Hrs	Dates	Staff
1. *Goals and Objectives*			
a. *Review legislative and internal materials* that define general goals and objectives	6	3-1/2	Mary
b. *Planning systems and procedures*			
• Document with narrative and/or flowchart	12	3-1/3-3	Bill
• Determine planning: long term and short term	4	3-3	Bill
• Review present plans: goals and objectives	4	3-3/4	Bill
• Review detail plans and reporting systems	6	3-4/5	Bill
	32		
2. *Budgets*			
a. Review budget process, as related to plans	3	3-8	Bill
b. Review budget justification procedures	2	3-8	Bill
c. Analyze budget reporting procedures:	6	3-8 to 3-10	Bill
• Budget versus actual			
• Flexible budgeting			
• Monitoring and controls			
	11		
3. *Organization Chart and Procedures Manuals*			
a. Obtain copy or prepare org chart and analyze	6	3-10/11	Betty
b. Obtain copy of procedures manuals and review	8	3-11/3-16	Betty
	14		
4. *Flowcharts*			
a. Familiarize with Purchasing Department procedures	4	3-8	Mike
b. Prepare general systems flowcharts of major systems and procedures	16	3-8/3-10	Mike
c. Analyze flowcharts	8	3-10/11	Mike
	28		

3.8 OPERATIONAL AUDIT ENGAGEMENT BUDGET

FIGURE 3.2. *(Continued)*

PLANNING PHASE

		Hrs	Dates	Staff
5.	*Reports*			
	a. Obtain copies of management/ operating reports	2	3-1/2	Mary/Cliff
	b. Discuss reports with appropriate personnel and write up description of each report	10	3-2/3-4	Mary/Cliff
	c. Review and analyze reports	6	3-4/5	Mary/Cliff
		18		
6.	*Personnel*			
	a. Obtain current job descriptions and review	4	3-8	Jane/Roy
	b. Review personnel folders; compare background to job description	6	3-8/9	Jane/Roy
	c. Analyze personnel functions: • Experience and training requirements • Determination of number of staff required • Formal or informal staff training • Employee evaluation procedures	8	3-10/11	Jane/Roy
	d. Prepare summary of positions and compare with: • Organization charts • Budgets • Job descriptions	6	3-11/12	Jane
	e. Observe employees at work	5	3-9/10	Jane/Roy
	f. Review employee statistics: • Turnover rate • Sick leave • Lateness • Overtime	4	3-11/12	Jane
		33		

AUDIT PROGRAM PHASE

FIGURE 3.2. *(Continued)*

PLANNING PHASE

		Hrs	Dates	Staff
7.	*Facilities*			
	a. Observe work layout and working conditions	4	3-15	Mike
	b. Prepare and analyze work layout flow diagram	4	3-15/16	Mike
	c. Review use of equipment	2	3-16	Mike
	d. Analyze general operating procedures	2	3-16	Mike
	e. Review fixed assets used in operations	4	3-15	Jane
		16		
8.	*Review of Planning Phase Results*	10	3-17/19	Betty
	Total Planning Phase Worksteps	162		
9.	*Preparation of Planning Phase Audit Program*	24	2-23/24	Betty/Cliff
10.	*Ongoing Audit Management*	40		Betty/Cliff
	Grand Total Budget	226		

It is important to understand the significance of the planning phase activities and not to look for audit budget shortcuts. A well defined and performed planning phase not only helps to focus correctly on the right operational activities to review during the field work phase, but it also helps to reduce unnecessary field work audit steps. Bear in mind that both of these audit programs are front-end estimates as to the necessary work steps and budget hours required. These are subject to change, based on actual conditions found to be in existence as a result of the performance of the audit work steps themselves. Accordingly, the audit work program could be changed dramatically upward or downward.

3.8 OPERATIONAL AUDIT ENGAGEMENT BUDGET

FIGURE 3.3. Sample operational audit budget: Purchasing function, field work phase.

FIELD WORK PHASE

	Hrs	Dates	Staff
1. *Company Policy and Organization*			
a. Organization Status of Purchasing Department			
• Organization chart and analysis.	20	3-25/30	Bill
• Employees' duties and responsibilities.	30	3-26/4-7	Bill
b. Responsibility for Purchasing			
• Purchasing functions and activities.	8	4-12/13	Bill
• Relations with vendors.	12	4-15/20	Bill
c. Authorization for Purchasing			
• Approval of purchases.	4	3-22/23	Jane
• Procedures: final cost exceeds PO amount.	3	3-23	Jane
• Procedures: quantity or spec changes.	3	3-23	Jane
d. Decentralized Purchasing			
• Policies and procedures.	6	3-25/26	Joe
• Review of decentralized operating units.	14	3-29/31	Joe
Total Company Policy and Organization	100		
2. *Purchasing Department Operations*			
a. Department Procedures			
• Purchasing department operating procedures.	8	3-29/30	Mike
• Flowcharts: purchase requisitions and orders.	32	3-30/4-6	Mike
• Bidding by vendors procedure.	10	4-5/4-6	Mike
b. Department Forms	20	3-31/4-5	Mary
c. Physical Facilities	12	3-29/3-30	Roy
d. Value Analysis Program	8	3-25/3-26	Cliff
e. Collateral Operations	16	3-29/4-1	Jane
Total Purchasing Department operations	106		

AUDIT PROGRAM PHASE

FIGURE 3.3. *(Continued)*

FIELD WORK PHASE

	Hrs	Dates	Staff
3. *Review of Purchase Transactions*			
a. Selection of Transactions	20	4-7/12	Joe/Beth
b. Examination of Purchase Transactions	30	4-13/20	Joe Beth
Total Review of Purchase Transactions	50		
4. *Records and Reports*			
a. Verification of Accuracy of the Records	12	4-20/22	Jane
b. Appraisal of Value to the Department	22	4-23/29	Jane
Total Records and Reports	34		
5. *Review of Field Work Results*	60	4-28/5-7	Betty/Cliff
Total Field Work Phase Worksteps	350		
6. *Development of Findings*	80	5-10/19	Betty/Bill Jane/Mary Cliff/Roy
7. *Oral Reporting*			
a. Preparation for Meetings	8	4-9,30	Betty/Cliff
b. Meetings with Client Personnel	12	5-20/21	Betty/Cliff
8. *Written Report: Draft and Final*	40	5-24/6-2	Betty, Bill, and Cliff
Total Audit Program Worksteps	490		
9. *Preparation of Audit Program*	40	3-17/19	All
10. *Ongoing Audit Management*	100	Ongoing	Betty and Cliff
Grand Total Budget	630		

3.9 ASSIGNMENT OF STAFF

The audit team needs to be flexible about shifting work steps to be performed, as well as the assigning of audit personnel, estimated budget hours, and scheduled start and completion times. This requires the exercise of proper and adequate management control over the operational audit engagement, together with sufficient reporting from operational audit staff to provide timely identification of any work scope changes. For the greatest effectiveness in conducting and controlling the audit program, there must be cohesive team effort between operational audit management, staff, and client personnel.

3.9 ASSIGNMENT OF STAFF

Once the audit program has been developed and work steps have been identified, the next step in the audit program phase is to assign appropriate staff personnel to conduct each work step. In a financial audit, assigning personnel to specific audit steps is a fairly simple matter, as there is great interchangeability between staff members in their ability to perform required audit procedures. In addition, many of the audit steps are repetitions of other financial audits and even from the same audit performed in previous years. But not so in an operational audit. First, some of the required audit steps for a particular operational audit may be one-time activities, whereby they are being performed for the first time and may or may not be done again.

Second, certain audit work steps may require specific specialized skills, such as analytical ability, communications skills, knowledge of specific systems and procedures, perceptual ability, organizational and personnel structure skills, and specific technical abilities.

Accordingly, it is extremely important in the performance of an operational audit to match the skills and abilities needed to perform effectively a specific audit work step with staff members' expertise in performing a particular work step. Theoretically, the closer the match between the skills needed for a particular work step and the skills possessed by the staff member doing the work, the greater the results. In reality, there is not always the luxury of having sufficient staff to assign to optimize such a matching of skills. What normally happens is that an effort is made to optimize such skills matching based on staff personnel available, while dealing with the constraint of having to perform audit steps requiring similar skills within the same time frame. The critical task of assigning the right staff members to the right work steps often becomes a case of "making the best of the situation."

3.10 OPERATIONAL AUDIT MANAGEMENT

The initial consideration in assigning staff to the operational audit is audit management. Where possible, it is always best to share such audit management responsibilities between the operational audit staff and the client's operational personnel. The operational audit staff manager should be clearly responsible for the technical content and timely completion of the operational audit work steps, while the client's staff person should be responsible for ensuring the cooperation of departmental management and operational personnel, as well as providing liaison, coordination, and integration between operational personnel and the operational audit staff. The specific individuals selected to manage the operational audit are extremely critical to its ultimate success. They should be selected most carefully, considering such attributes as:

1. Past performance on operational audits.
2. Knowledge and experience relative to the area being reviewed.
3. Ability to effectively manage for results.
4. Ability to recognize operational deficiencies, identify the causes, and recommend realistic improvements.
5. Communication skills with operational audit staff members, client management and operations personnel, and organizational decision makers.
6. Expertise or understanding in required technical skills such as interviewing, flowcharting, and so on.
7. Ability to work together with the operational audit team and client personnel.
8. Flexibility as to changes in identified critical areas, audit work steps, and audit staff assignments.
9. Persuasiveness required to convince client management to implement developed recommendations.

3.10 OPERATIONAL AUDIT MANAGEMENT

10. Organizational skills to keep the various pieces of the operational audit together in a cohesive and understandable framework.

The managers assigned to the operational audit—for example, Betty White, of the operational auditing staff, and Cliff Chambers, the purchasing supervisor from the client's operations—in our case study of the Example Company, would then be responsible for assigning the staff to work on the operational audit. In most instances, the starting point is to determine which audit staff members, client personnel, and outside technical assistance are available for assignment during the time required to conduct the operational audit.

The process then becomes one of scheduling the best fit between audit work steps and personnel attributes. For example, the audit staff available to perform the operational audit of the Example Company purchasing function are Joe Super, audit senior; Jane Plath, audit junior; Beth Herman, a new auditor; and Bill Brown, audit supervisor. Client personnel available to be assigned to this operational audit include Roy David, a Buyer II, and Mary George, the Standard Specifications Unit supervisor. In addition, Mike Clark, an outside consultant is available to provide assistance. Descriptions of each of these individuals and their availability are shown in Figure 3.4.

Based on these sketches of available personnel, the audit managers, Betty White and Cliff Chambers, must assign the appropriate staff to each proposed audit program work step. Note that the preparation of the planning phase audit program would most likely be done by the operational audit managers with additional assistance as requested (for example, other audit staff, client personnel, outside consultants), while the field work audit program would be prepared by all concerned. Many times the field work audit program must be submitted to management prior to the start of the operational audit. However, in most instances it will be changed as a result of the planning phase. The preparation and submission of field work audit programs prior to the completion of the planning phase is particularly difficult to achieve with any degree of accuracy. It is good practice to request that management wait until completion of the planning phase. This is even more critical for outside auditors, as they may be forced to provide budgets and fees before they are aware of the scope of the work.

Audit management would then assign the work steps of the planning phase and field work phase, based on the personnel available. It is good practice to document the operational audit team on an organization chart, showing reporting relationships and time availability, similar to that shown in Figure 3.5. To help audit managers assign staff to work steps based on

AUDIT PROGRAM PHASE

FIGURE 3.4. Operational audit, descriptions of personnel available: The Example Company.

1. Joe Super, operational audit senior who has reviewed the purchasing function's internal controls in the past and is known for his ability to get along with client management and operations personnel.
   Availability: March 22 to April 30.

2. Jane Plath, an experienced audit junior who is well respected for her ability to perform technical assignments in an orderly and timely manner.
   Availability: Immediately, through duration of audit, as her schedule allows.

3. Beth Herman, a recent addition to the audit staff who has proven to be conscientious and a hard worker but requires direct supervision.
   Availability: April 5 to May 20 on limited basis per schedule.

4. Bill Brown, an operational audit supervisor, with past experience and special expertise in the areas of planning and budget systems.
   Availability: As needed on limited basis, with exception of possible one-day schedule conflicts.

5. Roy David, a Buyer II in the Purchasing Department, with more than 15 years' experience with the organization, 8 of them in the Purchasing Department. He is extremely knowledgeable about the purchasing functions, particularly purchasing policies and procedures.
   Availability: Up to two days per week for the duration of the operational audit.

6. Mary George, the Standard Specifications Unit supervisor, who has worked in all of the Purchasing Department's functions during her 18 years with the organization.
   Availability: Up to two days per week for the duration of the operational audit, but normally not the same two days as Roy David is assigned to the operational audit.

7. Mike Clark, an outside consultant who has worked with the audit organization before in the performance of other operational audits. His special areas of expertise include systems and procedures, flowcharting, facilities layout and work flow, and data processing.
   Availability: As needed with exception of other client commitments.

3.10 OPERATIONAL AUDIT MANAGEMENT

FIGURE 3.5. Operational auditing: Purchasing function project team organization chart.

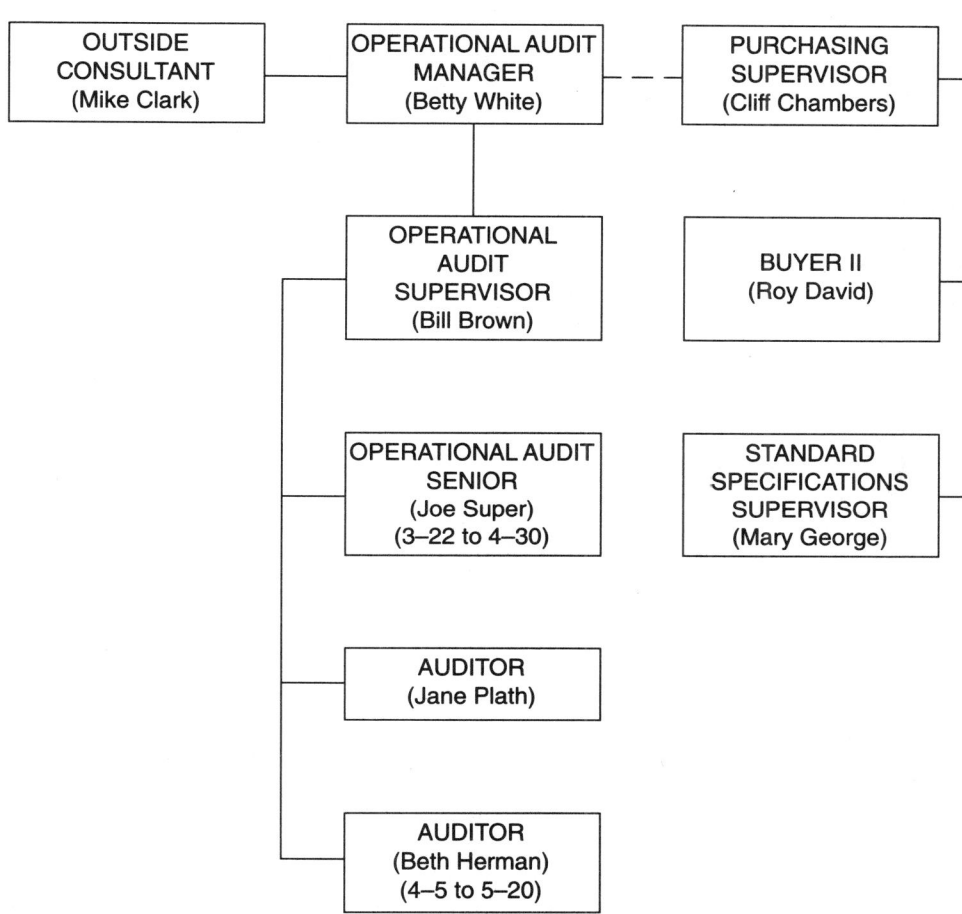

AUDIT PROGRAM PHASE

time availability, they could use an audit program calendar, as illustrated in Figure 3.6, showing the available work days.

Once staff assignments are made for the work steps, the planned dates for completion and the staff assigned to each work step are noted on the audit budget. Please refer to Figures 3.2 and 3.3; note that assignments have been based on personnel capabilities and time availability.

FIGURE 3.6. Operational auditing: Purchasing function audit program calendar.

	M	T	W	TH	F	
MARCH	1	2	3	4	5	⎫
	8	9	10	11	12	⎬ PLANNING PHASE
	15	16	17	18	19	⎬
	22	23	24	25	26	⎭
	29	30	31			
APRIL				1	X̶	⎫
	5	6	7	8	9	⎬ FIELD WORK PHASE
	12	13	14	15	16	
	19	20	21	22	23	
	26	27	28	29	30	⎭
MAY	3	4	5	6	7	⎫
	10	11	12	13	14	⎬ DEVELOPMENT OF FINDINGS AND REPORTING PHASE
	17	18	19	20	21	
	24	25	26	27	28	
	3̶0̶					⎭

3.11 OPERATIONAL AUDIT SCHEDULE CONTROL

The operational audit, including the planning, field work, and reporting phases of the purchasing function, is scheduled to be performed during the 14-week period of March 1 through June 2. The planning phase is scheduled for the 3-week period of March 1 through March 19; the field work phase is scheduled for the 7-week period of March 22 through May 7; and the development of findings and reporting phase is scheduled for the 4-week period of May 10 through June 2.

Note that the performance of the operational audit is not always a continuum, owing to staff scheduling conflicts, unavailability of needed client personnel, and so on. The audit program calendar (Figure 3.6) shows total elapsed time and does not necessarily imply that operational auditing work steps will be continually performed. Another tool that could be used in operational auditing staff scheduling is a Gantt chart. This type of chart graphically depicts the major audit work steps, their scheduled time frames and personnel assignments, and the interrelationships between work steps. Examples of Gantt charts for both the planning and field work phases are shown in Figure 3.7.

If Gantt charts are used, the completion of the chart with scheduled dates and personnel assignments allows audit management the ease of filling in the columns for scheduled dates and staff assigned on the operational audit budget forms (Figures 3.2 and 3.3). These two tools then act as effective scheduling control documents.

3.12 ENGAGEMENT CONTROL

Before starting the actual operational audit, the engagement manager should prepare some form of engagement control tool. Samples of such forms are shown as follows:

- Planning Phase Budget Hours Control, by personnel and time period—Figure 3.8.

- Planning Phase Budget Hours Control, by task and personnel—Figure 3.9.

- Field Work Phase Budget Hours Control, by task and personnel—Figure 3.10.

- Field Work Phase Budget Hours Control, by personnel and time period—Figure 3.11.

Any or all of these forms may be used for control purposes in conducting the operational audit, or original forms can be designed.

AUDIT PROGRAM PHASE

FIGURE 3.7. Operational auditing: Purchasing function, planning Field Work Phase Gantt charts.

Audit Work Steps	Budgeted Hours	Personnel Assigned
I. Goals and Objectives		
A. Review legislative/internal materials	6	Mary
B. Planning systems and procedures		
1. Narrative and/or flowchart	12	Bill
2. Determine extent of planning	4	Bill
3. Review present planS	4	Bill
4. Review detail plans	6	Bill
	32	
II. Budgets		
A. Review budget process	3	Bill
B. Review budget justification procedures	2	Bill
C. Analyze budget reporting procedures	6	Bill
	11	
III. Organization Chart and Procedures Manual		
A. Obtain copy or prepare organization chart and analyze	6	Betty
B. Obtain copy of procedures manual and review	8	Betty
	14	
IV. Flowcharts		
A. Familiarize with purchasing department and its operations	4	Mike
B. Prepare general systems flowcharts	16	Mike
C. Analyze flowcharts	8	Mike
	28	
V. Reports		
A. Obtain copies of management and operating reports	2	Mary/Cliff
B. Discuss reports and prepare written description	10	Mary/Cliff
C. Review and analyze reports	6	Mary/Cliff
	18	
VI. Personnel		
A. Obtain current job descriptions and review	4	Jane/Roy
B. Review personnel folders	6	Jane/Roy
C. Analyze personnel functions	8	Jane/Roy
D. Prepare summary of positions and compare	6	Jane
E. Observe employees at work	5	Jane/Roy
F. Review employee statistics	4	Jane
	33	
VII. Facilities		
A. Observe and analyze work layout	4	Mike
B. Prepare/analyze layout flow diagram	4	Mike
C. Review use of equipment	2	Mike
D. Analyze general operating procedures	2	Mike
E. Review fixed assets used in operations	4	Jane
	16	
VIII. Review of Planning Phase Results	10	Betty
IX. Preparation of Audit Program—By 3-1	24	Betty/Cliff
X. Audit Management	40	Betty/Cliff
Total Budgeted Hours	226	

3.12 ENGAGEMENT CONTROL

FIGURE 3.7. *(Continued)*

AUDIT PROGRAM PHASE

FIGURE 3.7. *(Continued)*

Audit Work Steps	Budgeted Hours	Personnel Assigned
I. Company Policy and Organization		
A. Organization status of purchasing department		
1. Organization chart analysis	20	Bill
2. Employee duties and responsibilities	30	Bill
B. Responsibility for purchasing		
1. Purchase functions/activities	8	Bill
2. Relations with vendors	12	Bill
C. Authorization for purchasing		
1. Approval of purchase	4	Jane
2. Final cost exceeds PO amount	3	Jane
3. Quantity or specification changes	3	Jane
D. Decentralized purchasing		
1. Policies and procedures	6	Joe
2. Review of decentralized units	14	Joe
	100	
II. Purchasing Department Operations		
A. Department procedures		
1. Operating procedures	8	Mike
2. Flowcharts: purchase reqs and orders	32	Mike
3. Bidding by vendors	10	Mike
B. Department forms	20	Mary
C. Physical facilities	12	Roy
D. Value analysis program	8	Cliff
E. Collateral operations	16	Jane
	106	
III. Review of Purchase Transactions		
A. Selection of transactions	20	Joe/Beth
B. Review of transactions	30	Joe/Beth
	50	
IV. Records and Reports		
A. Verification of accuracy	12	Jane
B. Value to the department	22	Jane
	34	
V. Review of Field Work Results	60	Betty/Cliff/Bill
VI. Development of Findings	80	Betty/Bill/Jane
VII. Oral Reporting	20	Mary/Cliff/Roy
VIII. Written Report	40	Betty/Cliff/Bill
Total Audit Work Steps	490	
IX. Preparation of Audit Program 3-17 to 3-19	40	All
X. Audit Management	100	Betty/Cliff
Grand Total Budget	630	

3.12 ENGAGEMENT CONTROL

FIGURE 3.7. *(Continued)*

Week Ending Date of Worksteps to Be Performed on Audit
3/26	4/2	4/9	4/16	4/23	4/30	5/7	5/14	5/21	5/28	6/2

FIGURE 3.8. Operational audit: Purchasing function, planning phase budget hours control by personnel and time period.

*B = Budget
A = Actual
D = Difference

Auditor's Name	*	3/1	3/2	3/3	3/4	3/5	3/8	3/9	3/10	3/11	3/12	3/15	3/16	3/17	3/18	3/19	Total Hours
Betty White—Manager	B								3	3	2	3	3	2	4	4	24
	A																
	D																
Bill Brown—Supervisor	B	4	6	8	5	3	6	5									37
	A																
	D																
Jane Plath—Auditor	B						3	4	4	6	4	4					25
	A																
	D																
Mike Clark—Consultant	B						6	8	8	6	4	6	6				40
	A																
	D																
Cliff Chambers— Purchasing Supervisor	B	1	2	2	2	2											9
	A																
	D																
Roy David—Buyer II	B						3	2	3	4							12
	A																
	D																
Mary George—Standard Specifications Supervisor	B	4	3	2	3	3											15
	A																
	D																
Totals	B	9	11	12	10	8	18	19	18	19	6	13	9	2	4	4	162
	A																
	D																

3.13 EXAMPLE COMPANY AUDIT PROGRAM PHASE

Consider again the Example Company to see how the audit program phase might work for the operational audit of its purchasing function. Several operational areas were identified in the planning phase for further review:

1. Organization concerns, including the function and authority of the Purchasing Department and personnel, and the function and necessity of specific job classifications.

2. Purchasing Department responsibility for processing regular purchase orders and processing outside the central Purchasing Department.

3. Purchase order processing procedures, including purchase requisitions, purchase order processing, open purchase order control, and work flow.

4. Purchase order preparation costs, including the cost to process a purchase order, its relationship to the amount of the actual purchase, such as under $50, $50 to $100, and $100 to $200; and the annual cost to process such small purchases.

Suggested audit work steps are shown for the completed audit program in Figure 3.12. Refer to the list of operational auditing field work techniques in Section 3.5.

3.14 CONCLUSION

These audit work steps will be followed up in the next chapter on the field work phase, but for now, remember: not all audit work steps developed in the audit program phase result in the development of significant operational audit findings. However, because the auditor does not know which audit steps will provide the most significant findings, all work steps in an audit plan must be followed through. The Example Company audit program will be followed through in the field work phase, and then identified findings will be developed and reported in succeeding chapters.

This concludes Chapter 3. However, before proceeding to Chapter 4, concerning the field work phase, review the operational auditing situation in Figure 3.13.

AUDIT PROGRAM PHASE

FIGURE 3.9. Operational audit: Purchasing function, planning phase budget control by task and personnel.

Audit Work Steps	Budgeted Hours
I. Goals and Objectives	
A. Review legislative/internal materials	6
B. Planning systems and procedures	
1. Narrative and/or flowchart	12
2. Determine extent of planning	4
3. Review present plans	4
4. Review detail plans	6
	32
II. Budgets	
A. Review budget process	3
B. Review budget justification procedures	2
C. Analyze budget reporting procedures	6
	11
III. Organization Chart and Procedures Manual	
A. Organization chart and analysis	6
B. Procedures manual and review	8
	14
IV. Flowcharts	
A. Familiarize: purchasing dept. operations	4
B. Prepare general systems flowcharts	16
C. Analyze flowcharts	8
	28
V. Reports	
A. Management and operating reports	2
B. Discuss reports and prepare written description	10
C. Review and analyze reports	6
	18
VI. Personnel	
A. Job descriptions and review	4
B. Review personnel folders	6
C. Analyze personnel functions	8
D. Prepare summary of positions	6
E. Observe employees at work	5
F. Review employee statistics	4
	33
VII. Facilities	
A. Observe and analyze work layout	4
B. Prepare/analyze layout flow diagram	4
C. Review use of equipment	2
D. Analyze general operating procedures	2
E. Review fixed assets used in operations	4
	16
VIII. Review of Planning Phase and Results	10
IX. Preparation of Audit Program	24
X. Audit Management	40
Total Budgeted Hours	226
Billing Rates	
Estimated Budget Dollars	$10,770

3.14 CONCLUSION

FIGURE 3.9. *(Continued)*

Betty White	Bill Brown	Jane Plath	Mike Clark	Cliff Chambers	Roy David	Mary George
						6
	12					
	4					
	4					
	6					
	3					
	2					
	6					
6						
8						
			4			
			16			
			8			
				1		1
				5		5
				3		3
		2			2	
		3			3	
		3			5	
		6				
		3			2	
		4				
			4			
			4			
			2			
			2			
		4				
10						
12				12		
24				16		
60	37	25	40	37	12	15
$80	$60	$30	$75			
$4,800	$2,220	$750	$3,000			

FIGURE 3.10. Operational audit: Purchasing function, field work phase budget control by task and personnel.

Audit Work Steps	Budgeted Hours
I. Company Policy and Organization	
A. Organization status of purchasing department	
1. Organization chart analysis	20
2. Employee duties and responsibilities	30
B. Responsibility for purchasing	
1. Purchase functions/activities	8
2. Relations with vendors	12
C. Authorization for purchasing	
1. Approval of purchasing	4
2. Final cost exceeds PO amount	3
3. Quantity or specification changes	3
D. Decentralized purchasing	
1. Policies and procedures	6
2. Review of decentralized units	14
	100
II. Purchasing Department Operations	
A. Department procedures	
1. Operating procedures	8
2. Flowcharts: purchase requisitions and orders	32
3. Bidding by vendors	10
B. Department forms	20
C. Physical facilities	12
D. Value analysis program	8
E. Collateral operations	16
	106
III. Review of Purchase Transactions	
A. Selection of transactions	20
B. Review of transactions	30
	50
IV. Records and Reports	
A. Verification of accuracy	12
B. Value to the department	22
	34
V. Review of Field Work Results	60
VI. Development of Findings	80
VII. Oral Reporting	20
VIII. Written Report	40
Total Audit Work Steps	490
IX. Preparation of Audit Program	40
X. Audit Management	100
Grand Total Budget	630
Billing Rates	
Estimated Budget Dollars	$29,280

3.14 CONCLUSION

FIGURE 3.10. *(Continued)*

Betty White	Bill Brown	Joe Super	Jane Plath	Beth Herman	Mike Clark	Cliff Chambers	Roy David	Mary George
	20							
	30							
	8							
	12							
			4					
			3					
			3					
		6						
		14						
					8			
					32			
					10			
								20
							12	
						8		
			16					
		8		12				
		12		18				
				12				
				22				
24	24					12		
8	18		22			12	10	10
10						10		
12	20					8		
54	132	40	82	30	50	50	22	30
12	8	4	4	2	2	4	2	2
80						20		
146	140	44	86	32	52	74	24	32
$80	$60	$40	$30	$30	$75			
$11,680	$8,400	$1,760	$2,580	$960	$3,900			

141

FIGURE 3.11. Operational audit: Purchasing function, field work phase budget hours control by personnel and time period.

Auditor's Name	*	3/26	4/2	4/9	4/16	4/23	4/30	5/7	5/14	5/21	5/28	6/2	Total
Betty White—Manager	B A D			3			11	16	4	8	6	6	54
Bill Brown—Supervisor	B A D	16	22	12	12	8	8	16	12	6	10	10	132
Joe Super—Senior	B A D	6	14	4	12	4							40
Jane Plath—Auditor	B A D	10	16			16	18		12	10			82
Beth Herman—Auditor	B A D			8	18	4							30
Mike Clark—Consultant	B A D		28	22									50
Cliff Chambers— Purchasing Supervisor	B A D	8		3			7	8	6	10	4	4	50
Roy David—Buyer II	B A D		12						6	4			22
Mary George—Standard Specifications Supervisor	B A D		16	4					6	4			30
Totals	B A D	40	108	56	42	32	44	40	46	42	20	20	490

*B = Budget
A = Actual
D = Difference

FIGURE 3.12. Purchasing function, operational auditing audit program: The Example Company.

I. *Organization*
  A. *Function and Authority of Purchasing Department*
    1. Obtain copy or prepare organization chart of the Purchasing Department. Determine to whom the head of the Purchasing Department reports.
    2. Document the functions of each of the Purchasing Department's units to ascertain their appropriateness and whether they are proper Purchasing Department functions.
  B. *Function and Necessity of Specific Job Classifications*
    1. Document the duties and responsibilities of the following job classifications, by obtaining copies of existing job descriptions and validation via interviewing and work observation.
      - Purchasing Supervisor
      - Buyers I and II
      - Clerk Supervisor
      - Clerical Supervisor
      - Clerk-Typist
      - Standard Specifications Unit
        - Standard Specifications Supervisor
        - Procurement Technician
        - Management Trainee
        - Clerk-Stenographer
        - Clerk
    2. Observe the actual work being performed and determine the necessity of all duties and responsibilities.

II. *Purchasing Department Responsibility*
  A. *Processing of Regular Purchase Orders*
    1. Obtain or prepare copy of Purchasing Department systems and procedures.
    2. Interview and observe work of Purchasing Department personnel responsible for purchase order processing to validate accuracy of systems and procedures.
    3. Prepare flowchart of the purchase order processing procedures, including related purchasing operations such as purchase requisitioning, preparation and placing of purchase orders, open purchase order control, and receipt of merchandise.
    4. Calculate the present cost of processing a purchase order, considering such things as:
      - Direct cost of operating the Purchasing Department.
      - Indirect costs related to the purchasing function.
      - Number of actual purchase orders processed.

FIGURE 3.12. *(Continued)*

    5. Analyze purchase orders processed, using purchase order reports provided by the Data Processing Department:
- Purchase orders processed by departmental source.
- Purchase order register by month in purchase order number sequence.
- Purchase register by month, showing purchases by department and type (account number).

    6. Stratify the number and amount of actual purchases as to:
- Under $50.00.
- $50.00 to $100.00.
- $100.00 to $200.00, etc.

Obtain a copy of the year-to-date purchase order detail data file maintained in data processing for the previous year. Develop and run computer audit program to analyze data file and print out results for above.

    7. Calculate the annual cost to process small purchases, using the present cost of processing a purchase order as calculated in work step 4 above, and the number of small purchases as determined in work step 6 above.

B. *Decentralized Purchasing*

    1. Obtain copy or prepare policies and procedures relative to purchases made outside the central Purchasing Department, such as:
- Emergency purchases.
- Direct purchases.
- Petty cash purchases.

    2. Select a number of such decentralized operating units for review. Analyze their operations as to compliance to existing company policies relative to decentralized purchasing.

III. *Purchasing Operations and Work Flow*

  A. Prepare a layout flow diagram of the Purchasing Department, depicting the personnel and work flow within the department. Analyze the flow diagram to identify any possible inefficiencies.

  B. Interview appropriate Purchasing Department personnel and observe related work flow to determine the extent and cause of identified operating deficiencies.

3.14 CONCLUSION

FIGURE 3.13. Defective merchandise returns.

A preliminary review of the operational audit disclosed the following deficiencies as related to the handling of defective merchandise returns:

Auditee's Return to Vendors
1. The auditee was paying return freight charges on almost 50 percent of defective merchandise returns. This practice was a result of noncompliance with established procedures, whereby return freight charges were not to be paid by the Traffic Department and other operating divisions.

Customer Returns to Auditee
2. Some of the auditee's local customers were returning defective merchandise in company trucks—contrary to auditee policy.
3. Cash discounts were being improperly handled when defective merchandise was returned by customers. The amount credited to the customer was the invoice price plus the cash discount. This is in violation of company policy and good business practice.

Questions and Solutions for Consideration
Document one audit step that the auditor would include in his or her audit program for each of the deficiencies noted above.

1. *Return Freight Charges*
   a. Analyze sample to determine incidence and amount of return freight charges.
   b. Review procedures in selected operating divisions to determine where practice is being performed.
2. *Returning Merchandise in Company Trucks*
   a. Analyze sample set of returns by local customers to determine extent of use of company trucks for this purpose.
   b. Review procedures in shipping to ascertain whether practices allow for the detection of returned merchandise in company trucks.
   c. Review the present policy of not using company trucks for the return of defective merchandise, and ascertain whether the current policy should be changed and whether this would be the most economical method for such returns.
   Note: This may be only indicative of the real problem: the amount of defective merchandise and the reasons underlying the situation, rather than the method of return.
3. *Cash Discounts Improperly Handled*
   a. Analyze accounting documents and records to determine the amount of cash discounts paid to customers for returned merchandise.
   b. Analyze the system, both manual and computerized operations, to determine whether controls can be established that will prevent this practice from continuing.

AUDIT PROGRAM PHASE

FIGURE 3.13. *(Continued)*

Note that the correction of these operating deficiencies resulted in an annual net savings of more than $140,000, as well as in identifying a significant problem area in the increasing amount of defective items returned by customers. The audit scope was therefore expanded to determine the causes for the increase in defective items, and a recommendation was made for major manufacturing and quality control systems and procedures changes.

CHAPTER FOUR

Field Work Phase

4.1 INTRODUCTION

The operational audit work done in the planning phase should produce indications of possible management weaknesses or significant operational areas for improvement in a particular area or activity. However, more information is usually needed to determine that there definitely is a management or operational weakness. The audit program, then, is the plan for conducting the operational audit steps in the field work phase. In this phase, additional information is gathered relative to management and operational controls and activities to identify those areas in which to expend time and effort on an in-depth examination. Then the operational audit work program steps are performed, and, as a result, areas are identified in which to develop specific findings to present to management.

If the operational audit team decides to proceed with an in-depth development of a finding, the information gathered in the field work phase provides a basis from which to proceed. Besides providing an understanding of particular inefficiencies within the organization or department being reviewed, field work also helps the audit team to understand the departmental organization and how it functions. Such an understanding is usually necessary in the event that additional information is needed in the development of the finding.

This chapter discusses the field work phase of an operational audit. It is in this phase that the audit work steps are performed, as defined in the audit program phase. The operational audit team makes a determination, based on the performance and results of these work steps, as to whether those areas of possible weaknesses identified in the planning phase are

FIELD WORK PHASE

worth going into in greater detail. If they are, any additional analytical work is done to fully develop the finding for presentation to management. There may also be additional critical areas discovered that require further analytical work. In addition, this chapter reviews some of the procedures and techniques that can be used by the operational audit team in the conduct of the field work phase.

This chapter will:

1. Increase understanding of the purpose of the field work phase in an operational audit.

2. Present various techniques that can be used in the field work phase.

3. Increase knowledge of how to use information gained in the field work phase in the further development of audit findings.

4. Describe field work phase documentation and audit file contents.

4.2 FIELD WORK CONSIDERATIONS AND TASKS

Based on the critical areas identified in the planning phase and the audit work steps designed in the audit program phase, the following two items are considered in the field work phase:

1. Whether the auditee's policies, and the related procedures and practices actually followed, are in compliance with basic authorities, statutes, and legislative intent, and

2. Whether the system of operating procedures and management controls effectively results in activities being carried out as desired by top management in an efficient and economical manner.

General tasks that would be performed to assist in reaching the correct conclusions include the following:

1. Fact-finding or verification; for example, are management procedures being followed?

2. Evaluation; for example, analyzing deviations from procedures and determining whether the cause is the policy or procedure itself, or other factors.

3. Review of findings; for example, meeting occasionally with the audit

supervisor and other members of the audit team to assist in getting a better understanding of matters requiring interpretation.

4. Recommendations as to the areas having sufficient significance to warrant a more detailed examination directed toward the development of an operational audit finding.

Operational audit recommendations resulting from effective field work are based on the auditor's determination as to the adequacy and effectiveness of management and operations.

4.3 FACTORS IN REACHING CONCLUSIONS

In reaching conclusions in the field work phase, the operational auditor needs to consider some specific factors, which include the following:

1. Management's use of standards or goals for judging accomplishment, productivity, efficiency, or utilization of goods and services. For example, the auditor may observe the use of net profit only, as a measure, as opposed to evaluating controllable results such as units shipped, goods returned, quality control, and so on.

2. Lack of clarity in written instructions, which may result in misunderstandings, inconsistent applications, or unacceptable deviations. An example is the purchasing policy of plus or minus 10 percent tolerances, as detailed in the operational audit situation described in Figure 2.22, in Chapter 2.

3. Capability of personnel to perform their assignments. For instance, the auditor may observe individuals who are unable to complete their assignments, such as a backlog of unprocessed purchase orders.

4. Failure to accept responsibility. For example, there may be persons who do not do what is expected of them in their functional job descriptions, such as preparing periodic reports.

5. Failure to properly control operations and activities. For example, there may be a work unit in which some individuals are overloaded and others are underloaded.

6. Duplication of efforts within departments and across departmental lines. An example might be account code checking by the purchase

requisitioner, by purchasing department personnel, and by accounting department personnel.

7. Improper or wasteful use of financial resources. An example could be the presence of data processing equipment and procedures, while the same operations are still being performed manually.

8. Cumbersome or extravagant organizational patterns, such as an overburdened hierarchy with multilevels of supervisors and managers or an excessive number of staff personnel.

9. Ineffective or wasteful use of employees; for example, the use of administrative assistants or staff personnel to perform functions that could and should be performed by the person to whom they report.

10. Work backlogs that are inappropriate to the activity. For instance, the auditor may find incompletely processed purchase orders, more than 6 months old, owing to an individual's processing the easy purchase orders first.

11. Necessity for, and effectiveness of, various operating and service units in relation to the costs of maintaining them. For example, the auditor may discover a purchasing specifications unit that was established at the outset of the company but is, for the most part, no longer used as there are very few changes made to purchase specifications.

12. Relevance and validity of criteria used by an auditee to judge effectiveness in achieving operating results. An example might be an oversupply of inventory, caused by the inability to change reorder points and reorder quantities for slow-moving items, or an undersupply of items selling far faster than they can be placed into inventory.

13. Appropriateness of methods used by an auditee to evaluate effectiveness of achieving results. For example, the auditor may observe insufficient reporting that does not relate the performance of activities to the achievement of results.

4.4 FIELD WORK TECHNIQUES

Many different field work techniques are used in the field work phase, depending on the particular circumstances of an engagement. However, the best tools are common sense and analytical ability. It is not necessary for the auditor to have mastered all the various technical tools before beginning an operational audit. But the auditor should be able to analyze problems logically, and, in many cases, this is the only tool needed.

The auditor can use various methods to gather the necessary information to identify weaknesses in management and operational systems. The auditor follows the previously mentioned adage: Whatever works, use it. However, there are certain tools and techniques that are used consistently from one operational audit to another. Some of the more common of these field work techniques are mentioned in Chapter 3 relative to developing audit program work steps. It is these work steps using these tools and techniques that are carried out in the field work phase. Often, however, further work steps are added in the field work phase. It is to the operational auditor's advantage to be familiar with as many of these techniques as possible. The more effective the technique, the more effective the audit results. Moreover, to be able to use a specific technique, the auditor needs to be familiar with it. These field work techniques and others are documented again in this chapter in Figure 4.1.

One or more of these techniques may be used in each audit step assignment. The techniques used will depend on the particular circumstances encountered and the objectives established for each audit step. Therefore, there are no hard and fast rules as to the work to be done or the techniques to be used in the field work phase. The most effective approach is to individualize the field work audit steps and related techniques to meet the needs of the particular situation. The operational auditor's expertise is to know under what circumstances which technique to apply to achieve desired results.

4.5 SPECIFIC FIELD WORK TECHNIQUES

Although there are many tools and techniques that can be used in the field work phase, there are a number that are used consistently. The operational auditor should be most aware of these techniques, which include the following:

Interviewing

Systems flowchart

Layout flowchart

Ratio, change, and trend analysis

FIELD WORK PHASE

FIGURE 4.1. Field work phase: Field work techniques.

1. Review of existing documentation, such as policy and procedures manuals.

2. Preparation of organization charts and related functional job descriptions.

3. Analysis of policies, systems, and procedures.

4. Interviews with management and operations personnel.

5. Flowcharting preparation:
   - Systems flowcharts, showing process of functional areas.
   - Layout flow diagram, showing physical layout of a work area and its related workflow.

6. Ratio, change, and trend analysis.

7. Questionnaires for auditor or client personnel use.

8. Surveys, by phone or in written form, for customers, vendors, etc., to respond to.

9. Questions within the audit program.

10. Review of transactions, in which the different types of normal and abnormal transactions are considered.

11. Review of operations by such techniques as observations, work measurement, time studies, and work performance forms or logs.

12. Forms analysis.

13. Analysis of results.

14. Review and analysis of management information systems and related reports.

15. Compliance reviews as to compliance with laws, policies, procedures, objectives, etc.

16. Use of EDP; using computer auditing "through the computer" techniques or analysis of computer-produced information.

4.5 SPECIFIC FIELD WORK TECHNIQUES

(a) Interviewing

As previously mentioned, interviews in the planning phase are generally limited to management, along with some interviewing of operations personnel. In the field work phase, however, interviews are not only not limited to management, but primarily include those employees who actually do the work so as to determine what is going on and why. Figure 4.2 provides some notes relative to the audit interview.

The purpose of the audit interview is to correlate practice and theory, to gather facts, opinions, and ideas, and to establish a positive image of the auditors in the minds of the client's personnel. To conduct a successful interview, there must be adequate preparation. The auditor should learn as much as possible about the operation through such sources as policies and procedures manuals, organization charts and functional job descriptions, internal and external reports, prior audit reports and working papers, and technical journals. It is the auditors' responsibility to do their homework prior to the interview, and not spend interview time asking questions to which they already know the answers.

(i) INTERVIEW AGENDA AND WHOM TO INTERVIEW As part of the auditor's interview preparation, an interview agenda is prepared which includes the major areas to be covered and the basic questions to be answered. The agenda is used as the auditor's guideline, not to share the details with the interviewee, but only the general areas to be covered. However, the auditor should be prepared to deviate from the agenda as required by answers obtained in the actual interview. The questions to be asked depend on who is being interviewed. For example, if the interviewee is decision management, the auditor would gather information relative to policies and objectives. If operating management, including department managers, supervisors, and the like, is being interviewed, the auditor might cover such things as work flow, interdepartmental relationships, present problems, and future improvements. And if operating personnel, the people responsible for a specific job, are being interviewed, the auditor might ask about the specific work flow and related systems and procedures.

(ii) SCHEDULING THE INTERVIEW Another significant issue is the proper scheduling of the interview. It is the auditor's responsibility to make advance arrangements as to the time and place, at the convenience of the interviewee. It is usually best to meet at the auditee's work area so that the person being interviewed is most at ease and the auditor can observe ongoing operations during the interview.

FIELD WORK PHASE

FIGURE 4.2. Operational audit interview.

I. *Importance of the Audit Interview*
    A. Correlates practice and theory.
    B. Gathers facts, opinions, and ideas.
    C. Establishes the auditor's image in the mind of the client.

II. *Preparing for the Interview*
    A. Learn something about the organization through:
        1. Policies and procedures.
        2. Operating manuals.
        3. Organization charts and functional job descriptions.
        4. Legislation: laws, charters, and ordinances.
        5. Reports: internal and external.
        6. Prior audit reports.
        7. Working papers.
        8. Technical journals.
    B. Prepare an interview agenda.
        1. Write out basic questions.
        2. Review and rephrase questions.
        3. Organize and consolidate questions.
    C. How and what the auditor asks depends on whom he or she is talking to.
        1. Decision Management: Aim at gathering information about policy and objectives.
            a. *Do:*
- Ask about policy.
- Ask about goals and objectives.
- Encourage free exchange of ideas.
- Sell yourself and the audit group.
- Concentrate on the "big picture."

            b. *Don't:*
- Use technical terminology.
- Get involved in great detail.
- Inject yourself in the middle of a story; let the auditee talk.
- Interrupt.
- Criticize the operation.

        2. Operating Management: Including department managers, supervisors, and the like. Some of the areas to be covered with this group are work flow, present problems, relationship to other departments, and future improvements.
            a. *Do:*
- Evaluate work flow.
- Document functions of departmental personnel.
- Sell yourself.
- Anticipate reluctance.

FIGURE 4.2. *(Continued)*

- Plan ahead and be prepared to discuss operations.
- Observe operations while you talk.

    b. *Don't:*
- Use technical terminology.
- Inject your ideas in the middle of a story; rather, direct the conversation.
- Be reluctant to stimulate the auditee to action.
- Ignore the day-to-day problems.
- Gloss over interdepartmental relationships.

  3. Operating Personnel: These include people responsible for a specific job.

    a. *Do*
- Have a list of questions.
- Know the general work flow.
- Be friendly and complimentary.
- Sell yourself.
- Concentrate on the areas of responsibility of the auditee.

    b. *Don't*
- Use technical terminology.
- Use words that can allow the interviewee to draw the wrong inference.
- Criticize the operations or personnel.
- Try to overpower the auditee.
- Allow the interview to deteriorate into a complaint session.

  D. Remember, never go into the interview cold and unprepared; do your homework before the interview.

III. *Scheduling the Interview*
  A. Make advance arrangements.
    1. Time and place; auditee's work area most desirable.
    2. Probable duration of meeting; limit to an hour or less.
  B. Arrange favorable hours and days.
    1. Avoid hours immediately before or after lunch.
    2. Avoid late Friday afternoon, day before or after a holiday or vacation.
    3. If possible, try for early morning, shortly after workday begins, or mid-afternoon.
  C. Share the agenda and request materials.
    1. Indicate generally the subject of the meeting.
    2. Request materials: sample forms, statements, etc.
  D. Keep interview generally one-on-one, with no supervisors or supervisees present.

FIELD WORK PHASE

FIGURE 4.2. *(Continued)*

IV. *Opening the Interview*
  A. Be punctual; it helps your image.
  B. Put the person at ease, but control the amount of small talk.
  C. State clearly the purpose of the interview.
  D. Assure the auditee you will protect his or her anonymity if desired and if possible.

V. *Conducting the Interview*
  A. Be open, objective, and reasonable.
  B. Convey to the other person that the audit is a matter of joint concern.
  C. Use your agenda to direct the interview and prevent undue wandering from the subject.

VI. *Questioning the Interviewee*
  A. Ask questions that require more than yes or no answers.
  B. Seek the other person's analysis of causes and effects; statements of things that are of concern to auditee.
  C. Do not ask loaded questions:
    1. Those that indicate you have already assumed an answer.
    2. Those that indicate what you would like to hear.

VII. *Note Taking*
  A. Never record complete minutes.
    1. Adversely affects other person.
    2. Not conducive to good listening; hence, you may not be able to separate material from immaterial items.

VIII. *Effective Listening*
  A. Ask the person to repeat or restate if you do not understand.
  B. Ask for concrete examples if language is general or vague.
  C. Summarize or rephrase in order to encourage elaboration.
  D. Ask the interviewee what he or she would do to correct or improve conditions.
  E. Allow periods of silence in which to think.
  F. Don't:
    - Debate or waste time in disagreeing over any point, no matter how important.
    - Be sarcastic.
    - Jump to conclusions.
    - Contradict a person in front of others.
    - Quote other people you have interviewed; the interviewee will not trust you to keep his or her responses confidential.

IX. *Closing the Interview*
  A. Stick to the time schedule even if you have not finished your agenda; simply arrange for another meeting.
  B. If the other person wishes to extend the interview, then do so; but let this be his or her option, not yours.

4.5 SPECIFIC FIELD WORK TECHNIQUES

FIGURE 4.2. *(Continued)*

    C. Before leaving, summarize the major facts obtained in the interview.
    D. Thank the interviewee for his or her time.
    E. Leave the door open for further questions or information.
X. *Recording the Interview*
    A. Review, organize, and record your notes as soon as possible after the interview; at least on the same day.
    B. Write out enough, so that conclusions are reasonably self-explanatory.
    C. Send a copy of your notes to the interviewee for his or her review and agreement, where appropriate.

There should be agreement on the length of time the interview will take—a good rule is to limit the interview to an hour or less. In scheduling the interview, the auditor should arrange for the most favorable hours and days. If possible, the interview should be conducted in the early morning, shortly after the beginning of the work day, or in the midafternoon, sometime between an hour after lunch and an hour before quitting. It is best to avoid those times immediately before or after lunch, first thing Monday morning, late Friday afternoon, and the day before or after a holiday or vacation.

(iii) SETTING UP THE INTERVIEW When setting up the interview, the auditor should indicate what the general agenda is to be, but should not share the actual agenda with the interviewee. If the auditor would like the interviewee to provide specific materials either before or at the time of the interview, the auditor asks for them at this time so that the interviewee has sufficient time to make them available—either prior to or at the time of the interview. The auditor should not wait until the time of the interview to request such materials. It should also be made clear to the interviewee that the interview should include just that individual and the auditor. This ensures confidentiality and helps the interviewee to feel free to speak, which might not happen in the presence of supervisors or supervisees. This also ensures getting more honest and correct information from both parties. It is also a good idea not to bring anyone else along—this only increases anxiety. A one-to-one interview can thus be more productive than an attempt to save time by talking to more than one person at a time.

(iv) STARTING THE INTERVIEW It is the auditor's responsibility to be punctual and to arrive at the interview site a little before the scheduled start time. While it might be inconsiderate of the interviewee to arrive late or to keep the auditor waiting, remember that it is the auditor's goal to get information from the other person during his or her work time, and therefore, sometimes the auditor will be inconvienenced. In addition, being on time helps to enhance the auditor's professional image and create a favorable impression.

From the outset, the interviewee should be put at ease. An effective icebreaker or small talk can be helpful, but the auditor should control the amount of time used for this purpose. An effective transition can be used to state clearly the purpose and general agenda of the interview. The auditor should assure the interviewee that his or her anonymity will be protected and confidentiality respected.

When conducting the interview, the auditor should be open, objective, and reasonable. The interviewee should be assured that the operational audit is a matter of joint concern and that the auditor's role is to help him or her to improve operations and make the job easier. The basic agenda is used to direct the interview, prevent unnecessary wandering, and ensure that all agenda items are covered. Note that the interviewee should not have a copy of the actual agenda. This keeps the auditor from being constricted by a written agenda if he or she wants to pursue more significant areas of concern that may arise.

(v) QUESTIONING PROCEDURES When asking questions, it is a good idea for the auditor to stay away from "yes or no" questions, as they limit the amount of information to be obtained. Rather, the auditor should ask questions that require the interviewee to analyze causes and effects, state matters of concern, and give opinions. The auditor should never ask "loaded" questions, those indicating that an answer is already assumed, or those indicating what the auditor would like to hear—for instance, "Your systems are really lousy, aren't they?"

(vi) NOTE TAKING While conducting the interview, the auditor should not take full notes or minutes as the interviewee is talking. Such note taking may adversely affect the other person, and no one wants to look at the top of another person's head. Moreover, such minute taking is not conducive to good listening; it can cause the auditor to be unable to separate material items from those having little impact. A good practice is to take abbreviated notes to trigger subsequent recall, including the recording of facts, source references, rough diagrams, quick flowcharts, key words, and so on.

(vii) EFFECTIVE LISTENING Since the purpose of the auditor is to gather information and learn more, it is important for him or her to be an effective listener and to make sure to get accurate facts and statements. People learn by listening, not by talking. A good technique to increase the effectiveness of listening skills is to ask the interviewee to repeat or restate items that are not completely understood.

However, this technique should not be overused, as it may turn off the interviewee. Nor should the auditor ask the interviewee to repeat something that can be found out easily elsewhere. Another good listening technique is to ask for concrete examples if the person's language is too general or vague. However, the auditor must be sure these are not areas that should have been known before the interview. Other techniques that can be used include summarizing or rephrasing what the interviewee has stated in order to encourage elaboration, or asking how the interviewee would correct or improve conditions.

During the interview, its good practice to allow periods of silence in which to think. It is not the auditor's responsibility to fill in the silent awkward periods. Often, the interviewee needs these silent periods to gather thoughts. It is also important not to antagonize the interviewee by debating a point, making sarcastic comments, jumping to conclusions, or contradicting him or her—particularly in front of others. Moreover, the auditor should never quote from past interviews with others, as this might get the other persons in trouble, while the present interviewee will not trust the interviewer to keep his or her responses confidential.

(viii) CLOSING THE INTERVIEW When closing the interview, the auditor must make sure to stay within the one-hour time agreement, even if the interview agenda is not finished. In this case, another interview can be arranged. However, if the interview can be completed in a short time—say within 10 minutes—and if the other person wishes to extend the interview, the auditor can do so, but allowing the decision to continue to be the interviewee's.

At the close of the interview, the auditor summarizes the major areas covered and the facts obtained to assure their completeness and accuracy. Then the auditor sincerely thanks the interviewee for his or her time, and asks cordially whether the person may be contacted again should there be additional questions or further information needed.

(ix) NOTE RECORDING After the interview, the auditor should review, organize, and record the notes taken as soon as possible, at least on the same day. This helps to ensure the accuracy of interview records. In recording interview notes, the auditor must be sure to write out sufficient details so that conclusions are reasonably self-explanatory. A good practice, where appropriate, is to send a copy of the interview notes to the

FIELD WORK PHASE

interviewee for review and agreement. This ensures accuracy and completeness while the interview is still fresh in his or her mind and provides more accurate data on which to base conclusions.

(x) SAMPLE INTERVIEW A sample interview between an operational auditor and a department manager is shown in Figure 4.3. To reinforce the materials covered on effective interviewing techniques, review and analyze the interview presentation and document any good or bad points identified. When a point is identified, try to think of how it affects the interview and later relations with the interviewee and the department. Some comments are provided in Figure 4.4.

(b) Systems Flowchart

Another technique that is widely used in the field work phase is systems flowcharting. The purpose of systems flowcharting is to document general and specific procedures to help the auditor understand operations and activities. Flowcharts show the work that is actually being performed, who is doing it, and how it is done. Flowcharting provides far more satisfactory results than reviewing operating manuals and documentation, because the auditor thus gains a better and more accurate understanding of operating activities. In addition, the process of flowcharting, which requires obtaining and documenting an understanding of operating systems, helps stimulate the auditor's interest, enthusiasm, and imagination, resulting in a more realistic identification of weaknesses.

The systems flowchart is a graphic representation of the sequence of operations in a process. It is especially useful in showing where documents, equipment, reference materials, files, and new paper work are introduced into the process. It documents what work is performed and how. A systems flowchart that could be prepared during the field work phase for a purchasing–receiving–payables–disbursement system is shown as Figure 4.5. It provides information relative to:

1. How operations are actually carried out,
2. The necessity or usefulness of the work steps included in processing the transactions, and
3. The effectiveness of the controls provided in the process.

4.5 SPECIFIC FIELD WORK TECHNIQUES

FIGURE 4.3. Sample interview.

1. **Auditor** *(Walks right into Department Manager's office—unannounced)* Hi, we're doing an operational audit of your area, so I thought you might answer some questions about the inventory system.
2. **Department Manager** *(Looks up and looks at watch)* What! You caught me by surprise. I have a meeting shortly, but I'll see what I can do for you.
3. **Auditor** *(Sits down next to Department Manager—picks up pencil from desk)* Can you tell me the status of the SRP program?
4. **Department Manager** Huh?
5. **Auditor** *(Louder)* SRP program—surplus removal program.
6. **Department Manager** Oh. We haven't used that in months.
7. **Auditor** I know. Can you describe the program?
8. **Department Manager** *(Obviously disturbed)* I told you, its not currently being used.
9. **Auditor** Could you just describe it?
10. **Department Manager** *(More annoyed)* Okay. The purpose was to transfer surplus inventory to another location where it was needed. We dropped it because we couldn't establish an effective reporting system between locations where we could tell . . . *(cut short)*.
11. **Auditor** Uh huh. So, you have to correct your reporting system for SRP to work. What type of inventory records do you keep?
12. **Department Manager** We use an on-line computerized record.
13. **Auditor** I see. It's my experience that whatever records you use, it's almost impossible to effectively control inventory. In fact, most inventory operations are extremely sloppy. I suppose I'll see for myself how good yours are.
14. **Department Manager** *(Shocked—sits back in chair)* Uh huh.
15. **Auditor** What vehicles do you have in your delivery fleet?
16. **Department Manager** *(Looks confused and disturbed)* Two panel trucks, one pickup, one station wagon.
17. **Auditor** *(Writes down answer and asks manager to repeat)* Run that by me again.
18. **Department Manager** *(In very annoyed tone)* Two panel trucks, one pickup, and one station wagon.
19. **Auditor** Is that all?
20. **Department Manager** *(Extremely annoyed)* Yeah, that's all!
21. **Auditor** Who schedules the deliveries?

FIELD WORK PHASE

FIGURE 4.3. *(Continued)*

22. **Department Manager** Chief storekeeper schedules deliveries and dispatches drivers.
23. **Auditor** Is the schedule formally written?
24. **Department Manager** No, its not formal! Its just a day-to-day type thing.
25. **Auditor** Do you have any delivery records and time spent on them?
26. **Department Manager** *(Really disturbed)* No!
27. **Auditor** Have you ever calculated the cost to make a delivery?
28. **Department Manager** No!
29. **Auditor** That's funny—Tony Maroney, the assistant storekeeper told me that they keep detailed records and costs of all deliveries. He thinks we could save a bundle of money if we got out of the delivery business.
30. **Department Manager** *(Quite disturbed—turns away)* You don't say.
31. **Auditor** Where do you get your authority over inventories?
32. **Department Manager** *(Picks up large loose-leaf binder)* Look, its right here in the *Company Policies and Procedures Manual (flips through the book).* Here are the sections.
33. **Auditor** That's okay. I'll read my copy when I get back to the office. Do you have an organization chart I can have?
34. **Department Manager** Sure, just a minute. I'll call my assistant. *(Calls out)* Al, get me a copy of our organization chart.
35. **Al** *(Enters room)* I have a chart you can have, but its about three years old.
36. **Auditor** You don't have a current organization chart? How can you run your department without one?
37. **Department Manager** *(Upset and embarrassed; pauses and stutters)* We'll, uh, I'll get you a copy when we update it *(nods to Al, who leaves)*.
38. **Auditor** *(Starts to gather up his papers—puts the Department Manager's pencil in his bag)* Uh, I've written down the forms I'd like to have copies of *(hands piece of handwritten paper to Department Manager)*.
39. **Department Manager** *(Looks over paper)* Uh huh, Order and Bill, Log of Filled Orders, Manufacturing Order, Inventory Addition Record, Inventory Status Report, Completed Order, Shipping Documents. Look, I can't get them for you now *(looks at watch)*. I'm already 20 minutes late for my meeting. I'll have to send them to you.
40. **Auditor** Okay. I didn't think it was that much trouble *(grabs paper back and copies down forms on pad)*.
41. **Department Manager** *(Gets up to leave)* If you have any more questions, contact my secretary *(leaves the office with the auditor still sitting there)*.

4.5 SPECIFIC FIELD WORK TECHNIQUES

FIGURE 4.4. Sample interview comments.

Overall Weak Point
The interview was not planned; it skips from one area to another without any logical sequence. The question of authority over inventory is asked at the end of the interview, instead of at the beginning, which would be the most logical place.

1. No appointment was made. The auditor called on the department manager without making an appointment, establishing a time limit, or reviewing the general agenda. This is a result of lack of proper planning. If the department manager was contacted in advance and given the general agenda or areas to be covered, he or she could have been prepared for the interview. In addition, the department manager might have been able to raise some points the auditor may not have thought about.

2. The department manager mentions having a meeting shortly but will see what he or she can do. However, the auditor not only fails to respond to this issue, but offers no apology for just stopping by unannounced, producing an immediate negative image of the auditor and the audit group.

3 to 6. The auditor jumps right into the interview with no preliminary ice breaking, again putting the department manager ill at ease. In addition, the auditor starts out with the SRP program—obviously a sore point in the department. This creates a good possibility of putting the department manager immediately on the defensive.

7. The auditor's question, "Can you describe the program?" is the type of open-ended question to be asked in an operational audit interview. However, there is the point of whether this might not be a too detailed question for a department manager and whether the auditor could have acquired such detailed information prior to the interview.

8 to 10. The department manager, although obviously disturbed, starts to respond to the question quite adequately, providing good information. However, the auditor cuts the department manager short and jumps immediately to a conclusion. Had the auditor allowed the department manager to continue, instead of being presumptuous and dismissing his or her opinions, the auditor might have gained some valuable information and recommendations.

11. The auditor, after cutting the department manager short, jumps right into another area (inventory records) without properly concluding the discussion on the SRP program or introducing the new discussion area.

12 and 13. After the department manager responds that the department uses an on-line computerized record, the auditor interjects his or her own poor opinion of any and all inventory operations—again putting the department manager on the defensive. As the interview is unfolding, the department manager will probably hold back and not provide as much and complete information as possible.

FIELD WORK PHASE

FIGURE 4.4. *(Continued)*

14. The department manager, although shocked, allows the interview to continue.

15 to 18. The auditor does not properly close the discussion on inventory records, but instead jumps right into the delivery fleet. The auditor writes down what the department manager says about the delivery fleet and then asks him or her to repeat. This can be annoying and distracting, especially to a department manager. Such detailed information should be obtained from someone other than the department manager, and prior to the interview.

19 and 20. The auditor asks the department manager, "Is that all?" This again implies displeasure and the point that there should be more. The department manager is justifiably "extremely annoyed."

21 and 22. The question "Who schedules the deliveries?" is again detail data that should have been known prior to the interview. This type of question only puts the person on the spot, implying, "You should know the answer, or how can you be running the department?"

23 to 28. These questions tend to be of the yes or no type, allowing the department manager to offer no additional information, opinion, or analysis. In addition, the staccato-style questioning suggests a scene in which a bright light might be shone on the department manager as the interrogation gets heavier.

29 and 30. The question "Have you ever calculated the cost to make a delivery?" is a setup, and the department manager provides the expected "no" answer. The auditor, however, rather than pick up on the thread of the discussion and ask for an analysis or opinion of why not, disputes the department manager's information by bringing another employee's (Tony Maroney) input into the discussion. This is not only a breach of confidentiality of the other employee, but it also undermines the confidence of the department manager being interviewed. For, if the auditor is that quick to bring someone else's opinion into the discussion, he or she will do the same with the present discussion. In most instances, the other person will be either a supervisor (as in this case) or a supervisee; such a situation creates possible trouble and conflict. This practice also destroys the interviewee's trust in the auditor and inhibits the openness of the interview.

31 and 32. The auditor asks, "Where do you get your authority over inventories?" This question should have been asked at the beginning of the interview. In addition, it points to the auditor's having done insufficient advance preparation. When the department manager offers to show the *Policies and Procedures Manual,* the auditor says, "That's okay. I'll read my copy when I get back to the office." This not only discounts the department manager's offer, but also reemphasizes the lack of preparation.

4.5 SPECIFIC FIELD WORK TECHNIQUES

FIGURE 4.4. *(Continued)*

33 to 37. The auditor asks for an organization chart, which should have been requested at the time the interview was scheduled or obtained from other sources prior to the interview. What results here is the necessity to engage someone else in the interview (Al, the assistant), ultimately resulting in the auditor's criticizing the department manager in front of the supervisee. This causes the department manager to become upset and embarrassed, certainly not conducive to a good working relationship, which is necessary for the rest of the operational audit.

38. The auditor begins to end the interview by gathering up papers and walks off with the department manager's pencil—rude on both counts. The auditor then requests certain forms via a handwritten piece of paper. Note that any forms or documents needed should be requested at the time the interview is scheduled. This allows the department manager to have them ready so as to explain their use at the interview. The auditor should know what to request by proper planning and research in preparation for the interview. Should other items come up in the interview, of which the auditor was not aware, these could be legitimately asked for.

39. The department manager needs to read the handwritten note to make certain of the request and responds that he or she will have to send such copies to the auditor, which is quite doubtful based on the content of the interview thus far.

39. The department manager also says, "I'm already 20 minutes late for my meeting". Remember, the department manager had originally stated that he or she had a meeting to go to shortly. However, the auditor has shown no regard for the department manager's needs during the entire interview.

40. The auditor's response, "Okay. I didn't think it was that much trouble," is probably the last straw. Not only has this final comment sent the department manager out the door, but the auditor has also not left the door open for the future.

41. The department manager's closing, "If you have any more questions, contact my secretary," while cordial under the circumstances, is more likely a brush-off; and the chance of the department manager's cooperating with the auditor in the future is remote.

FIGURE 4.5. Systems flowchart: Purchasing–Receiving–Payables–Disbursement system. Page 1 of 6

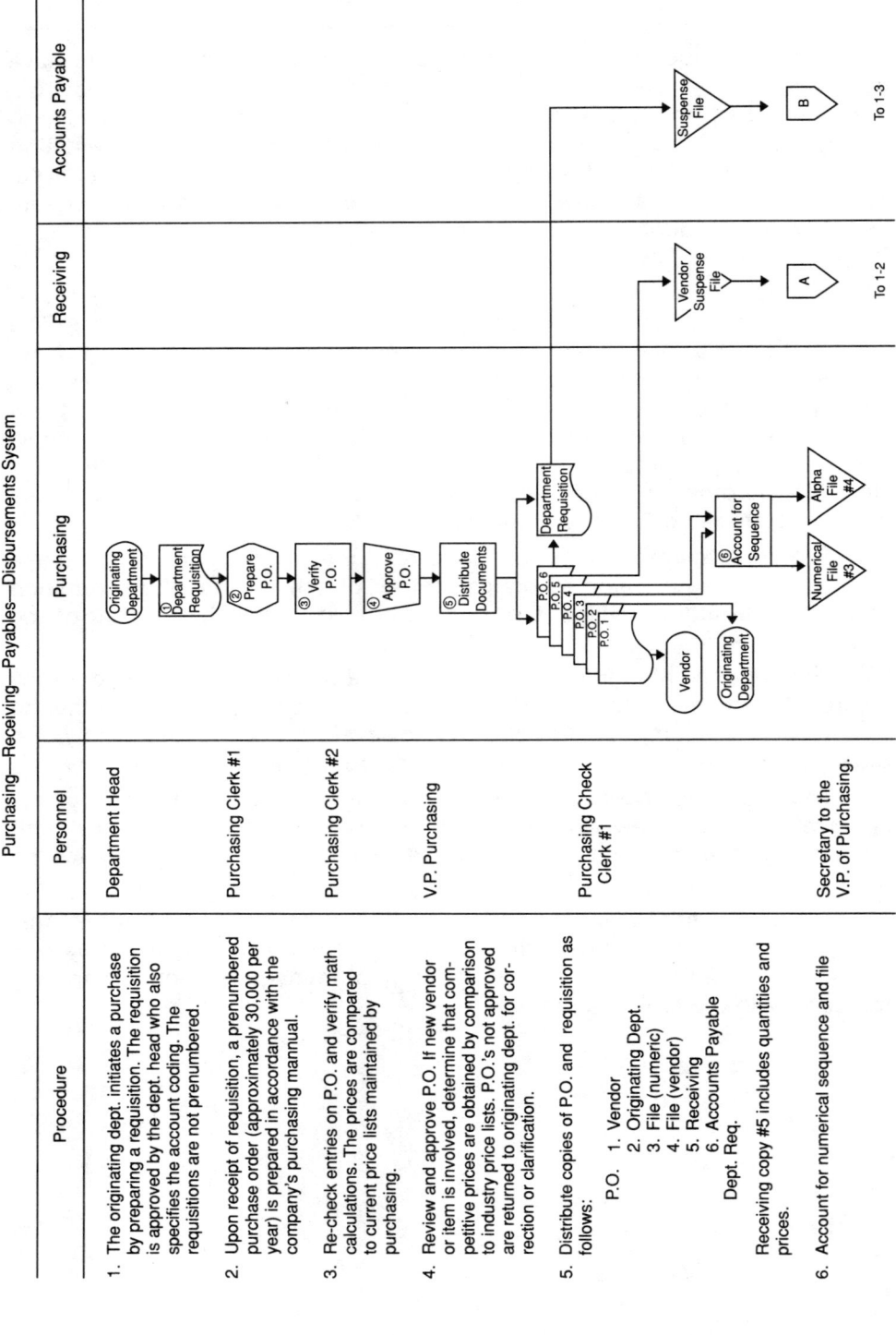

FIGURE 4.5. *(Continued)*

Purchasing—Receiving—Payables—Disbursements System

Page 2 of 6

Procedure	Personnel	Receiving	Production Control	Accounts Payable
7. When goods are received, count and check for damaged items. (See separate narrative write-up.) Prepare, sign, and date three part prenumbered receiving report. Attach to bill of lading and P.O.5.	Receiving Clerk #1			
8. Review and compare receiving report, bill of lading and P.O.5 for completeness and any discrepancies. Distribute as follows: P.O.5. Production Control B of L. Production Control R.R.1. Production Control 2. Accounts Payable 3. Head of receiving dept. Note: the two receiving clerks may rotate steps 7 & 8 as both are involved.	Receiving Clerk #2			
9. Check numerical sequence of receiving report. Prepare daily listing of receiving reports and forward to accounts payable.	Head of Receiving dept.			
10. Update inventory records. (See separate flowchart on inventory system for detailed discussion.)	Inventory Control Clerk #1			

FIGURE 4.5. *(Continued)*

Purchasing—Receiving—Payables—Disbursements System

Page 3 of 6

Procedure	Personnel	Accounts Payable	Orig. Dept.
11. Match all related documents and hold in suspense file pending receipt of vendor invoice.	Accounts Payable Clerk #1		
12. Vendor invoices are forwarded from the mail room daily. Duplicate invoices are stamped as such. Match vendor invoices with other documentation.	Accounts Payable Clerk #1		
13. Review file of unmatched invoices and receiving reports daily. Notify V.P. Purchasing of unmatched items over 10 days old for his follow-up.	Head of Accounts Payable dept.		
14. Approve invoice for payment when all documents have been received and matched. Exceptions are brought to the attention of the head of Accounts Payable dept, who is responsible for corrective action. Upon resolution, the documents are returned to the head of the originating department for approval.	Head of originating dept.		

FIGURE 4.5. *(Continued)*

Purchasing—Receiving—Payables—Disbursements System

Page 4 of 6

Procedure	Personnel	Accounts Payable	Cash Disbursements
15. Match invoice and supporting documentation to related entry on daily listing of goods received and indicate that items have been matched by initialing the list. Check all documentation, verify math computations, agree quantities, check for proper discount, verify account distribution, check for approval, and indicate work by initials. At end of month, prepare accrual on the basis of open items on daily receipts list. 16. Prepare prenumbered voucher (approximately 35,000 per year). Includes all information necessary for posting to accounting records and preparation of check by E.D.P. Accumulate net amount of vouchers on adding machine tape as a control total for each day's transactions. A supply of prenumbered checks is given to computer operator.	Accounts Payable Clerk #2 Cash Disbursement Clerk #2	From 1-2 (D) → From 1-3 (F) → (15) Match to List of Receipts; Verify Calculations, Coding, Etc. → Daily List of Receipts → E.O.M. → Prepare Accounts Payable Accrual → Chron File; Dept. Req., P.O. 6, P.O. 5, B of L, R.R. 2, R.R. 1, INV 2, INV 1	Locked File of Blank Checks → (16) Prepare Vouchers → Voucher Blank Checks → J (To 1-5), I (To 1-5); Control Total → H (To 1-6); G (To 1-6)

FIGURE 4.5. *(Continued)*

Purchasing—Receiving—Payables—Disbursements System

Page 5 of 6

Personnel	Procedure
Data Terminal Operator	E.D.P. documentation consists of the source programs, operator instructions and record layouts.
	17. The vouchers are entered via data terminal in E.D.P. An interactive edit routine is performed as data is entered.
Computer Operator (all operators are capable of running this series of programs)	18. Computer operator processes data file through an edit program. The edit program checks that all numeric fields are numeric and checks for missing voucher numbers. The conversion process is verified by the use of record counts. Any vouchers which are detected as errors are returned to cash disbursements clerk #1. The voucher is corrected within two days and sent back to E.D.P. for reprocessing.
Computer Operator	19. The daily transaction data file is used to prepare the checks and the check register. In addition, a month-to-date transaction file of checks issued is maintained to accumulate and prepare the monthly posting to the general ledger by account. The data file has internal header and trailer labels which are tested by the program. The daily transaction data file and the month-to-date file are maintained for one week. The final MTD file is kept for 13 months.
Computer Operator	20. End of the month procedure: The end of month file is processed to prepare a summary of the checks issued which serves as the source document to post the journal entry in the general ledger.

FIGURE 4.5. *(Continued)*

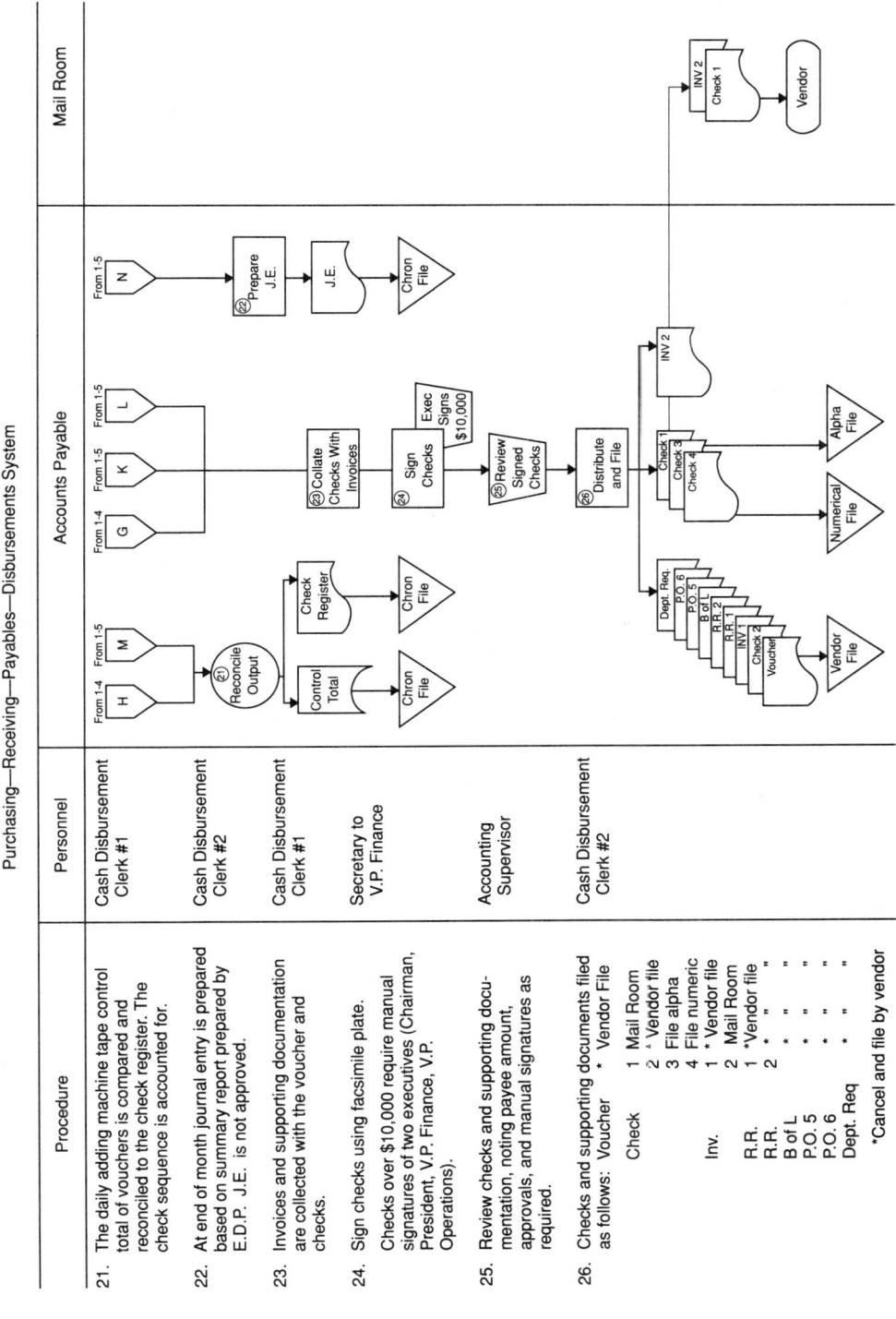

The systems flowchart also helps the auditor to identify the system's inefficiencies, such as the following:

- Unnecessary handling
- Inefficient routing
- Unused information on documents or records
- Inadequate planning or delegation
- Inadequate instruction
- Insufficient or excessive equipment
- Poor use of data processing facilities
- Poorly planned reports
- Inadequate or improper scheduling

The detailed operating procedures demonstrated in the systems flowchart example in Figure 4.5 do not represent recommended procedures but, rather, procedures that the auditor might uncover in an operational audit. Consequently, the auditor's focus should not be on these detailed procedures, but on how the flowchart is structured, to identify strengths and weaknesses in the operations by classifying procedures by departments and relating their flow across departmental lines. Although it is important that the auditor know how to prepare such systems flowcharts, it is equally important to know how to analyze them. A sample analysis of the systems flowchart is shown in Figure 4.6.

(c) Layout Flowchart

A layout flowchart is a schematic diagram of the existing or proposed physical arrangement of a work area to which has been added the flow lines of the principal work performed there. This type of chart is used to document the existing layout and paths of movement of people, paperwork, or materials.

The layout flowchart also enables the auditor to disclose certain inefficiencies in the system, such as the following:

1. Unnecessary handling of certain documents
2. Inefficient routing of certain documents

4.5 SPECIFIC FIELD WORK TECHNIQUES

3. Inadequate planning or delegation of work
4. Inadequate instruction to employees
5. Insufficient or excessive office equipment
6. Poor use of data processing facilities
7. Poorly planned reports
8. Bad work scheduling
9. Inefficient work area layout

In addition, the layout flowchart enables the auditor to identify certain potential personnel roadblocks to economical, efficient, and effective operations. Among these are the following:

1. *Isolates*—individuals or work units that appear to be unconnected to the rest of the work area,
2. *Controllers*—individuals whose major function appears to be controlling or overseeing the work of others without any appreciable value added, and
3. *Dispatchers*—individuals or work units whose main purpose is to receive work from one work unit or individual and pass it to another work unit or individual without appreciably adding to the work.

In addition, the auditor should be aware of hierarchical pyramids, in which there is a reporting relationship either upward or downward, and in which the individuals appear to be mainly reviewing and/or redoing the work that was passed to them prior to passing it further up or down the pyramid. Most organizational pyramids are constructed so that each higher level can police and control the lower level, while often providing no other benefits than to ensure that the lower levels do their work. If these hierarchical levels can be eliminated, it can greatly reduce the cost of operations without sacrificing results; in fact, results are often increased. What is really needed is to motivate each worker's self-disciplined work behavior; in effect, to make the worker responsible for results.

An example of a layout or flow diagram is shown in Figure 4.7. Note that the solid lines between numbered blocks represent direct reporting relationships and the dotted lines represent indirect relationships. Inefficiencies or potential personnel roadblocks are shown in Figure 4.8.

FIELD WORK PHASE

FIGURE 4.6. Analysis of systems flowcharts: Suggested responses.

1. a. Procedure and control question as to whether the department heads should be doing the account coding (is this the best use of time?). Normal procedure calls for the requisitioner and/or an account coding clerk to provide such coding. This may also be a situation suggesting a larger problem—an organizational pattern of management performing clerical tasks.
   b. Purchase requisitions are not prenumbered. Numerical control over purchase requisitions ensures that all purchases are processed by the Purchasing Department and no requisitions are processed more than once. Normally, such control is exercised by the requisitioning department and, accordingly, must be performed uniformly throughout the organization.
2. Approximately 30,000 purchase orders are prepared annually by one Purchasing Clerk. This appears to be a large number for one person to handle. The auditor would want to analyze the procedures for preparing purchase orders to clarify this situation.
3. a. Another Purchasing Clerk rechecks entries on the purchase order and verifies math calculations. The preparation of purchase orders (particularly for 30,000 per year) is usually done on a computerized basis with today's technology. If so, this step could be eliminated. This may also suggest a larger problem, in which computer equipment and resources are available, but not properly utilized.
   b. The prices are compared with current price lists maintained by the Purchasing Department. The operational auditor should note this as an area for further analysis to determine accuracy and up-to-dateness of the price list.
4. a. The V.P. of Purchasing reviews and approves all purchase orders, which again is not the best use of management time.
   b. If a new vendor or item is involved, the V.P. determines that competitive prices are obtained by comparison with industry price lists. This is another area for further analysis.
   c. Purchase orders not approved are returned to the originating department for correction or clarification. The operational auditor should determine what reasons constitute disapproval.
      There is also no mention of whether a check is made against the approved plan/budget prior to the preparation of the purchase order. Other than this, there would not appear to be any other reason to return purchases to the issuing department, particularly after the purchase order is prepared.
5. Distribute copies of purchase order and requisition.
   a. The purchase requisition should be returned to the issuer as proof of processing (or some other method of notification), and not to accounts payable.

FIGURE 4.6. *(Continued)*

    b. The originating department needs to receive notification of its open purchases, but not necessarily a copy of the purchase order. With a computerized system this could take the form of a data file or open purchase listing. These data are then used to control the processing of open purchase requisitions and subsequent open purchase orders.

    c. Two copies of the purchase order (one maintained in numeric sequence and one in alphabetic sequence) are kept in the Purchasing Department. Again, with a computer system, only one copy (filed numerically) is needed, as the computer system can enable the user to go from numeric to alphabetic and back.

    d. The receiving department normally receives a copy of the purchase order as its authorization to receive the goods. However, it has no reason to have prices on its copy. Quantities usually are on the receiving copy, so that the receivers know what is authorized for receipt and proper control is maintained over partial receipts. Another method is not to provide quantities, thereby forcing receivers to count everything. However, this method does not provide an open item quantity with which to reconcile to the actual receipt. The operational auditor should determine which method works best in a specific situation.

6. The secretary to the V.P. of Purchasing accounts for numerical sequence of the purchase orders and files both the numerical and alphabetical copies. The computer system should maintain strict numerical sequence and eliminate the sorting and filing of alphabetical copies. In addition, at the present time this does not appear to be a function that needs to be done by the secretary to the V.P. of Purchasing.

7. a. Damaged items procedure. This is an area for additional analysis to determine whether proper control and handling is exercised for damaged items upon receipt.

    b. Prepare a three-part receiving report. Good business practice is never to re-record information that already exists in the system. In this instance, receiving data are already shown on the purchase order copy. Therefore, this document should be used as the receiving report without any unnecessary re-recording. At all times, the open purchases awaiting receipt should equal the open purchases maintained in the Purchasing Department.

        For partial receipts (where the full quantity of an item or all the items on the PO are not received at the same time), a copy is made of the purchase order to be used as the receiving copy, the partial shipment data are noted on the original copy of the receiving PO, and the original PO is refiled as a purchase awaiting receipt for the remaining open items.

FIELD WORK PHASE

FIGURE 4.6. *(Continued)*

8. Review and compare the receiving report and the PO copy. With the use of the PO itself, there is of course no need to compare with receiving reports.
9. Check numerical sequence of receiving reports and prepare daily listing of receiving reports by the head of the Receiving Department. This step would also be eliminated by the use of PO receiving copies, greatly reducing the amount of paper within the system.
10. Update inventory records. At present this is done on a manual basis independent of other updating. This inventory updating should be integrated and simultaneously processed within a computer system.
11. Match all related documents and hold them in a suspense file pending receipt of vendor invoice. This step is necessary; but notice the number of documents already accumulated in the process.
12. Vendor invoices are forwarded from the mail room. The auditor may want to review mailroom procedures to determine whether this is the most efficient manner of receiving and processing vendor invoices. An effective alternative might be to receive vendor invoices directly by the Accounts Payable Department or via a lock-box system.
13. Review unmatched invoices and receiving reports. Analyze the current situation and determine whether unmatched items are proper. Note that unmatched invoices more than 10 days old may indicate the nonreceipt of receiving reports from the receiving department (inefficiency in the receiving department); and unmatched receiving reports may indicate the nonreceipt of vendor invoices from the mail room (inefficiency in the mail room). In addition, this is not a function that the head of accounts payable, nor the V.P. of Purchasing, needs to be involved with.
14. a. Approve invoice for payment. This is a necessary step; however, note the number of documents that need to be reviewed and filed.
    b. Exceptions brought to the attention of the head of accounts payable for corrective action. Analyze what types of exceptions are being experienced and how they are being corrected.
    c. Upon resolution, the documents are returned to the head of the originating department for approval. This step is unnecessary, and the documents should not leave the accounts payable department.
15. a. Matching invoice and support documentation and verifying math, discount, account distribution, etc. This procedure should be tested on a sample basis to determine the accuracy of such operations.
    Consider reduction and elimination of these procedures by changes in receiving procedures and computerization.
    b. End-of-month accrual based on open items on daily receipts list. Computer system should provide this automatically.
16. a. Prepare prenumbered voucher (approximately 35,000 annually). As the purpose of the voucher is to provide the necessary data in an

4.5 SPECIFIC FIELD WORK TECHNIQUES

FIGURE 4.6. *(Continued)*

orderly manner for subsequent data entry, alternative procedures might be considered for this purpose, such as circling the original document, recording data onto a rubber stamp impression directly on the document, etc.

b. Data entry control procedures should be reviewed to ensure that the present process of controlling by the total net amount of the vouchers is the most efficient and best.

Reference to EDP documentation:

This is the first indication in the system that data processing procedures are in existence. The operational auditor should determine the extent of data processing used, the overall capability of present EDP resources, the effectiveness of use, and the efficient use for present systems concerns. In this situation, the operational auditor might recommend the increased use of EDP procedures for the present system under review to provide for the economies, efficiencies, and effectiveness previously discussed.

In the development of his or her recommendations for the increased use of EDP procedures, the operational auditor should consider the providing of an EDP systems design for the implementation of recommended EDP procedures. The systems design document should include items such as input formats, off-line and on-line controls, data record layouts, processing procedures, information and report layouts, etc.

With regard to the present procedures being reviewed on the systems flowchart, the operational auditor should:

17. Review data terminal operations to determine that proper EDP controls exist to ensure that only authorized transactions are processed and no others, that error identification and correction procedures are adequate, and that edit routines contain all necessary checks and validations.
18. a. Review edit routines embedded in the computer edit program to ensure that all edit checking is proper and that there are not other edits that should be included in the program.

    The edit program should also be tested (possibly "through the computer") to determine that it is working as documented.

    b. Review all internal processing controls, such as the use of record counts in the conversion process, to ensure that no data records are lost, added, or suppressed during processing.

    c. Review error detection and correction procedures to ensure that all error conditions are properly identified, controlled, and resubmitted back into data processing correctly. This is an extremely critical area, as it is subject to abuse and laxity if not properly controlled.
19. The present systems flow within data processing should be reviewed as to efficiency and the production of necessary operating and management

FIGURE 4.6. *(Continued)*

information. The various data files used in EDP and their physical and processing controls and purposes should also be reviewed.

As part of this review, EDP procedures relative to system run-to-run controls should be determined as to their operating properly. In addition, off-line control total procedures should be reviewed to ensure that the EDP system is being properly controlled by the users.

20. The end-of-month procedure consists of EDP preparing a monthly check summary listing. This listing then serves as the source document for reinputting the same data for EDP posting to the general ledger. This is an indication of the improper use of EDP, as the principle to be applied is to use the same data sources for all integrated purposes. In this case, EDP should be automatically posting to the general ledger without such reinputting.
21. Off-line daily control procedures to reconcile the results of EDP processing should be reviewed to determine that controls over the results of computer processing are adequate.
22. An end-of-month journal entry is prepared, based on the summary report prepared by EDP. This processing should be done automatically by EDP with integrated processing procedures.
23. Invoices and supporting documentation are collected with the voucher and checks. This is another point at which the auditor should look at the accumulation of documents and determine what can be eliminated.
24. a. Sign checks, using a facsimile plate. The controls and safeguards for the use of this plate should be reviewed.
    In addition, review the check-signing procedure and determine whether the secretary to V.P. of Finance needs to be involved.
    b. Checks for more than $10,000 require manual signatures of two executives. Determine whether this is a proper limit and whether procedure is working.
25. Review of checks and supporting documents by Accounting Supervisor. Determine whether this step is necessary and, if so, whether the Accounting Supervisor needs to be involved.
26. Checks and supporting documents filed. As can be seen, the present systems and procedures have created an enormous amount of paperwork necessary for the purchasing, receiving, payables, and vendor payment functions. Each document that can be eliminated results in the reduction of forms cost, preparation costs, handling time, filing time, and file costs. In looking at the documents to be disposed of, the following could be considered for elimination:
    - Voucher
    - Check copies
    - Receiving report
    - Department requisition

4.5 SPECIFIC FIELD WORK TECHNIQUES

FIGURE 4.7. Example of layout or flow diagram.

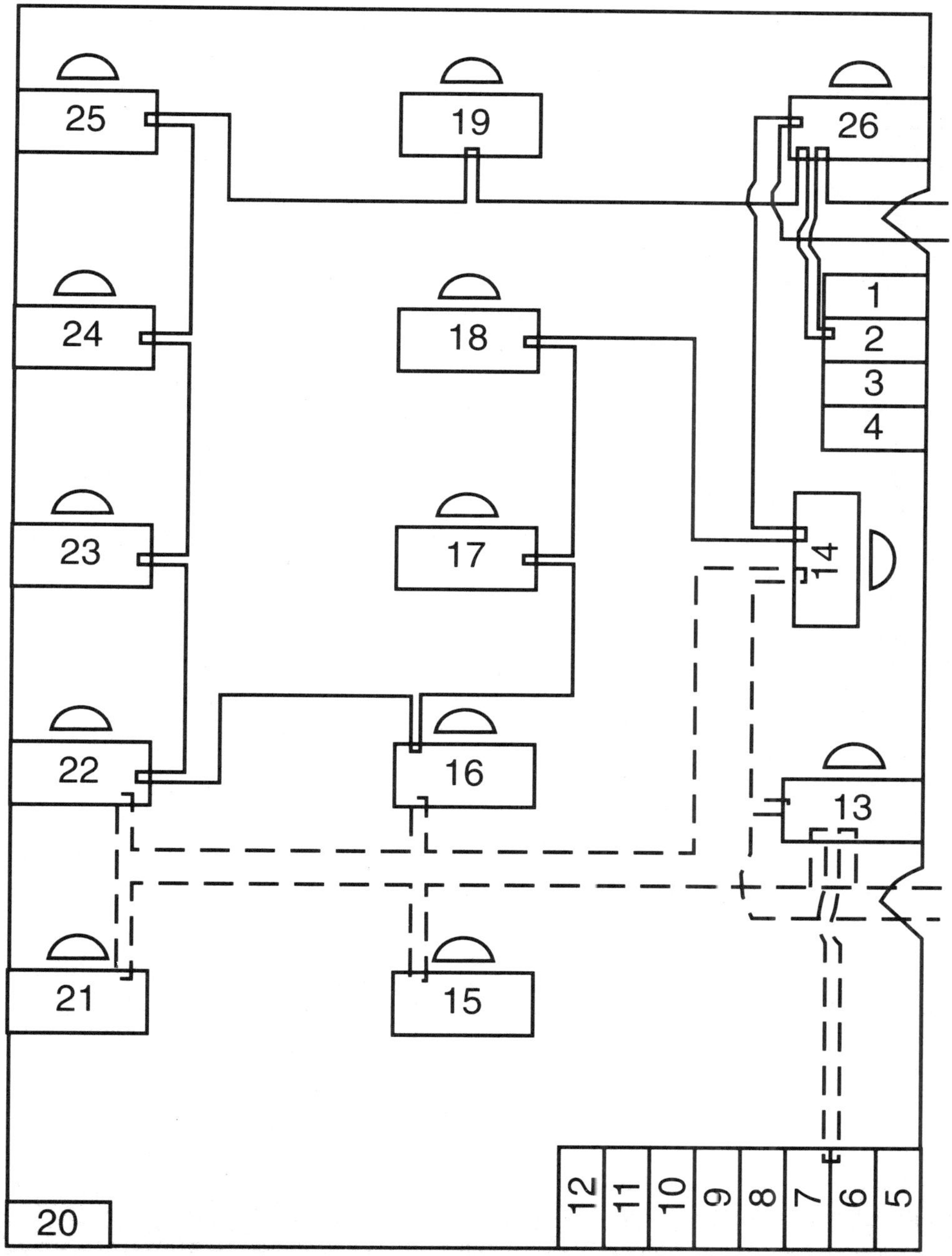

FIGURE 4.8. Analysis of the layout flowchart: Suggested responses.

Note: The following responses correspond to the numbers shown on the layout flowchart for each person/job function.

1 through 4: These employees all appear to be performing the same function, with #2 most likely being the titular "supervisor" or head worker. This function should be reviewed for efficiency. In addition, reporting relationships should be analyzed, including their reporting to #26, who appears to be acting as a controller.

5 through 12: These employees appear to be performing an off-line or staff function in an "isolate" capacity to the remainder of the work group. Their only reporting, which is indirect (as shown by the dotted lines), appears to be with #13, who appears to be performing the role of "dispatcher."

13: This employee is performing the role of dispatcher—on an indirect basis. He or she is interfacing in this capacity with #5 through #12, #14, and #21. The detailed tasks of this function should be looked at as far as necessity.

14: This employee is performing the role of "controller." He or she is controlling materials from #22 and #16 on an indirect basis, and from #26 and #18 on a direct basis, and is then routing to #13 on an indirect basis. The operational auditor should determine whether there is any value-added effort being made or whether this is strictly controlling.

15: This employee appears to be an "isolate" with only an indirect interest in materials coming from the outside and from #13, who is then routing them on to #21.

16 through 18: There appears to be an inverse pyramid, with materials coming from #14 and then distributed downward from #18 to #16. The function being performed should be reviewed as to the necessity of all three employees. #16, at the bottom of the pyramid, relates to #22 on a direct basis, and to #22 and #14 on an indirect basis.

19: This employee is performing the role of "controller" between #26 and #25. This is a typical role for a manager over two supervisors. That is, there is a review of one area's output prior to routing it to another area. This is often an expensive and unnecessary function.

20: This employee is an absolute "isolate," bearing no direct or indirect relation to anyone else in the work area. This could be a staff resource person who is sometimes necessary and sometimes just a nice luxury.

21: This employee appears to be an "isolate" with only indirect relation to #22 and #15. Ask, again, is this a necessary function?

22 through 25: This is another inverse pyramid similar to #16 through #18. Work is routed by #19 to #25, who then appears to distribute the work downward through #24, #23, and #22. #22 relates directly to #16 (the auditor should find out what is happening here) and indirectly to #21.

26: This employee performs the role of "controller," receiving work from #2 and from the outside and routing it back to the group of employees #1 through #4 and, when satisfactory, routing the work to either #14 or #19.

4.5 SPECIFIC FIELD WORK TECHNIQUES

(d) Ratio, Change, and Trend Analysis

Ratio, change, and trend analysis is another technique used in the field work phase to strengthen and supplement other operational audit tools and procedures. Using this technique, the auditor critically examines, interprets, and explains relationships between sets of operating and financial data at a given point in time by comparing them over a number of periods. Ratios have no intrinsic significance; they are primarily useful in highlighting significant changes and relationships. They do not, in and of themselves, form a basis for reaching informed decisions.

Ratio, change, and trend analysis may be used for a variety of purposes. For example, investors may be interested in financial strength, creditors in solvency, management in performance and deviation from what was planned or considered normal. Within the scope of operational auditing, the auditor uses ratio, change and trend analysis to identify managerial and operational problems and trouble areas.

The identification and analysis of a problem situation is the initial step in developing an effective solution. Ratio, change, and trend analysis helps the auditor to detect problem areas for further analysis. The auditor should consider for ratio, change, or trend analysis those areas in which most significant change has occurred and those of greatest vulnerability. In applying these techniques, the goal is to determine and measure changes and interrelationships in data, and then to examine critically and evaluate the changes revealed and their significance.

In using ratio, change, and trend analysis, the auditor considers each situation individually and develops the ratios to use accordingly. There are two prime sources of reference to be used in applying this technique:

1. Comparison with historical internal data and budget data, and

2. Comparison with external data, such as industry statistics, functional standards, and work performance standards.

In using internal data, it is important to make sure that such data are accurate and collected and reported properly. It must also be determined that such data are recorded on a consistent basis from period to period. When using budget data, the auditor must determine that budgets are constructed in relationship to organizational and departmental plans and that actual data are not just compared with budgets, but that actual and budget numbers are what they should be from the standpoint of economy, efficiency, and effectiveness.

For external data to be used effectively, they should be objective and independent, derived from similar and comparable operations, and if current, reflect experience during a comparable period with similar common economic factors and conditions. Note that in using such external data there are no two organizations that are exactly the same—even within the same company structure. Accordingly, the auditor uses external comparisons as a yardstick or indicator, not as a finite measure. These results can indicate possible trouble spots and further field work to be performed.

Incidentally, ratios are but one tool available to the auditor to determine changes. Others that can be used are indexes, percentages, relationships, variable budgets, correlation analysis, and so on. These tools are often used in conjunction with one another.

The development of ratio, change, and trend analysis as related to an audit finding is not an end in itself. Such analysis must be evaluated, integrated, and interpreted as one factor in the development of an operational audit finding. Typically, more analysis and field work are required to develop the full dimensions of the audit finding. The results of ratio, change, and trend analysis provides a measure of significance.

There are two situations in our operational audit of the Example Company where we found the use of ratio, change, and trend analysis helpful in the measurement of changes and their significance. The first situation relates to the apparent use of petty cash funds to circumvent the policy

FIGURE 4.9. Ratio, change, and trend analysis: Petty cash fund review

Situation:

A work unit in the Example Company that should be processing its purchases through the Purchasing Department was found to have a petty cash fund of $3,000.

In 19XX, it was found that total reimbursements for the year totaled $102,000.

An analysis of a sample of 200 petty cash vouchers in 19XX disclosed that 150 of them were for amounts between $40 and $50, and that 130 of the 150 vouchers were for books. Of the other 50 vouchers, 30 were found to be from repetitive vendors who, as a practice, submitted their charges on a vendor's invoice for subsequent payment. These 30 vouchers averaged more than $32. The remaining 20 vouchers were for cash payments, with an average amount of $8.46.

The total number of petty cash payment vouchers in 19XX was 3,200.
Analysis of Purchasing Department policies revealed the policy that "all purchases over $50 must be processed by the central Purchasing Department via a purchase requisition procedure."

4.5 SPECIFIC FIELD WORK TECHNIQUES

that all purchases over $50 be processed by the central Purchasing Department. The second situation relates to the present status of inventory, where a relatively large number of zero usage items and increased usage items were found from one year to the next. The facts of these situations are presented in Figures 4.9 and 4.11. Suggested responses are provided for each of these situations in Figures 4.10 and 4.12.

FIGURE 4.10. Ratio, change, and trend analysis: Petty cash fund review suggested responses

---

RATIOS

Petty Cash Turnover
$102,000 total / $3,000 petty cash fund = 34 times per year. *Note:* A petty cash fund is normally set up for low-amount and/or cash emergency purchases. Within this framework, it is normally expected that the fund will be replenished about once a month. In this situation, it is being replenished about every week and a half, which is far too often.

Average Amount of Petty Cash Payment Voucher
$102,000 / 3,200 vouchers = $31.88
As mentioned, the petty cash fund should be for low-amount purchases. The present average amount of $31.88 appears to be too large for normal petty cash purposes.

Petty Cash Vouchers Between $40 and $50
Sample: 150 / 200 = 75%
Extrapolation: $102,000 × 75% = $76,500 estimate of vouchers between $40 and $50.
Books: 130 / 150 × $76,500 = $66,303 for books between $40 and $50.
Other Vouchers: $102,000 − $76,500 = $25,500 less than $40.
Vendor Invoice Type: 30 = 60% × $25,500 = $15,300.
Remainder: Cash Type: $25,500 − $15,300 = $10,200.
Turnover: Remainder: $10,200 / $3,000 = 3.4 times.

Estimated Monthly Reimbursement:
320 vouchers @ $8.46 = $2,707 estimated annual reimbursements. $2,707/ 12 = $225 petty cash fund based on monthly reimbursement.

Conclusion: Petty cash fund could be substantially lowered to about $225 on a monthly reimbursement basis if vouchers that appear to be legitimate central purchasing items (particularly those for books) were combined and processed correctly through the central Purchasing Department. This would allow the company to invest less of their funds in petty cash (this practice may also exist in other work units) and achieve the economies of central purchasing. You might also want to analyze whether the policy of all purchases over $50 going through central purchasing is appropriate.

FIELD WORK PHASE

FIGURE 4.11. Ratio, change, and trend analysis: Inventory usage review

Situation
The Example Company raw materials inventory approximated 6,000 items valued at about $350,000 at December 31, 19XX. An operational audit test, based on accepted statistical sampling procedures, of 113 listed raw material inventory items disclosed the following:

1. Total value of tested items: $15,000
2. Total zero-usage items: 20
3. Total December 31, 19XX, value of zero-usage items: $4,000
4. Total number of items whose December 31, 19XX, usage was greater than 1½ times their prior year's usage: 45
5. Total value of items in #4: $6,200

FIGURE 4.12. Ratio, change, and trend analysis: Inventory usage review suggested responses

Zero-Usage Items
Number of Items: 20 / 113 = 18% × 6,000 items = 1,080 items
Dollar Value: $4,000 / $15,000 = 27% × $350,000 = $94,500
Conclusion: 18% of 6,000 inventory items, estimated at 1,080 items, had no usage during the year. 27% of inventory value, estimated at $94,500, had no usage for the year. These data could be used to determine the cost of carrying inventory and the company's return on investment to determine the cost of carrying such a relatively high percentage of inventory having no usage.

Analysis could also be made as to why so many items with no usage were allowed to build up in inventory during the past year. These items should also be reviewed as to disposition: used in the future, sold, returned to vendor, or scrapped.

Usage Greater Than 1½ Times Prior Year
Number of Items: 45 / 113 = 40% × 6,000 items = 2,400 items.
Dollar Value: $6,200 / $15,000 = 41% × $350,000 = $143,500.
Conclusion: Approximately 40% of inventory items, estimated at 2,400 items and a dollar value of $143,500, had more than 1½ times usage over the prior year. These facts, coupled with the high increase in zero-usage items, could indicate a change in product lines manufactured, without corresponding changes in raw material forecasting and ordering.

Therefore, further analysis could be made to determine whether reorder points and reorder quantities have been changed to reflect accurately the recent increase in usage. Analysis could also be made to determine the number of resultant stock-outs and the related cost to the company.

4.6 FIELD WORK: EXAMPLE COMPANY

Figure 3.12 in Chapter 3 illustrates an operational audit program for the Example Company's purchasing function. As part of the operational audit of the Example Company, the following areas were defined for performance in the field work phase.

1. Organization
   - Function and authority of the Purchasing Department
   - Function and necessity of specific job classifications
2. Purchasing Department Responsibility
   - Processing of regular purchase orders
   - Decentralized purchasing
3. Purchasing Operations and Work Flow

Some of these work steps have already been accomplished through previously considered techniques such as:

- Obtaining or preparing copy of organization chart
- Determining authority for purchasing: policies and procedures manual
- Determining functions of each work unit: for example, work observation
- Interviewing: for example, determining job duties and responsibilities
- Obtaining or preparing copy of systems and procedures
- Determining purchase order processing procedures: for example, using systems flowchart
- Decentralized purchasing: for example, reviews of petty cash procedures
- Determining work flow: for example, using layout flow diagram

Additional work steps that need to be accomplished to complete the audit work program include the following:

Function and authority

Cost to process a purchase order

Sample of small purchases

(a) Function and Authority

One objective of the audit program for the Example Company was to determine the specific functions, responsibilities, and authority of each personnel position. Therefore, the auditor desires to document the duties and responsibilities of the following job classifications:

- Purchasing Supervisor
- Buyers I and II
- Clerk Supervisor
- Clerical Supervisor
- Clerk-Typist

- Standard Specifications Unit
  Standard Specifications Supervisor
  Procurement Technician
  Management Trainee
  Clerk Stenographer
  Clerk

The auditor has obtained copies of existing job descriptions (which were found to be quite sketchy and inaccurate) and has attempted to validate them through interviewing and direct work observation. To assist in these efforts, a Job Responsibilities Questionnaire was developed for each employee to fill out and return to the auditors. Such a questionnaire is used to help accumulate a large amount of information in a relatively short period of time and to obtain relevant nonthreatening data from each employee to substantiate actual duties and responsibilities.

The auditor then analyzes the data to identify problem areas, intra- and interdepartmental patterns, indications of organization-wide personnel-related issues, and so on. An example of the Job Responsibilities Questionnaire developed is shown in Figure 4.13.

(b) Cost to Process a Purchase Order

The audit program for the Example Company's Purchasing Department defined work steps to determine the cost to process a purchase order, considering such elements as the direct cost of operating the Purchasing Department, indirect costs related to the purchasing function, and the number of actual purchase orders processed. The data required to calculate the cost of processing a purchase order are given in Figure 4.14. The completed calculation is shown in Figure 4.15.

4.6 FIELD WORK: EXAMPLE COMPANY

FIGURE 4.13. Job responsibilities questionnaire

Instructions

The purpose of this form is to help you describe the duties and responsibilities of your job and the jobs of your supervisees. A separate questionnaire is to be completed for each employee under your supervision, as well as one for your own job. In the event that two or more employees perform identical duties, only one questionnaire need be completed. However, the names of all employees covered by the questionnaire should be included in the identification section. Please read the entire questionnaire carefully before answering any questions; type or print your answers clearly.

PLEASE RETURN THIS QUESTIONNAIRE TO:
Mr. Cliff Chambers
by April 30, 19XX

Identification

Employee Name _____ Title _____

Division _____ Department _____

Name of Immediate Supervisor _____

Title of Immediate Supervisor _____

Your Name _____ Date _____

A. *Description of Regular Duties and Tasks*

Describe each of the duties and responsibilities in the employee's regular routine, in two or three sentences. The first sentence in each case might tell what the employee is supposed to do, and the next sentence might tell how it is done. Do not refer to previous job descriptions or attempt to describe what you think the job *should* be. Write what is *actually* done. In addition, enter the number of hours usually spent on each duty or responsibility in either the "Daily," "Weekly," or "Monthly" column.

If you do not have enough room to describe the job duties and responsibilities, you can complete them on the back of page 2 or on a blank piece of paper, which should then be attached.

		Time	
Duties and/or Responsibilities	Daily	Weekly	Monthly
1. _____	_____	_____	_____
_____	_____	_____	_____
2. _____	_____	_____	_____
_____	_____	_____	_____

FIELD WORK PHASE

FIGURE 4.13. *(Continued)*

| | Time | | |
Duties and/or Responsibilities	Daily	Weekly	Monthly
3. _____	_____	_____	_____
4. _____	_____	_____	_____
5. _____	_____	_____	_____
6. _____	_____	_____	_____
7. _____	_____	_____	_____
8. _____	_____	_____	_____

B. Difficulty of the Job
What, in your opinion, is the most difficult feature of the job, and why is this so?

_____

_____

_____

_____

C. Description of Contacts
List the persons (by general job title, not name) with whom the employee comes in contact in the performance of normal job duties. Contacts may be either (1) within the employee's own department or division or (2) within other divisions of the firm. Under the heading "Frequency," indicate whether these contacts (conversations, correspondence, meetings, etc.) are made "not often," "moderately often," "very often," or "constantly."

FIGURE 4.13. *(Continued)*

Contacts Within Your Own Department or Division	Reason for Contact	Frequency

Contacts with Other Divisions of the Firm	Reason for Contact	Frequency

FIELD WORK PHASE

FIGURE 4.13. *(Continued)*

D. *Work Flow*

The purpose of this question is to determine where the employee's work originates and where the results of employee's contributions to the work terminate; i.e., where do the data for completing a form originate, and where copies of the form are sent.

Form Title	Data Source	Frequency (No. Forms/Week)
_____	_____	_____
_____	_____	_____
_____	_____	_____
_____	_____	_____

	Form Destination					
Form Title	Copy A	Copy B	Copy C	Copy D	Copy E	Copy F
_____	____	____	____	____	____	____
_____	____	____	____	____	____	____
_____	____	____	____	____	____	____
_____	____	____	____	____	____	____

E. *Additional Remarks*

State here additional information that you believe would help in describing or understanding the duties of this job.

_____
_____
_____
_____

FIGURE 4.13. (Continued)

F. *Types of Employees' Jobs Supervised*
List the job titles of employees supervised and the number in each classification.

_____

_____

_____

_____

_____

_____

_____

_____

_____

_____

_____

_____

(c) Sample of Small Purchases

Another audit program work step was to analyze the purchase order volume for small purchases: under $50, $50 to $100, and $100 to $200. Remember, in the planning phase it was determined that many small purchases were being processed by the Purchasing Department and many small purchases were circumventing central purchasing procedures. In addition, the cost to process a purchase had not been updated in many years. The objective of this work step is to determine the impact of processing small purchases on the Purchasing Department.

The results of an analysis of a selected sample of purchase orders showing small purchases are given in Figure 4.16. These results will be used in the next chapter to develop an audit finding related to small purchases and the corresponding cost to process a purchase order.

FIGURE 4.14. Data: Cost to process a purchase order: The Example Company.

Number of Regular Purchase Orders	18,100
Purchasing Department:	
Payroll	$384,587
Elements directly associated with purchase order preparation	
Other Direct Costs	243,264
Other costs directly associated with purchase order preparation	
Indirect Costs	95,059
Allocated to purchase order preparation on basis of percentage that above payroll costs relate to total Purchasing Department payroll	
Fringe Benefits: Estimate (percentage of payroll)	28%
Other Expenditures: Allocated to Purchasing	101,000
Other company costs that can be directly attributable to purchase order preparation	

FIGURE 4.15. Calculation: Cost to process a purchase order.

Purchasing Department	
Payroll Costs	$384,587
Other Direct Costs	243,264
Indirect Costs	95,059
Fringe Benefits (28% × $384,587)	107,684
Other Expenditures: Allocated to Purchasing	101,000
Total Preparation Cost for Functions Directly Associated with Purchase Order Preparation	$931,594

Cost to Process a Single Purchase Order =
Total Cost (approximate) / Annual Number of Purchase Orders
$931,594 / 18,100 = $51 per Purchase Order

FIGURE 4.16. Sample of purchase orders: Purchase order volume of small purchases.

	Volume		Dollar Value	
	Number	% Total Sample	Amount	% Total Sample
Purchase Orders Processed for:				
Under $50	17	2.9	460.74	.03
$50 to $100	43	7.4	3,173.03	.20
$100 to $200	76	13.2	16,022.55	1.00
Total $200 and under	136	23.5	19,656.32	1.23
Over $200	442	76.5	1,574,395.93	98.77
TOTAL	578	100.0	1,594,052.25	100.00

Total dollar value of purchases for the year was $48,158,617. The above distribution was arrived at by taking samples of two groups of purchase orders, consisting of approximately 300 each (actually 578 in total owing to canceled orders). The first sample was chosen randomly, using tables of random numbers. Purchase orders in this first sample group were dated March and April 19XX. A second group of approximately 300 purchase orders was chosen from a later month, November 19XX, to be examined for their distributions of $0 to $200 and over $200.

4.7 OTHER TECHNIQUES

There are many other tools and techniques that the operational auditor can use in the field work phase, depending on the situation and the objective of the work step—too many to cover in this book. However, two significant techniques of which the auditor should be aware are tests of transactions, and reviewing performance versus plans.

(a) Tests of Transactions

The operational auditor, in testing transactions, examines the procedures actually applied to specific transactions or items, from beginning to end. The transactions selected for review should represent the operations involved. The character or type of transactions selected is more important than the number of transactions selected. Operational audit tests of transactions should be limited in the number of transactions used, but must be representative of actual transactions processed.

In addition to the information provided in flowcharting, the test of transactions provides the auditor with information relative to the results of transactions in terms of management's objectives, specific requirements, and common sense practices. The operational audit program given in Chapter 3, Figure 3.1, shows a selection of transactions and an examination of transactions selected as sample audit program work steps.

(b) Performance Versus Plans

A review of performance versus plans allows the auditor to examine existing plans that relate to the area being audited and the methods that operations management follows, to compare actual performance with the plans. This technique can provide direct insight into the ability of management to effectively plan for the organization, as well as the relative strength and effectiveness of management control. This is a good technique to use in most operational audits, to help analyze management controls over operations—primarily to help ascertain how management personnel themselves determine whether plans, policies, and procedures are being followed, and whether they are effective and efficient.

In many organizations that come under operational audit, there exist no effective planning procedures whatsoever. These organizations are typified by "seat of the pants" and crisis-type management, which attempts to operate without adequate short-term detail plans and, in many instances, without a budget. Those organizations that are found to have budgets often use the budget as a constraining and punitive tool, rather than as part of a helpful system. In these instances, this practice not only constitutes an audit finding, but also makes it incumbent upon the auditor to help management develop an effective planning and budgeting system. This is often one of the first steps of the operational audit, as the definition of planning goals and objectives are necessary to effectively evaluate the results of operations.

4.8 WORKPAPERS

During the course of the operational audit, various procedures are followed which are aimed at ascertaining what was found, what was measured against, what was the effect, why did it happen, and what does the auditor recommend. To carry out this program in a systematic fashion, to have a record of what was done, and to accumulate the data, the auditor must prepare workpapers. These are the principal records of the work actually

4.8 WORKPAPERS

performed to substantiate the operational audit report. Therefore, the audit workpapers must be complete and self-explanatory. They are the tangible means of measuring the operational audit team's professional skill.

Information obtained on an assignment is of little or no continuing value if it is accumulated only mentally by staff members. To minimize errors and omissions, information given orally must be recorded in the workpapers as soon as possible.

Workpapers serve as the basis on which operational audit work programs and reports are prepared and as a connecting link between work done and the report. Workpapers provide systematic evidence of how audit responsibilities in specific assignments were carried out.

Any questions that may arise concerning the operational audit must be answered by reference to the workpapers. As a result, any omission of information may have serious consequences.

(a) Use

Workpapers are used:

1. As the repository of the information obtained.

2. To identify and support problems, events, or actions occurring during the engagement, findings, meetings, and the like.

3. To give support to discussions with operating personnel.

4. To provide support for the report.

5. As a line of defense when facts, conclusions, and recommendations are challenged.

6. As a basis for supervisory review; to provide evidence that work was performed according to the audit plan and consistent with auditor's understanding of what was to be done.

7. As a basis for appraising an auditor's technical ability, skill, and working habits.

8. As background and reference for subsequent review.

(b) Identification

Each workpaper supporting the operational audit must be properly identified. A completed workpaper should contain the following:

FIELD WORK PHASE

1. Title
   A complete title consists of:
   - Department or unit number, entered in the upper left-hand corner of the paper.
   - Department or unit name, entered in the center of the paper on the first line.
   - A description of the workpaper, entered in the center of the paper on the second line. (The third line may also be used.)
   - The period covered in the workpaper, entered in the center of the paper on the third line. (The fourth line may also be used.)
2. Reference index number—center of the paper, last line.
3. Initials of the preparer and date prepared.
4. Initials of the reviewer and date reviewed.
5. Source (person, data processing output, book, periodical, etc.) of information.
6. Indication of the review or verification of material received from the department or unit being audited.
7. Names of all persons present at conferences or discussions.

(c) Sample Table of Contents

The following are the sections that should be included in the current operational audit workpaper files:

1. Working paper index
2. Audit program
3. Audit checklist
4. Time control
5. Engagement status reports
6. Supervision notes
7. Correspondence (both in and out)
8. Minutes of meetings
9. Planning papers
10. Fact-finding: statement of condition

4.9 EVIDENCE

11. Fact-finding: establishment of criteria
12. Analysis and conclusions
13. Development of recommendations: alternatives
14. Development of recommendations: final
15. Presentation outline: oral reporting
16. Written report: draft
17. Written report: final copy
18. Bulk material

4.9 EVIDENCE

The operational auditor is also responsible for accumulating sufficient competent and relevant evidence to support opinions, conclusions, and recommendations.

(a) Types

The types of evidence that should be considered in the operational audit include the following:

1. Physical—Observations, photographs, slides, and so on
2. Testimonial—Interviews, personal statements, and so on
3. Documentary—Letters, contracts, grants, records, and so on
4. Analytical—An analysis of information

(b) Attributes

The basic attributes of evidence are as follows:

- Sufficiency—Presence of enough factual, adequate, and convincing material to lead a prudent person to the same conclusion as the auditors. This is a judgmental decision.

- Competence—Is the evidence reliable and the best obtainable through the use of reasonable audit methods?

- Relevance—The evidence must provide a logical relationship to the issue at hand.

(c) Evidence in the Workpapers

To reflect the basic attributes of evidence, the workpapers that generally constitute the evidence must be complete and accurate. They must express the intended message clearly, so that reviewers and report writers can understand it. They must have a purpose, and must explain the nature and the scope of the work done and the preparer's conclusions. It is important that workpapers be concise, and it stands to reason that they should be legible, neat, and restricted to matters that are material and useful, with reference to the objectives established for the audit.

4.10 CONCLUSION

Those items identified as significant in the field work phase are further developed as operational audit findings in the next phase. Before proceeding to Chapter 5, review the operational auditing situation in Figure 4.17.

FIGURE 4.17. Clerical procedures.

During the preliminary review of the planning phase of the operational audit, the auditor observed that the office area of the Purchasing Department appeared to be grossly overstaffed. Accordingly, the audit staff wanted to perform operational audit procedures during the field work phase and included such techniques in their audit program.

Although the office manager agreed that there might be a little overstaffing, she pointed out that a recent company report showed their office expense per purchase order processed was no higher than that of other similar companies, including those operating in lower cost areas.

Question and Solution Consideration
What audit steps would you perform in the field work phase to substantiate your preliminary finding of overstaffing in the office area?
Some of the audit steps that could be performed include:

1. Expanded audit of office payroll to verify total office payroll costs being reported, and to make sure all costs are being included (for example, the office manager being charged to the executive payroll).
2. Interviews with each of the employees to determine exactly what tasks they perform and to what extent.
3. Layout/flow diagram of the office area and major operations to determine smoothness of operational flow.
4. System flowcharts for each operating procedure to determine whether procedures could be simplified, steps eliminated, and duties realigned.
5. System flowcharts and layout/flow diagrams of proposed systems for increased efficiency with reduced staff.

Note: As a result of these audit steps being performed, it was determined that office costs were understated by $84,000 and that in actuality overall costs were more than similar companies'. You should be aware that such comparisons are only to be used as yardsticks and do not actually measure the economy, efficiency, and effectiveness of the entity being audited.

The performance of these audit steps during the operational audit provided the following results:

- Purchase order processing simplified.
- Manual procedures eliminated which were the same as EDP.
- Number of reports eliminated where information was duplicated.
- Personnel duties realigned, resulting in increased efficiency.
- Overall staff able to be reduced by six positions.
  (Note that it is not the operational auditor's responsibility to identify specific personnel to be dismissed, but only to document job positions or functions that can be eliminated. It is auditee management's responsibility to decide what to do at that point; i.e. reassign personnel, change responsibilities, dismiss employees, etc. The dismissal of good employees is to be discouraged.)

The total net annual savings resulting from these operational audit findings and conclusions amounted to more than $250,000.

CHAPTER FIVE

Development of Audit Findings

5.1 INTRODUCTION

The operational audit team, considering the critical areas identified in the field work phase for further analysis, begins to develop its significant audit findings. During the course of the operational audit engagement, the audit team may have identified certain findings that required no additional analysis. In those instances, the team would have prepared their findings and presented them directly to management. It is not good practice to hold such audit findings for the final report. As findings are identified and/or developed, they should be reported to management, so that if management agrees, remedial action can be taken as soon as possible.

Every operational audit finding, whether requiring additional analysis or not, has certain common structural characteristics—just as every building, no matter how different from other buildings, has a roof, walls, floor, and so on—which can be regarded as building blocks. The operational auditor must use these basic building blocks to construct a complete audit finding, one that gives the reader all the information needed to understand the finding and the reason for the recommendations.

This chapter discusses the development of effective and convincing operational audit findings. Using the audit work steps performed in the field work phase, the operational audit team identifies those findings it believes to be most significant. For these findings, the operational audit team develops the necessary elements to convince management that a deficiency ex-

DEVELOPMENT OF AUDIT FINDINGS

ists and that there is need to take corrective action. These findings are not intended to be critical, but to help management improve its operations. Establishing a constructive atmosphere helps to ally management with the auditing team and to ensure greater receptiveness of such findings. Moreover, if operations people are part of the audit team, the findings will be more binding. This chapter reviews the attributes of a well-developed, convincing operational audit finding and discusses how the operational audit team can put the relevant principles into practice.

This chapter will:

1. Increase understanding of the importance of the proper development of an operational audit finding.

2. Familiarize the auditor with the five operational audit attributes—statement of condition, criteria, cause, effect, and recommendation—and their significance in the development of audit findings.

3. Increase knowledge as to how to use proper audit finding presentation as an effective reporting tool.

4. Provide hands-on experience in the development of operational audit findings.

The most important single element of the operational audit is the development of specific audit findings—this is the heart of the operational audit. Furthermore, the acceptance and implementation of these findings by management is the yardstick for measuring operational audit success. A good rule of thumb is that if the audit team can persuade management to accept at least 50 percent of its findings and recommendations, then the team has been successful. Developing audit findings involves:

1. Data collection, to get as much pertinent, significant information about each finding as is realistic, and

2. Evaluation of the finding, in terms of cause, effect, and possible courses of corrective action.

In developing such specific audit findings and conclusions, the auditor must do the necessary amount of analytical work, along with accumulating all appropriate evidential supporting data.

5.2 ATTRIBUTES

To develop a specific operational audit finding, the auditor should be aware of, and use effectively, the following attributes or building blocks:

Statement of Condition,

Criteria,

Cause,

Effect, and

Recommendations.

These attributes have been summarized in Figure 5.1.

FIGURE 5.1. Operational audit finding attributes.

1. *Statement Of Condition*
   What did you find?
   What did you observe?
   What is defective, deficient, or in error?
   This is the what-when-where-how step.
2. *Criteria*
   What should it be?
   What do you measure against?
   What is the standard procedure or practice?
   This is the step comparing what is with what should be.
3. *Cause*
   Why did it happen?
   What is the underlying cause of the deficiency?
   Why have operations become inefficient or uneconomical?
   This is the step for identification of the cause and not the symptom.
4. *Effect*
   So what?
   What is the effect of the finding?
   What is the end result of the condition?
   This is the step to determine the present or potential impact on the operations.
5. *Recommendations*
   What is recommended to correct the condition?
   What recommendation is practical and reasonable for acceptance?
   Who should implement the recommendation?
   This is the step to determine what needs to be done to correct the situation.

(a) Statement of Condition

In determining the present condition of an operational audit finding, the auditor should address the following questions:

What did you find?

What did you observe?

What is defective, deficient, or in error?

Is the condition isolated or widespread?

All operational audits involve initial fact-finding in the field work phase. When fact-finding is used to determine the statement of condition, the auditor examines and verifies as much of the operations and related data as necessary to establish clearly all pertinent facts. The audit work steps performed are those that best fit the situation. In an operational audit, this fact-finding process is really the "what-when-where-how" step. The statement of condition provides a reference point to the finding as it relates to established criteria.

One difficulty in performing operational audits is that the condition disclosed by the detailed audit work in the field work phase often does not turn out to be quite the same as initially indicated in the planning phase. Thus, developing the audit finding sometimes turns out to be an evolutionary process in actual practice, which requires the audit program to be evolutionary as well. It is in the field work phase that these changes take place, causing the audit program to be revised as facts are discovered.

The auditor should be able to reach agreement with appropriate management on the correctness of the facts, even though there may be disagreement on the reasons, significance, and need for corrective action. The auditor's failure or inability to agree on the facts with management does not, however, stop the audit team from reporting a finding if team members are reasonably certain that the information developed is correct. Bear in mind that although it may be reported to top management and financial management, the operational audit finding is really intended for operations management.

Note, too, that the condition (or the problem or the finding itself) is always presented in the singular. However, the related criteria, causes, effects, and recommendations may be multiple in nature. Although there is no absolute order, the attributes of an operational audit finding are normally presented in this order: condition, criteria, cause, effect, and recommendation. The auditor may decide to present operational audit findings in a different order, but always starting with condition and ending with recommendation.

(b) Criteria

In analyzing present conditions, the operational auditor must be aware of what conditions are expected to meet organizational goals and objectives. In determining the proper criteria for a specific condition, the auditor reviews such areas as relevant legislation and laws, existing contracts, policy statements, systems and procedures, internal and external regulations, responsibility and authority relationships, standards, schedules, plans and budgets, principles of good management and administration, and so on. In determining the correct criteria for a specific audit finding, the auditor answers the following questions concerning the stated condition:

What should it be?

What is it measured against?

What is the standard procedure or practice?

Is it a formal procedure or an informal practice?

This is the "comparing what is to what should be" step.

In evaluating procedures and practices, the auditor should be aware that procedures are formal methods of doing things. Such procedures are documented, usually in writing, and prescribed by management. Practices are the actual ways in which work activities are performed and are rarely documented in written form.

Essentially, in developing the audit finding criteria, the auditor compares what is, with what should be. The audit team has taken the first step toward developing an audit finding when it has identified a difference between what actually exists and what should be or what the auditors think is correct or proper.

Examples of criteria that can be used for such comparison purposes include:

1. Written requirements, such as laws, regulations, instructions, policies and procedures manuals, directives, and so forth.

2. Stated goals and objectives of the organization and/or department or work unit.

3. Verbal instructions.

4. Independent opinion of experts.

Some other measures or standards that are used to compare an operational condition with what it should be are shown in Figure 5.2.

(i) ALTERNATIVE CRITERIA In many cases, criteria may not be available and must be developed. This is one of the operational auditor's challenges. In the absence of standards or other effective criteria with which to evaluate performance, three alternative approaches are available to the operational auditor:

1. Comparative analysis.

FIGURE 5.2. Operational auditing criteria standards.

a. Internal to the Organization:
- Organizational policy statements
- Legislation, laws, and regulations
- Contractual arrangements
- Funding arrangements
- Organizational and departmental plans: goals and objectives
- Budgets, schedules, and detail plans

b. Developed by the Operational Auditor:
- Performance of similar organizations
- Industry or functionally related statistics
- Past and present performance of the auditee organization
- Engineered standards
- Special analysis or studies
- Auditor's judgment
- Sound business practices
- Good common business sense

Example:
Objective: To provide meaningful, accurate, and timely financial information.
Criteria:
1. Information provided is relevant to management's needs.
2. Information supplied is accurate.
3. Information is received in sufficient time after the reporting period to be useful for its intended purpose.
4. Information is easily understood.

2. The use of borrowed standards.

3. The test of reasonableness.

Comparative Analysis Comparative analysis is the technique that can be used, where there are no specific standards for comparison, to compare the audited circumstances to similar situations. This analysis can be accomplished in two ways:

1. Current performance can be compared with past performance, and

2. Performance can be compared with that of a similar organization.

Comparing current performance with that of past periods has the advantage of possibly disclosing trends in performance. For example, if the cost per employee procedures manual rises from year to year, the auditor might question whether (1) prices have risen, (2) inefficiencies in manual preparation have increased, (3) employees are being given larger quantities, or (4) material of better quality is being used. The auditor can then analyze the situation further to determine exactly why the cost per procedures manual has increased. In this example, the criteria by which actual performance is evaluated are not part of a predetermined plan or a formal set of performance standards, but simply derived from what was done in prior years. Using such comparisons does not provide sufficient data to tell whether the rise in procedures manual prices per employee is good or bad, or whether costs are too high. This method does, however, identify the causes so that management can judge performance as it occurred. Although trends can be noted and examined by this method, meaningful comparisons of alternative methods or procedures cannot usually be accomplished.

The comparison of two similar organizations normally provides the opportunity for the auditor to evaluate different approaches to operations management. By determining the results of different operational approaches, the auditor can make some helpful recommendations for improving efficiency and effectiveness.

There are, however, some disadvantages in comparing two separate but similar organizations. The major disadvantage is the auditor's possible failure to recognize factors that justify differences between the two organizations. For example, it is difficult to compare two manufacturers, because no two manufacturers have exactly the same type of manufacturing systems, hire the same type of employees, use the same type of equipment, or have the same proximity to materials and other essentials. Most manufacturers would, however, have many of the same types of problems, regardless of their differences. The similarity of problems can enable the operational auditor to analyze how each management group handles them. The auditor can then analyze alternatives for improving the efficiency and effectiveness of operations, and the resultant recommendations can reflect his or her judgment, based on the results produced by each alternative.

The Borrowed Standard Many groups and organizations throughout the country, such as manufacturers, hospitals, and banking associations, provide uniform and comparable standards for evaluating performance. These borrowed standards can then be used to compare performance of organizations in similar endeavors. Although such comparisons may make performance evaluation quicker and easier for the operational auditor, there are some disadvantages to this procedure as well.

One disadvantage is that national averages and broad-based statistics hardly ever relate to specific situations. Thus, while such statistics provide some indications of the organization's performance, they cannot be used for precise measurement or evaluation. Another disadvantage is that very few national averages or uniform statistics actually exist. In those cases where such statistics do exist, such as by standard industry code, for hospitals, banks, service industries, schools, libraries, and so forth, they either relate to only a small portion of the areas subject to operational audit, or are limited to very restricted areas and are of minimal use to the auditor.

The auditor should be more critical when thinking of using these borrowed standards or statistics, than when using the performance standards established by the organization itself. The auditor should use borrowed standards only when and if they are found to be relevant and appropriate.

The Test of Reasonableness When there are no internal standards, and comparisons with other organizations are impossible or borrowed statistics are unavailable, the auditor can still test organizational performance on the basis of reasonableness. Through experience, auditors have become familiar with how things are done economically, efficiently, and effectively in other organizations. The auditors should be able to relate these experiences to the current operations under audit.

Accordingly, the auditor can often spot operational irregularities and weaknesses that might escape the notice of others without such a background. In operational auditing, perceptions of a situation are in the eyes of the beholder—in this case, the cumulative experience of the individual operational auditor. In addition, there exist what may be termed "general standards of society" that apply to good management in any field, public or private. For example, the auditor can often spot work being done in a loose, unsatisfactory, and inefficient manner, even in the absence of specific standards. Often this work has been considered acceptable—"That's the way we've always done it."

Obsolete inventory, excessive supplies, personnel who are continually absent from work, abuse of resources such as automobiles and expense accounts, and negligence in processing documents or handling cash funds—all are examples of items that can be evaluated through the test of reasonableness. The auditor can also use the test of reasonableness as an appropriate tool to quickly review operating areas not subjected to detailed analysis. Even where the audit team has analyzed in detail, the auditors should still examine their conclusions for reasonableness. This ensures that the auditors have not become so engrossed in statistics that they have overlooked important items or put too much weight on minor ones. The test of reasonableness can also be viewed as the operational auditor's application of good common sense or prudent business practice to the situation.

(c) Cause

The operational audit finding is not complete until the auditor has fully identified the reason or cause for the deviation from the criteria. To analyze the cause, the operational auditor must answer the following questions:

Why did it happen?

What are the reasons for the operational deficiency?

The most important factor of an operational audit finding is the underlying cause of the deficiency. This cause is the reason that operations have become inefficient or uneconomical. The auditor's responsibility is to report what must be done to correct the situation and prevent recurrence of the adverse effect.

Developing the underlying cause of an audit finding requires a good amount of judgment on the auditor's part. If the auditor analyzes the cause of a problem too deeply, the conclusion may be impractical. Moreover, the auditor must make sure to identify the cause, not the symptom.

Audit tests and procedures should normally be sufficient to show whether the condition is isolated or widespread. This determination is necessary to:

1. Reach a proper conclusion about the significance of the deficiency.
2. Propose adequate recommendations for corrective action if the condition is widespread and/or likely to recur.

The auditor must be careful in identifying a specific cause, as it often appears to be specific individuals who are the cause. Normally, the auditor's responsibility is to identify the underlying reasons for resultant deviations from expected criteria, not specific individuals. The audit team is wise to avoid identifying specific individuals as the cause of a problem. The real cause could be such things as improper orientation or training, unclear instructions and expectations, poor hiring practices, ineffective supervision and management, or inappropriate systems and procedures. Remember, the task of the operational auditor is to help achieve improvements in the operation, and finger pointing at employees may jeopardize the audit team's ongoing credibility.

Some possible types of causes include the following:

- Ineffective or lack of adequate planning systems and procedures.

- Confusing, ineffective, or faulty organizational structure.

- Superfluous or unwieldy organizational hierarchy.

- Lack of effective delegation of authority, commensurate with related responsibilities.

- Inability or unwillingness to change, as exemplified by resistant attitudes: "We've always done it that way"; "It's industry practice."

- Lack of effective or sufficient management or supervision.

- Inadequate, misleading, or obsolete policies, procedures, directives, standards, and so on.

- Lack of effective personnel procedures relative to hiring, orientation, training, evaluation, promotion, and firing.

- Ineffective use of computerization.

- Inadequate management and/or operational reporting systems.

- Lack of effective communication.

- Personal inadequacies such as negligence, carelessness, unfamiliarity with expected requirements, failure to use good sense or judgment, dishonesty, lack of effort or interest, and so on.

- Inadequate resources, including people, equipment, materials and supplies, and facilities.

- Ineffective operating systems and procedures.

5.2 ATTRIBUTES

- Deviation from expected standards or criteria.
- Lack of knowledge that a problem or condition exists.

(d) Effect

One of the primary goals in conducting the operational audit is to persuade operations management to take positive action to correct the findings of operational deficiencies the audit team has identified. To help management determine just how seriously the condition affects its operations, the auditor should quantify the effect to the extent possible. As discussed earlier, economy, efficiency, and effectiveness are good measures of effect. They can usually be stated in quantitative terms, such as *dollars, time, production, number of items or transactions,* etc. Sometimes, when past effects cannot be fully determined, the auditor may want to present future effects.

In determining an operational audit effect, the auditor should answer the following questions:

So what?

What is the effect of the finding?

Effect represents the end result of the condition, actual and/or potential. Effect should convince management either that:

1. Its policies are working out well and its goals are being achieved, or
2. Its goals are not being achieved, and therefore something needs to be done.

The operational auditor should, whenever possible, quantify the financial effects or loss. Such determinations demonstrate to management the need for corrective action, as well as help convince management in the operational audit report.

Such quantification may consist of the following:

1. Actual or estimated monetary losses or potential cost savings,
2. Uneconomical or inefficient use of resources,
3. Actual or estimated loss of potential income,
4. Not achieving as effective operating results as possible,
5. Job expectations not being met as well as they could be,

6. Information system not useful or meaningful, resulting in poor decision making, and

7. Decrease in employee morale and organizational atmosphere.

A list of possible indicators for quantifying effect is shown in Figure 5.3.

(e) Recommendations

The successful completion of the operational audit finding is the development of recommendations as to the action that should be taken to correct the present undesirable condition. The recommendations should logically follow an explanation of why the present condition exists, the underlying causes, and what should be done to prevent its recurrence. The auditors' recommendations should be practical and reasonable, so that management will easily see the merits of adopting them.

In developing recommendations, the auditor should answer these questions:

What could be recommended to correct the situation?

Is this recommendation based on a logical connection to the present condition, criteria, and causes?

Is the recommendation practical and reasonable for implementation?

In many cases, a workable recommendation seems to suggest itself, but at other times the auditor may need some ingenuity to come up with a recommendation that is sensible and has a reasonable chance of being adopted. Operational audit recommendations should be as specific and helpful as possible, not simply that operations need to be improved, controls need to be strengthened, or planning systems need to be implemented. Auditing team members should do their best to make certain that their recommendations are practical and acceptable to those responsible for taking action.

Each recommendation should be directed to a specific management member, so that it is clear who should take the necessary action to implement the recommendation. In addition, the auditor should always weigh the cost of carrying out a recommendation against its expected benefits.

5.2 ATTRIBUTES

FIGURE 5.3. Effects of operational audit findings: Possible indicators.

1. Management and Organization
   - Poor planning and decision making
   - Too broad span of control
   - Badly designed systems and procedures
   - Excessive crisis management
   - Poor channels of communication
   - Inadequate delegation of authority
   - Excessive organizational changes
2. Personnel Relations
   - Inadequate hiring, orientation, training, evaluation, and promotion procedures
   - Lack of clearly communicated job expectations
   - Idle, excessive, or not enough personnel
   - Poor employee morale
   - Excessive overtime and/or absenteeism
   - Unclear responsibility/authority relationships
3. Manufacturing and Operations
   - Poor manufacturing methods
   - Inefficient plant layout
   - Excessive rework, scrap, or salvage
   - Idle equipment and/or operations personnel
   - Insufficient or excessive equipment
   - Excessive production or operating costs
   - Lack of effective production scheduling procedures
   - Poor housekeeping
   - Excessive, slow moving, or obsolete inventory
4. Purchasing
   - Not achieving best prices, timeliness, and quality
   - Favoritism to certain vendors
   - Lack of effective competitive bidding procedures
   - Not using most effective systems such as blanket purchase orders, traveling requisitions, telephone ordering, etc.
   - Excessive emergency purchases
   - Lack of a value analysis program
   - Purchase of unnecessarily expensive items
   - Unmet procurement schedules
   - Excessive returns to vendors
5. Financial Indicators
   - Poor profit/loss ratios
   - Poor return on investment
   - Unfavorable cost ratios
   - Unfavorable or unexplained cost/budget variances

DEVELOPMENT OF AUDIT FINDINGS

FIGURE 5.3. *(Continued)*

6. Complaints
   - Customers: bad products or poor service
   - Employees: grievances, gripes, or exit interview comments
   - Vendors: poor quality or untimely deliveries
   - Production: schedules not met, material not available, deliveries not on time, quality poor, etc.

5.3 AUDIT FINDINGS DEVELOPMENT

The operational audit team is responsible for the effective development of the audit findings. To help them in developing adequate and complete audit findings, auditors can use a checklist such as the following:

1. Are any of the audit finding attributes—statement of condition, criteria, cause, effect, recommendation—missing? Why? What can or should we do about it? Is it a presentation defect or a symptom of an incomplete audit?

2. Are attributes mixed up with one another in a way that impedes clarity? Are facts distinguishable from opinions?

3. Is the *condition statement* valid? Have we indicated that it is a fact or that it was told to us?

4. Are the *audit criteria* unclear or unconvincing? Are they weak or unsound from a professional standpoint? Do they contain subjective bias?

5. Have we explained the *cause*? Have we given the real cause, or is it a symptom? Is the information on the cause incomplete? Superficial? Does it get to the heart of the matter?

6. Has *effect* been understated? Exaggerated? Quantified when possible?

7. Is the *recommendation* unnecessarily vague? Too rigid? Does it take care of the past but not the future? Is it punitive rather than constructive? Is it out of harmony with the cause?

5.4 IDENTIFYING ATTRIBUTES

Auditors who do not use an approach such as utilizing the operational audit finding attributes, as suggested, tend to prepare confusing and incomplete findings. This contributes to management's resistance and lack of follow-through on findings. To ensure greater success in acceptance, auditors should become proficient in identifying and documenting audit finding attributes. To provide some practical experience in identifying operational audit attributes, there are two examples to look at:

- Finished Goods Shipments (Figures 5.4 and 5.5).
- Identification of Attributes (Figure 5.6).

5.5 APPROACH TO DEVELOPING AUDIT FINDINGS

There are, of course, many different and varied operational auditing situations. Thus, there is no one approach to use consistently to perform the operational audit and develop audit findings. However, the following steps can be considered a basic approach:

 1. Review and analyze operating policies, systems, and procedures and the practices actually being followed to determine whether they will produce the desired results if performed correctly and adequately. If they will not, the operational auditor can proceed directly to quantifying the effect and determining the cause.
 2. Accumulate valid evidence on the operational area under review and its corresponding transactions. This is done by gathering available documentation such as written correspondence, contracts, authorized forms; through interviews with management and operations personnel; and through systems analysis such as via systems flowcharts, layout flow diagrams, work observation, and so on.
 3. Compare actual transactions with systems and procedures to determine whether procedures are being followed correctly and desired results achieved. If so, the auditor stops here, ceases spending any more audit time, and stops reviewing this area. If procedures are not being followed and results are not being achieved, then the auditor continues with the development of the finding and identification of the attributes.
 4. Quantify the effect in terms of dollars lost, or ineffectiveness resulting from the failure to achieve desired results. If the effect is insignificant, the

DEVELOPMENT OF AUDIT FINDINGS

FIGURE 5.4. Identifying operational auditing attributes: finished goods shipments.

You are the supervisor of finished goods warehouse operations for an electrical component manufacturer. At the end of each day, shipments are set up for effective loading onto company and private carrier trucks the following morning. Each planned shipment is palletized and waiting in the correct truck loading dock or position. As the trucks arrive as scheduled, the corresponding pallets are at the front of the line for efficient loading via mechanized forklift equipment. This system has been in effect for more than a year and has worked quite effectively. As long as planned shipments are prepared the night before and the trucks arrive according to schedule, the system will continue to function properly.

This morning when you arrived, you found that the proper shipments were all in the correct loading position. It was less than 15 minutes before the arrival of the first trucks, and the forklifts should have been moving the items from the warehouse onto the loading docks. You were greatly concerned, as there was no forklift available for any of the 16 loading docks. If the materials were not ready, private carriers would not wait and would most likely charge the company for the time anyway. Your own company trucks could wait; however, it would cost the company to pay its drivers for waiting. In addition, the entire day's schedule would be out of whack, and items out of place or not picked up would have to be juggled around in the warehouse—and some customer orders would not be delivered.

You immediately went back to the forklift area and found all 16 pieces of equipment with dead batteries. A new policy had recently been installed to economize on the use of electricity, whereby all forklift equipment was to be recharged overnight, with the corresponding circuit breaker thrown by Hank, the forklift supervisor, prior to his leaving each night. However, last night Hank had to leave early, and no one else was directed to throw the circuit breaker.

Listed in the chart on Figure 5.5. are some thoughts you might have related to this situation. An X has been placed in the column of the attribute (if it is an attribute) that corresponds to each of your thoughts.

5.5 APPROACH TO DEVELOPING AUDIT FINDINGS

FIGURE 5.5. Identifying operational auditing attributes, finished goods shipments: Relating thoughts to attributes—Suggested responses.

Thought	Condition	Criteria	Cause	Effect	Recommendation	None
This makes me angry.				X		
Let's borrow the three batteries from the raw materials storeroom forklifts.					X	
The forklifts won't start.	X					
We'll mess up the schedule.				X		
There should be system backups.		X				
It's too early in the morning.						X
The circuit breaker wasn't thrown.			X			
Hank never told anyone what to do.			X			
I knew not to trust this system.						X
The first trucks are due.						X
Customers won't get their orders.				X		
Let's use the four new batteries in the storeroom.					X	
My boss will be angry.				X		
Critical items should have sufficient spares available.		X				
The batteries are dead.	X					

217

FIGURE 5.6. Identification of attributes.

Each of the following statements has been excerpted from an actual operational audit finding. To the left of each statement is the attribute of an audit finding that would be associated with it: A = Condition, B = Criteria, C = Cause, D = Effect, E = Recommendation.

A   1. In fact, the total project cost was $16,685 on May 30, 19XX, with the
&   institution sharing $2,302 of the total cost, which was more than the
B   required 10 percent of the total project cost.

C   2. The above conditions existed because the property custodian did not have adequate control over the receipt of equipment.

C   3. Furthermore, procedures were not established to make a review of the activities of these employees.

E   4. The necessary ledger accounts should be established and maintained on a current basis to provide control over funds.

D   5. We believe that these procedures also result in wasted effort and unnecessary costs in maintaining duplicate records.

B   6. The Internal Revenue Service, Circular E, Employer's Tax Guide, states that students working for a school, college, or university are eligible for federal income tax withholding.

A   7. We were told that there were only oral contracts between the department manager and the individual performing the service.

B   8. In our opinion, timely and accurate final expenditure reports from local offices are essential to proper management and control of funds.

D   9. As a result, we estimate that the administrative costs of the department were overstated by $287,584.

B   10. The approval of project proposals is one of the Director's most impor-
&   tant responsibilities, and we believe that management should take
E   whatever action is necessary to improve review procedures.

---

auditor curtails spending any more time in further audit finding development. Nevertheless, the auditor may decide to report the area to management and may spend some additional time to develop reporting details.

5. If desired results are not being achieved, determine the cause, together with appropriate and sufficient evidence. Note that it is possible that the policy or procedure is faulty and the practice correct, in which case it may be that the policy or procedure needs to be changed.

6. Develop recommendations on improving the situation for economy, efficiency, and effectiveness. If the cost of the proposed recommendations

5.5 APPROACH TO DEVELOPING AUDIT FINDINGS

exceeds the projected dollar savings, the auditor may conclude that the recommendation is not warranted. This situation is not usually the case. Operational audit recommendations are not always considered solely on an economical basis. They may also provide for increased operational effectiveness, improved decision making, increased organizational efficiency, higher personnel morale, and so on.

Having completed the steps in this approach, the operational auditor would then be ready to present the audit finding to auditee management, using the audit finding attributes. This approach is summarized in Figure 5.7.

To reinforce the previously discussed principles of developing operational audit findings and the use of the audit program and field work steps, look at the case situation included in Figure 5.8.

FIGURE 5.7. Approach to developing operational audit findings.

1. *Review and analyze policies, procedures, and practices.*
   a. Determine whether policies are appropriate, consistent with goals and objectives.
   b. Determine whether procedures and practices are appropriate, resulting in attaining desired goals and objectives.
2. *Accumulate evidence and determine its validity.*
   a. Analyze a number of different types of transactions.
   b. Analyze a number of individual transactions.
   c. Ascertain results: statistical sample, decision making, questioning, etc.
3. *Compare transactions to prescribed procedures.*
   a. Test transactions versus procedures.
   b. Are procedures followed properly?
   c. Analyze results of following or not following procedures.
4. *Quantify the effect.*
   a. Calculate the dollars lost (amount of savings).
   b. Determine other factors, such as ineffectiveness, etc.
   c. Establish total effect.
5. *Determine cause.*
   a. Determine why results are not being achieved.
   b. Document with appropriate and sufficient evidence.
6. *Develop recommendations.*
   a. Determine how to improve the situation—i.e., economy, efficiency, and effectiveness.
   b. Document how to implement recommendations: practical and reasonable.

FIGURE 5.8. Equipment maintenance audit: Case situation.

As part of the operational audit of the production facilities at the Example Company, you have identified equipment maintenance as a significant and critical area for review. You found that equipment maintenance costs skyrocketed over the past few years, from $180,000 to $340,000 annually. In addition, the amount of manufacturing equipment downtime increased in like amounts. The objective in reviewing and analyzing this situation is to determine whether operating economies can be achieved while at the same time decreasing the amount of equipment downtime.

During the review of this situation, you analyzed the inventory control system and related storage procedures for equipment maintenance items. Based on this analysis, it was found that for more than 70 percent of the 800 items in inventory, on average there were enough equipment maintenance parts and materials for the next 30 months, based on current rates of usage. For the other 30 percent or approximately 240 inventory items, it was found that more than 90 were out-of-stock, more than 40 were below reorder points, and the other 110 were mainly low-usage items.

You believe that such poor inventory control methods and results constitute a substantial area for which to develop an operational audit finding. Not only should improved systems and procedures result in reduced costs, but they should also assist in improving the equipment downtime situation.

The audit steps that you might consider for inclusion in your audit program, the suggested responses, and the related attributes are as follows:

Audit Step	Attribute
1. Determine authority as to requisition and purchase items.	Criteria
2. Analyze whether anyone exceeded that authority.	Condition
3. Determine what the goals are for Equipment Maintenance (i.e., to keep equipment functioning at the least cost without unnecessary equipment downtime).	Criteria
4. Determine policy as to how much of each item to maintain in inventory.	Criteria
5. Determine how much of each item needs to be in stock and any overages from that quantity.	Criteria & Condition
6. Calculate cost savings from inventory reductions to more reasonable levels, including any items that need to be increased.	Effect
7. Analyze the inventory control and storeroom operations as to meeting the desired results.	Cause
8. Investigate improvements in inventory control methods and procedures necessary to correct the situation.	Recommendation

5.6 AUDIT FINDING DEVELOPMENT: EXAMPLE COMPANY

In the planning and field work phases, the auditors learned that the Example Company Purchasing Department processed 18,100 regular purchase orders annually, and that the policy is not to issue a purchase order where the cost to process a purchase is greater than 25 percent of the value of the purchase. It was also found that this policy has not been changed since it was issued 12 years ago, when the cost to process a purchase order was $11.80. In the field work phase, the auditors found the present cost to process a purchase order to be approximately $51. In addition, two sample groups of purchase orders were analyzed, and it was found that approximately 23.5 percent of all purchase orders amounting to only 1.23 percent of the total cost of purchases were for $200 or less.

Based on existing Purchasing Department policy, all of these purchases should be eliminated from regular purchase order processing, as the cost to process each purchase order would be greater than 25 percent of the value of the purchase ($200 divided by 4 = $50).

Given these data, the auditor needs to quantify the effect of this practice—in other words, what is it costing to process purchases that, economically, should not be going through the central Purchasing Department. The auditor accomplishes this by calculating the annual cost to process purchase orders for $200 or less by the Purchasing Department. The facts needed to perform this calculation are summarized in Figure 5.9.

In the process of quantifying the economical effect of processing purchase orders for $200 or less, the audit team determined that at least 75 percent of the present processing costs of $216,903 (or $162,677) could be saved by diverting their processing from the Purchasing Department. Note that the auditors should always state their effects (and savings) on the

FIGURE 5.9. Annual cost to process purchase orders for $200 and less.

DATA:
- 18,100 Regular purchase orders processed annually
- $51 Cost to process a purchase order
- 23.5% of all purchase orders are for $200 and less

Analysis:
- 18,100 Purchase orders (annual)
- 23.5% % of orders for $200 and less—from sample
- 4,253 Purchase orders for $200 and less (estimate)
- $51 Processing cost of a purchase order
- $216,903 Annual processing cost for purchase orders of $200 and less

DEVELOPMENT OF AUDIT FINDINGS

conservative side and should be able to prove them easily. This approach has a psychological advantage in that it avoids overwhelming and putting managers on the defensive. It also ensures the ease of managers' achieving such savings—in fact, setting them up to beat your estimates and make them look good. Normally, there is more than enough savings and inefficiencies to cite to convince management to take action without having to overstate the situation.

The audit team now has sufficient data to develop and document an operational audit finding using the five basic attributes: statement of condition, criteria, cause, effect, and recommendation. A recommended response as to the actual finding is documented in Figure 5.10. Note that it is good practice to submit such findings as they are developed, and to request management's response. If agreed upon, action should be started immediately. If findings are reported this way, the final report becomes mainly a summary of the audit and its accomplishments.

5.7 DEVELOPMENT OF AUDIT FINDINGS: EXAMPLES

The development of audit findings is the most critical element of the operational audit—this is the mechanism to convince and persuade management to take action. To reinforce the process of developing operational audit findings using the five attributes, another two situations uncovered during the operational audit of the Purchasing Department of the Example Company can be reviewed.

(a) Employee-Leased Automobiles

During the course of the operational audit of the Purchasing Department, the auditors analyzed the procedures performed by one of the Buyer IIs relative to the administration and control of employee-leased automobiles. The details of the situation, as well as a suggested operational audit finding in response to this situation, are documented in Figure 5.11.

(b) Low Dollar and Local Purchases

During the course of the operational audit, the audit team decided to expand the audit scope to include purchasing procedures at other locations and divisions. As a result of this review at an independent operating subsidiary, ABC Pipe Supply, the auditors found great misuse of Example Company central purchasing procedures related to processing low-dollar purchases and the overuse of local vendors. The facts and suggested audit finding are documented in Figure 5.12.

5.7 DEVELOPMENT OF AUDIT FINDINGS

FIGURE 5.10. Document operational audit finding: Annual cost to process purchase orders for $200 and less recommended response.

A. *Statement of Condition* (What did you find?)
   - 23.5% or 4,253 of 18,100 purchase orders were for $200 or less (based on our sample).
   - $51 cost to process a purchase order.
   - $216,903 estimated annual processing cost for purchase orders of $200 or less.
B. *Criteria* (What should it be?)
   Based on present Purchasing Department policy, purchase orders should not be issued where the cost to process a purchase is greater than 25% of the value of the purchase. Accordingly, since the present cost is $51 to process a purchase order, all purchase orders under $200 should be processed in a more efficient and economical manner.
C. *Cause* (Why did it happen?)
   Present purchasing policy states that all purchases for items charged to specific accounts for more than $50 should be processed as a regular purchase order. This policy has been continued since it was effected 12 years ago, when the cost to process a purchase order was calculated at $11.80. This cost has not been recalculated since that time, and the policy has remained the same.
D. *Effect* (So what? What is the effect of the finding?)
   The processing of purchase orders for under $200 results in unnecessary purchasing procedures and resultant costs. As a result of present practices, it is costing an estimated amount of $216,903 to process these purchase orders. We believe we can realize at least 75%, or $162,677, of this $216,903 in savings as well as increase the efficiency of purchasing systems and procedures.
E. *Recommendation* (What is recommended to correct the situation?)
   We recommend that the policy be changed to process all purchase orders under $200 either as petty cash or direct purchases, as appropriate.

Note: The details for the cost to process a purchase order, amount of savings claimed, and the recommended direct purchase system would be documented in the auditor's workpapers and reviewed with management. They need not be part of the actual documented finding, which would tend to clutter the finding.

Management Response:

DEVELOPMENT OF AUDIT FINDINGS

FIGURE 5.11. Development of audit finding: Employee-leased automobiles: The Example Company.

As part of the operational audit of the Purchasing Department, procedures were reviewed as performed by the Buyer II responsible for administering and controlling automobile leasing arrangements and the use of the cars by assigned staff personnel for the fiscal year 19XX. Analysis of the 87 leased cars disclosed that 24 cars were being used consistently for only short distances each day. In addition, 37 employees' personal cars, although not driven on company business every day, were still driven sufficiently on company business each month to justify using a leased car as opposed to reimbursing such employees at the rate of 28 cents per mile. Analysis of the entire situation, along with recommendations as to the reassignment of leased cars, demonstrated that the Example Company could realize a savings of more than $44,000 per year.

The operational audit response to this situation was as follows:

1. *Statement of Condition*
   Our analysis of the use of leased cars by your assigned personnel for the fiscal year 19XX disclosed the following:
   a. Of 87 leased cars, we found that 24 of these were not being used sufficiently to justify the lease payment. It would be more economical for the company to allow these employees to use their own personal cars and reimburse them at the current rate of 28 cents per mile.
   b. For 37 employees who presently use their personal cars and are reimbursed at 28 cents per mile, the total reimbursement for the fiscal year exceeds the cost of leasing an automobile.
2. *Criteria*
   It is normal business practice to lease automobiles for employees in situations where the cost of the lease is expected to be less than the reimbursement for the use of their own cars.
3. *Cause*
   We found that a procedure does not presently exist whereby the use of leased cars and personal automobiles on a reimbursement basis is analyzed periodically. Accordingly, the present situation has evolved over a number of years.
4. *Effect*
   The present situation has resulted in the company's paying excess costs of more than $44,000 per year, as shown in Schedule C.
5. *Recommendation*
   We recommend that a procedure be implemented to analyze the use of leased and personal automobiles on an ongoing basis. To correct the present situation, we recommend the reassignment of leased cars according to Schedule D, which will result in a present savings to the company of over $44,000 per year.

5.7 DEVELOPMENT OF AUDIT FINDINGS

FIGURE 5.12. Low dollar and local purchases: The Example Company.

As a result of an operational audit of the purchasing function at the ABC Pipe Supply subsidiary, the following audit findings were uncovered:

1. Twenty percent (20%) of all purchase orders issued were for a value of less than $25.
2. Thirty-two percent (32%) of all purchase orders issued were for a value between $25 and $50.
3. Sixty-six percent (66%) of all purchase orders were issued to local vendors.

The cost to process a purchase order in the Example Company central Purchasing Department has been calculated at $51. Present Example Company policy states that all outside purchases (including those from subsidiaries) of more than $50 should be processed through the central Purchasing Department. Although the Purchasing Department has the authority to alter this policy, this has not been done for ABC Pipe Supply.

The suggested operational audit finding is as follows:

1. *Statement of Condition* (What did you find?)
   - 20% of all purchase orders were for less than $25.
   - 32% of all purchase orders were for $25 to $50.
   - 66% of all purchase orders were issued to local vendors; should be part of another finding.
2. *Criteria* (What should it be?)
   In our opinion, purchase orders should not be issued for purchases under $50 by ABC Pipe Supply, as it costs $51 to process a purchase order in the Example Company central Purchasing Department.
3. *Cause* (Why did it happen?)
   The above conditions exist because present company policy states that all outside purchases over $50 must be processed through the Example Company Purchasing Department. The Purchasing Department, however, has the authority to allow operating departments and subsidiaries to purchase directly for amounts under a certain limit (i.e., $50). Such delegation of authority has never been made. Accordingly, the ABC Pipe Supply purchasing function presently processes all purchases as purchase orders, regardless of the amount.
4. *Effect* (So what? What is effect of the finding?)
   The processing of purchase orders by ABC Pipe Supply for under $50 results in unnecessary purchasing, overstaffing in the purchasing function, excessive paperwork, and wasted time in the purchasing/receiving cycle. As a result, we estimate a realizable savings of approximately $87,000 (less the costs of alternative procedures) of purchasing function costs by eliminating the need for purchase orders for purchases under $50. (The auditor should provide the data to show the actual savings and what can realistically be reduced or eliminated, as well as the cost of recommended alternative procedures.)

DEVELOPMENT OF AUDIT FINDINGS

FIGURE 5.12. *(Continued)*

5. *Recommendations* (What is recommended to correct the situation?)
We believe that such a high proportion of small-value purchase orders (52% under $50) warrants consideration of a more economical ordering system. We recommend that you consider the use of a telephone ordering system for purchases under $50. This system does not require the processing of a purchase order, but rather, the order is placed directly over the telephone from a copy of the purchase requisition.

We estimate that this system will reduce the cost of processing a purchase order by at least 60% of present costs, resulting in an annual savings of $52,200, as shown on Exhibit A.

5.8 DEVELOPING RECOMMENDATIONS

As mentioned earlier, the development of audit findings is the most critical element of the operational audit. Furthermore, the development of practical and reasonable recommendations that persuade management to implement them is sometimes the most difficult element of the finding. Good, workable recommendations are a result of the collective audit team's experience. The more alternative systems and procedures team members are aware of, the better the chance to arrive at the optimum recommendation. In developing recommendations, the audit team should consider all sources: audit team members, outside consultants, departmental personnel, other employees, other audit staff, other organizations, professional associations, and so on.

Often the best recommendations come from operating personnel, who need only the auditor's channel of communication to be heard by decision making management. In these instances, the auditors must make sure that such operating personnel are given credit for identifying and/or developing the recommendations. The more involved operation personnel are in developing recommendations, the more committed they will be to make them work most effectively. The auditors' goal is to identify the systems and procedures for recommendation that will optimize savings, be least costly and most efficient to use, and achieve maximum results, regardless of where they come from.

Audit team members also need to be aware that management might ask them to assist in implementing their recommendations. Whether or not this is possible in a given situation, the audit team should use this situation as a test of their recommendations; that is, the auditors might

5.8 DEVELOPING RECOMMENDATIONS

ask themselves: "If we are asked to implement our recommendations, would we be able to?" If the auditors document their recommendations adequately as to the process for implementation and the results to be expected, there is a good chance for success. On the other hand, if recommendations are stated in general terms, not only will management tend to shy away from them, but there is a good chance that results will be sabotaged.

The audit team should work toward developing a cooperative atmosphere with management and operating personnel, whereby the auditor's role becomes that of helper and change agent. In such a working relationship, there is a much greater likelihood that management will accept the auditors' recommendations. Operational auditors will be much more successful in this situation than in the typical auditor versus management adversarial relationship.

To reinforce the process of identifying and developing good recommendations, there are two case situations presented that may help to sharpen the auditor's skills in this area:

- Shipping and Receiving Procedures (Figure 5.13).
- Accounts Receivable and Collections (Figure 5.14).

FIGURE 5.13. Operational audit situation: Developing recommendations: Shipping and receiving procedures.

During the course of an operational audit at a plant location, the auditors reviewed the shipping and receiving functions. As part of this review, they observed that freight cars at the plant location siding in shipping and receiving were loaded and unloaded by eight employees (two four-person teams).

Shipping Procedures
The auditors observed that products to be shipped were all similarly boxed and stored on pallets in the storeroom. A forklift operator would pick up the loaded pallets and bring them to the appropriate shipping area. The eight-employee crew would then unload the pallet and stack the boxes in the freight cars, returning the pallets for reuse. This was in accordance with company policy, not to use pallets in shipping, as there had been past incidences of many lost pallets.

Upon checking with the client's 12 major customers (accounting for over 80% of total sales), the auditors found that 10 of these customers were reversing the client's procedure (unloading the railcar onto pallets) and would be willing to provide the client with pallets so they could use palletized shipments.

FIGURE 5.13. *(Continued)*

Receiving Operations
The auditor's review of receiving operations disclosed that the bulk of freight car receipts were for commodities in 50-pound bags, 55-gallon drums, standard-size boxes, etc. All of these were shipped in full railcars and stacked one on top of another. The eight-person crew would unload the railcar by stacking the items onto pallets. The forklift operator would then pick up the loaded pallets and take them to the appropriate storage area.

The auditors checked with the client's four major suppliers (more than 80% of material purchases) and found that each of them transported the product from its storeroom to the railcar on pallets and then had the product taken from the pallets and placed on the railcar—similar to what the client's plant location was doing with shipments as described above.

The operational audit recommendations are as follows:

Shipping Procedures
1. Palletize shipments for the 10 major customers who are willing to provide pallets, and who wish to have palletized shipments.
2. Conduct further review and study as to palletizing shipments for other customers who order in sufficient quantities and where palletizing would be appropriate.

Receiving Procedures
1. Provide the four major material suppliers with sufficient pallets to cover those that would be in transit, so that they can ship product to the client on pallets.
2. Initiate a policy to analyze all other receiving (and shipping) situations for the possibility of using palletized shipments whenever possible and appropriate.

The net cost savings of these recommendations for the initial year were estimated at $80,000 annually.

FIGURE 5.14. Operational audit situation: Developing recommendations: Accounts receivable and collections.

A group of auditors, performing an operational review of the accounts receivable and collection functions at a bank credit card operation, found that the policy for sending out delinquent payment notices was as follows:

- First notice: 10 days after payment due date
- Second notice: 10 days after first notice
- Third through eighth notices: every 5 business days
- After 60 days: to credit department for further action

Each overdue payment notice was prepared automatically by the computer system as long as the customer had any amount overdue. The last 60-day notice, prior to credit department intervention and credit card cancellation,

FIGURE 5.14. *(Continued)*

was hand signed by the Accounts Receivable manager and sent "Certified Mail, Return Receipt" at a cost of $2.00 each.

The auditors' review and analysis disclosed that many overdue accounts, approximately 28%, were of that status as the customer was questioning an item(s) on the bill and Customer Service was investigating. The client's policy was that the customer did not have to pay for an item under investigation. However, there was no mechanism to code the customer's account on the computer system, so as not to send out delinquent payment letters. Generally, customers would phone Customer Service when they received the overdue letters, and Customer Service would tell them to ignore the letters until the situation was cleared up.

As part of the operational review, the auditors also discovered that another 24% of these delinquent payment accounts were for account balances of less than $20. The primary reason for most of these (more than 90%) was the questioning by the customer or improper recording by the computer system of finance charges accumulated while a customer's account was being investigated by Customer Service. Bank policy prohibited the waiver of any finance charge without proper approval by Accounts Receivable management.

The operational audit recommendations are as follows:

1. Reappraise the philosophy of credit card operations being in the "short-term loan" business, thus increasing emphasis on customers' paying down bills plus finance charges rather than on nonpayment of bills. The credit card operation probably makes more money on finance charges than on retailers' fees for using the charge card service (which does not usually cover operating costs). This is an area for further analysis.
2. Eliminate the practice of sending out delinquent notices for overdue accounts of less than $20 (calculated as the approximate cost to process and follow up a delinquent notice).
3. Revise the delinquent payment notice schedule to allow customers sufficient time to remit payments. For example: first notice 30 days after delinquency, second notice after 60 days, third notice after 90 days, fourth notice = termination.
4. Make the necessary changes to computer processing so that accounts under investigation by Customer Service can be properly identified, so as to eliminate the preparation of delinquent notices and the calculation of finance charges for those items under investigation.
5. Initiate additional study of the calculation routine for finance charges, to determine whether the computer program might be miscalculating finance charges—as might be indicated by the large number of customer complaints regarding improper calculations.
6. Change the existing policy requiring Accounts Receivable management to approve the waiver of all finance charges. Allow for the delegation of these finance charge waivers to appropriate Accounts Receivable and Customer Service staff for amounts under a certain limit (for example, $20).

The net cost savings of these recommendations were estimated at $140,000 per year.

5.9 CONCLUSION

If the operational audit team is successful, many of the findings will be accepted as the auditors progress through their operational audit. The auditors present their findings to management as they are identified and developed. Management responds to each finding by agreeing and proceeding with the implementation of the recommended action, by agreeing but requesting further clarification, or by disagreeing. Because many, if not all, of the audit findings are disposed of through this process as the operational audit transpires, they do not need to be restated as part of a final report. If the operational audit is conducted in this way, the final report becomes a summary of what has happened.

The following chapter discusses the next and final phase of the operational audit, the reporting phase.

CHAPTER SIX

Reporting Phase

6.1 INTRODUCTION

In the reporting phase of an operational audit, the auditing team communicates the results of its operational audit work to the intended operating and management personnel. The principal objectives of the operational audit report are to:

1. Provide useful and timely information on significant operational deficiencies and other matters, and

2. Recommend improvements in the conduct of operations.

The audit report is the operational audit team's opportunity to get management's undivided attention—an opportunity to show management the benefits of the operational audit and what the operational auditing organization has to offer. Accordingly, the operational audit report has two functions:

1. To communicate the results of the operational audit, and

2. To persuade and, when necessary, sound a call to action.

This chapter discusses the principles and techniques of good reporting in an operational audit. The operational auditor normally prepares both an oral and written report for management review, based on the significant operational audit findings developed during the field work and audit finding development phases. As discussed in Chapter 5, specific audit findings have been identified and developed for management review during the course of the audit. If the audit has been performed correctly, the operational audit team has already presented these findings to management during the field work phase, and operations personnel have already begun to implement those steps necessary to correct the identified deficiencies. The audit report then becomes more a summary of the operational audit, documenting the following:

1. What the operational audit team has accomplished,
2. What was found during the course of the operational audit,
3. The extent of operational deficiencies, and
4. What operations personnel have done thus far to correct the situation.

In some instances, however, where operational audit findings have not been addressed during the course of the audit, the audit report (both oral and written) becomes the operational auditor's vehicle to convince and persuade management to take corrective action. This is appropriate for operational audits of short duration, of perhaps less than two weeks, or for a general overview type of audit, where there is not sufficient elapsed time to present findings during the course of the audit. Otherwise, the audit team should present its findings as they are identified.

This chapter reviews the principles of good operational audit reporting that should ensure the operational audit team greater success in getting operations management and staff to implement recommended operational improvements. Remember, to be successful, the operational audit team does not need to convince management to follow all recommendations—action on more than 50 percent of the significant findings is usually adequate.

This chapter will:

1. Increase understanding as to the purpose of good operational audit reporting.
2. Increase knowledge of the types of operational audit reporting— oral and written, informal and formal.
3. Increase understanding of the basic characteristics of good operational audit reporting.
4. Increase ability to decide the significance of findings—what to include in the formal report and what to report informally.

5. Increase understanding of the types of information to be included in the operational audit report.

6. Increase understanding of the relationship of developed operational audit findings to the reporting phase.

7. Increase knowledge of positive factors related to more effective written communications.

8. Increase understanding of the format of a completed operational audit report by presenting a sample letter and regular report.

6.2 INTERIM REPORTING

Operational audit reports may be either informal or formal, and oral as well as written. The operational audit staff should issue a signed written report to appropriate management and staff and other interested parties after the field work is completed, as a record of the completed operational audit. However, there is a need for reporting the progress of the audit to management during the course of the audit.

These interim reports may be oral or written, depending on the circumstances, and may be transmitted formally or informally. It is a good practice to review and submit audit findings to operations personnel in the five-attribute format as they are identified during the actual operational audit. This can be done by using the format shown in the audit finding examples in Chapter 5, either showing the actual titles "Statement of Condition," " Criteria," "Cause," "Effect," and "Recommendations" or by merely separating each attribute into paragraphs. The audit team can use a standard form or merely a free form, leaving space to record management responses and comments. This gives operations and management personnel an opportunity to respond to the audit findings and recommendations quickly and to take whatever appropriate action is required—either to begin to implement the recommendations or to question some part of the finding.

In either case, this approach allows action to be taken when necessary, as opposed to waiting for the formal report to be issued and reviewed. This practice also allows the audit team to include the views of management and operating staff in their final formal written report, both agreeing and opposing views. In addition, for balanced reporting, the auditors' formal written report should acknowledge any outstanding accomplishments or any corrective action that operations has taken prior to completion of the operational audit and issuance of the audit report.

Note that the auditors' can now refer to the detailed findings and recommendations previously issued and reviewed with operations in the formal report, or attach them as an appendix to the report. In effect, the final written report becomes a formal summary of actions already taken by operations personnel.

6.3 ORAL REPORTING

Oral reports or briefings should be given to operations and management personnel periodically, as determined by the length of the audit and whether there is anything significant to report. For instance, an operational audit scheduled for a three-month period might include periodic oral reporting on a biweekly basis. These progress reports should be specified in the original proposal or letter of understanding and included as part of the audit team's budget. There is, of course, no need to hold such a meeting if there is nothing to report.

Oral reports are usually less formal than written reports and include a greater use of visuals such as photographs, slides, charts, and graphs. Oral reporting requires effective oral communication and presentation skills on the part of all audit team members. To be most effective in communicating issues to operations personnel, those audit team members involved in conducting the field work and developing the audit findings should make the presentation—not just audit management.

Oral reports have some distinct advantages over written reports for example:

1. Oral reports are immediate. They give prompt attention to current information to allow for timely corrective action.

2. Oral reports evoke face-to-face responses. They can disclose client attitudes and convictions that could be important to the auditors in finalizing their findings and recommendations.

3. Oral reports allow the auditors to counter operations' arguments and provide additional information that operations personnel may require.

4. Oral reports can reveal inaccuracies in the audit team's thinking, which can be corrected before decisions become final.

The audit team may, in some cases, give oral briefings to operations personnel at various stages of the audit. In most operational audits, the auditors present at least one internal oral briefing in addition to the final oral presentation. These oral briefings may take the form of scheduled periodic progress meetings or may be called at the option of audit or operations management when there is something significant to discuss or report.

These presentations must be made professionally, as they are golden opportunities to convince management as to the merits of operational auditing and the auditors' competency. This is the auditors' chance to persuade operations management to take the proper action so as to improve operations immediately—without waiting for a more formal written report. Often the audit findings are presented at these briefings in attribute format.

6.4 WRITTEN REPORT

The audit team does not generally close out the operational audit with a final oral presentation alone, but normally will issue a written report as well. The more formal written report benefits operations personnel, as well as audit team members. The written report provides official recognition of completion of the operational audit and highlights, in writing, the results of the audit. For audit team members, the written report serves as a source of information concerning the work done and as a resource for future operational audits.

Operations management judges the completed operational audit work, in large part, by the quality of the reports. Operational audit reports must be prepared according to certain basic principles to maintain high professional standards of operation and to effectively meet reporting objectives. A poor job of written reporting can discredit the auditors' work accomplished on the operational audit. It can also discredit the audit staff and put them in a bad position for additional work, no matter how competently they performed the other aspects of the audit.

The writer of the audit report must keep in mind the intended recipients and other readers. A good rule to follow in achieving this objective is to present the report in a simpler format than the perceived reader's comprehension level. In conjunction with this principle of simplicity, the auditors should consider using familiar words and phrases, specific descriptive examples, and visual displays such as charts, graphs, and flowcharts to enhance reader understanding.

A good way to ensure that responsible management personnel comprehend and understand the primary concerns is to develop the written report in an inverse format—that is, going from concepts to more specific details. Most people, particularly senior managers, do not want to read through all of the specific details and individual issues and concerns. They want to understand the top-level considerations and what action needs to be taken to correct a given operational deficiency or to make operational improvements. Therefore, the auditors present the broad overview, the purpose and objectives of the operational audit, and their opinions and the benefits to be derived, in conceptual terms.

The auditors' findings should be specific and to the point, emphasizing the present effect and future benefits of implementing the recommendations. The auditors' recommendations should clearly state what actually needs to be done. Ideally, the auditors' documented findings and related recommendations should be specific enough to give the person responsible for implementing the recommendation a clear description of what needs to be done. Remember too, the auditors may be asked to help implement.

Whether at the oral briefing or in the written report, each finding and recommendation should be reviewed in complete detail with operations management and staff to be sure of accuracy and understanding. This ensures mutual agreement on all reported findings and actions to be taken.

6.5 CHARACTERISTICS OF GOOD REPORTING

There are many characteristics of good reporting. Some of the most basic are the following:

Significance

Usefulness and timeliness

Accuracy and adequacy of support

Convincingness

Objectivity and perspective

Clarity and simplicity

Conciseness

Constructiveness of tone

Organization and positiveness

(a) Significance

The matters included in the operational audit report must be sufficiently significant to justify reporting them to operations and management person-

6.5 CHARACTERISTICS OF GOOD REPORTING

nel. The usefulness, and therefore the effectiveness, of operational audit reports are decreased by the inclusion of insignificant matters. These tend to distract the reader's attention from the truly important matters reported. To decide what is significant enough to report, the auditors have to consider a number of factors, including:

1. The degree of interest by others in the operations or activities being audited;
2. The importance of the operations or activities, judged by such measures as the size of expenditures, investment in assets, and amounts of revenue;
3. The relative newness or experimental nature of the operations or activities;
4. The opportunity to provide useful and timely information to help staff improve the effectiveness, efficiency, or economy of their operations;
5. The frequency of occurrence of an adverse condition, the possibility of its occurrence elsewhere, and the relative dollar amounts of loss or additional cost involved (actual or potential); and
6. The failure of operating staff members to take necessary actions to correct weaknesses or improve operations.

(b) Usefulness and Timeliness

Operational audit reports must be structured to meet the interests and needs of the audience; that is, they must be useful. However, it is a mistake to assume that the audience for such reports is limited to management. The operational audit report should be written so it will be clear to any reasonably intelligent, well-informed persons, even though they may not be familiar with the particular operations, activities, or even the areas involved.

Timeliness, like usefulness, is essential to effective reporting. A brilliantly written audit report may be of little value to operations management if it arrives too late to fully consider, and act on, the information and recommendations being reported.

The auditors can often trace problems that affect the timeliness of their operational audit reports to unresolved problems that they should have taken care of during the field work phase. To minimize this risk, the auditors should have their audit findings completely developed before leaving the field work phase.

In most operational audits, before the final report is written the auditors should have already discussed the major findings and reviewed them with management and staff, who, in turn, should have taken appropriate action. In these instances, the final operational audit report becomes more a summary of what has taken place, the significance of the results obtained, and the corrective actions that have been implemented.

(c) Accuracy and Adequacy of Support

The audit team should apply all of its operational audit report preparation, review, and processing procedures to the objective of producing reports that contain no errors of fact, logic, or reasoning. In addition, all facts presented and conclusions reached must be backed up by the documentation of audit work done.

The need for accuracy in operational audit reports is based on the need for the auditors to be fair and impartial in their reporting and to assure report users and readers that what is reported is reliable. One inaccuracy in the audit report can cast doubt on the validity of the entire report and can divert attention from the auditor's objectives. Accuracy helps to maintain the reader's positive attitude toward the reporting and the auditors' integrity.

All of the factual data, findings, and conclusions presented in the operational audit report must be adequately documented by sufficient objective evidence in the audit workpapers to support the existence, accuracy, and reasonableness of the matters reported. If operations personnel question any item being reported, the auditors must have adequate support available.

The opinions and conclusions that are included in the audit report should be clearly identified as such and must be based on sufficient audit work to support them. In most cases, one example of a deficiency will not be enough to support a broad conclusion and a related recommendation for corrective action.

(d) Convincingness

Audit findings must be presented in a convincing manner, and the related conclusions and recommendations must follow logically from the facts presented. The information offered must be adequately supported to persuade those who read the report that the findings are significant, the conclusions reasonable, and the implementation of the recommendations important.

6.5 CHARACTERISTICS OF GOOD REPORTING

The data presented must be convincing enough to move management to action.

The auditors cannot take the attitude, "It's so, because we say it's so." The burden of proof is on the audit team, not on those being audited. If audit findings are questioned, the audit team must be able to provide sufficient support to convince operations personnel of their correctness.

(e) Objectivity and Perspective

Every operational audit report should present the audit findings in an objective and unbiased manner. The report should include sufficient information on the subject to give its readers proper perspective. The objective of good report writing is to produce reports that are impartial and fair, not misleading, and that emphasize those matters that need attention. The auditors, as the report writers, must not however, exaggerate or overemphasize deficient performance.

The following are examples of the types of information that the auditors should include in their operational audit report to provide proper report balance:

1. Appropriate information as to why the auditors made the particular examinations on which they are reporting.

2. Clear statements of the nature and scope of their operational audit examinations. The audit reports, where applicable, should clearly state that the primary emphasis of the operational audit was the analysis of matters apparently needing attention, and not an evaluation of the department's total activities or operations.

3. Information on the size and nature of the operations and activities to which the audit findings relate. This provides proper perspective in judging the significance of the findings.

4. Correct and fair descriptions of audit findings to avoid reader misinterpretation and misunderstanding. The report should identify all significant relevant factors, even though some may contradict the findings. Information on the size of audit tests and the methods of selecting items to test should also be included so that readers may relate such information to the audited areas' total operation and the findings.

An effective way to ensure that operational audit reports are complete and objective is to obtain advance reviews and comments, prior to final issuance, by personnel whose operations are discussed in the report. This enables the auditors to produce a report that shows not only what the auditors found and what they think about it, but also what the operations personnel think about it and what, if anything, they are going to do about it. This kind of report is usually more useful to those receiving it.

(f) Clarity and Simplicity

Operational audit reports must be presented as clearly and simply as practicable, to effectively communicate to report recipients. It is unwise to presuppose any detailed technical knowledge of the subjects by the readers. Where technical terms and unfamiliar abbreviations must be used, they should be clearly defined. Efforts at "style" should be aimed at clear meaning. Flowery expressions aimed at impressing the reader must be avoided.

To achieve report clarity, it is essential to properly organize the audit report material. The writer should be concise in stating facts, analyzing them, and drawing conclusions. The audit report should be so well organized that everything that is pertinent to a given subject is covered in one place.

The use of visual aids—pictures, charts, graphs, and maps—whenever possible, can make the report more easily understood and therefore more useful. Readers are more inclined to take the time to look at such visuals than to read lengthy narrative.

(g) Conciseness

Operational audit reports should be no longer than necessary to communicate the required information. They should not contain words, sentences, paragraphs, or sections that do not clearly tie in with the report message. Too much detail detracts from the report and may even conceal the real message or confuse or discourage readers. The reader will appreciate getting the point directly.

Although there is a certain amount of judgment involved in determining the exact content of the audit report, the auditors should understand that reports that are complete, but concise, are more likely to get attention. Those who receive the report are usually busy people who may not want to wade through unessential details to get to the essential points. The auditors should try to determine the audience and what type of reporting will get the most attention.

(h) Constructiveness of Tone

The auditors' basic objective in performing the operational audit and reporting its results is to help improve the operation of audited activities. Accordingly, the tone of the auditors' report should encourage favorable reaction to their audit findings and recommendations.

The titles, captions, and texts of the report should be stated in constructive terms. Although audit findings should be presented in clear, concise terms, the objective of obtaining favorable reaction must be kept in mind. This objective can best be accomplished by avoiding language that unnecessarily antagonizes those the audit team is trying to help and causes them to become defensive and resistant.

Although it is often necessary to criticize past performance to demonstrate the need for some management or operational improvement, even then the primary emphasis in the audit report should be on the needed improvements rather than on criticism.

(i) Organization and Positiveness

Two other areas of which the operational audit report writer should be aware are organization and positiveness. One of the most significant problems that report writers face is how to organize their material. The auditors must present the information in a logical order or the reader may become confused. They must get the attention of the reader immediately and retain it throughout the report. They must stimulate interest by starting with the most important findings, not burying their important comments in the middle of the report. Forcing management personnel to hop, skip, and jump around in their thinking reduces the effectiveness of the report.

The auditors should think and write positively. Their aim in the report is to help management improve operations. This requires a good deal of concentration by the auditors to keep the tone of their report positive. Auditors tend to use negative words such as *deficiencies, weaknesses, errors, delinquent, inefficient,* and *inaccurate* to describe operating practices and procedures. Words of this type immediately put management personnel on the defensive, and so they start to defend the situation for which they feel they are being criticized. Experience has proved that people will be more cooperative if the auditors express their opinions positively. The auditors should try to use words such as *strengthening, improving,* and *increasing* to make it more difficult for management to disagree with their audit finding suggestions and comments.

A manager who does not favor improving his or her operations is not an effective manager. Most managers will be responsive to the auditors if they are able to describe or explain how their suggestions will help achieve the manager's objectives. Keep in mind that the operational auditor is a helping agent and a catalyst for change, and the audit report (both oral and written) is the communication tool for convincing and persuading operations management to take the proper action.

(j) Summary

It should be clear from everything stated about the need for clarity and conciseness in operational audit reports that conducting and reporting on operational audits requires effective communication skills on the part of the operational auditor. However, operational auditors rarely have the executive authority to take the action necessary to correct the deficiencies noted. This means that the operational auditors must communicate effectively with those who do have such authority and persuade them to take action. Then they must also be ready to assist management in making positive changes and improvements if called upon.

The audit report should be as brief as possible. Auditors' comments should be factual, adequate, pertinent, and clearly and precisely worded. The audit report should include any statements or promises management made that pertain to the correction of the deficiencies noted. To be most effective, the report must be completed promptly after the conclusion of the field work. Figure 6.1 shows examples of unclear writing together with suggested clearer rewrites.

6.6 REPORTING AUDIT FINDINGS

As discussed in Chapter 5, well-developed audit findings, regardless of subject matter, have certain common attributes (statement of condition, criteria, cause, effect, and recommendations).

Audit findings can be reported separately as identified and developed in the field work phase, held for reporting until the final formal report, or both. Proper reporting practice calls for separate reporting of audit findings in the field work phase, with a summary of findings in a final report that either references the previously submitted individual findings or includes them as an appendix.

6.6 REPORTING AUDIT FINDINGS

FIGURE 6.1. Examples of reporting operational audit results.

Each of the following three examples relates to the reporting of an operational auditing result. An example of unclear writing is shown for each example, together with a rewrite done in clearer more easily understood language. Remember, reporting needs to be objective, clear, concise, and understandable. The reader needs to know what is actually being reported; for instance what is wrong and what needs to be done.

Example 1: Inadequate Facts
The Purchasing Department, many times could not process purchase requisitions due to inadequate controls and procedures relative to the proper recording of account charges by the various operating departments.

Rewrite:
The Purchasing Department has been delegated the authority to process all departmental purchase requisitions for purchases over $50. However, each operating department is responsible for proper coding of account charges per the company's approved chart of accounts. Purchasing Department personnel do not have the authority to change any incorrect account charges recorded at the departmental level, but are required to review them for completeness and accuracy and return any improper purchase requisitions to the originating department for correction. We analyzed 364 purchase requisitions submitted by various operating departments, and found 146 to have incorrect account coding.

Example 2: Use Of Internal Or Technical Jargon
Inventory requirements in the ASP are determined by the use of RP and EOQ formulas. IC is responsible for updating these formulas, together with related min and max levels.

Rewrite:
Inventory requirements for items included in the Accelerated Surplus Program (ASP) are determined by the use of reorder point and economic order quantity formulas. The Inventory Control Unit is responsible for updating these formulas, together with the establishment of quantity on hand minimum and maximum levels.

Example 3: Unclear Conclusion Or Recommendation
The existence of an in-house equipment and maintenance unit cannot be justified as related to the economies of using an outside service organization.

Rewrite:
The present in-house equipment maintenance unit is costing the company over $280,000 per year. Based on our analysis of completed equipment main-

FIGURE 6.1. *(Continued)*

tenance work orders for last year, we found the work load of the equipment maintenance unit to be less than 40% of total available work hours. This has resulted in many of the 8 employees assigned to the equipment maintenance unit being idle a good part of their working hours. In addition, our analysis of completed work orders disclosed an average overage of 160% of standard. By contracting with an outside service firm at an annual cost of $60,000 to handle the present equipment maintenance workload, the company can obtain a net savings of $220,000 per year. The present 8 person equipment maintenance unit should be re-assigned to production units where needed, such as production scheduling, inventory control, sub-assembly, and assembly operations.

There are some aspects for the operational auditor to consider relative to these attributes and reporting audit findings in the reporting phase:

Statement of condition

Criteria

Effect

Cause and recommendations

Inclusion of all attributes

(a) Statement of Condition

All operational audits involve fact-finding. But what is a fact? Suppose someone involved in operations tells the auditor that something has happened. Is that something a fact? Or is the fact only that the person told the auditor it is a fact? For facts that make up the statement of condition, the auditor must obviously make sure that the information is accurate, well supported, and worded as clearly and precisely as possible. Each fact must be adequately supported in the auditors' workpapers to the extent that it cannot be questioned.

(b) Criteria

The auditor's selection of criteria in judging the statement of condition requires experience and wisdom. Many of the audit findings stand or fall on the criteria used. If the auditors apply or interpret the criteria incorrectly, their initial comparison process is defective and they will have compounded the problem. It is the auditor's responsibility to convince the reader that the audit finding criteria are valid.

(c) Effect

Effect is probably the most important attribute of audit findings. Effect quantifies the impact of the deficiency and encourages management to take the proper corrective action. The significance of a deficiency is judged by effect.

Efficiency, economy, and effectiveness are useful measures of effect and frequently can be stated in quantitative terms such as dollars, times, units of production, numbers of procedures and processes, or transactions. In addition, where possible, any potential future effects should be presented.

(d) Cause and Recommendations

The remaining attributes of an audit finding, cause and recommendations, are normally interconnected and should be reported as such. Constructive recommendations usually depend on the correct identification of the cause of the operational deficiency. When the auditors know why something has happened, they can more readily consider how to prevent it or continue it, as the case may be. If it is not practical to recommend a specific or best way to correct a situation, the auditors may propose a more general recommendation or suggestion—but only in isolated instances.

The auditors must make sure that the reader fully understands the reasons for their recommendation—that is, what it is correcting and what benefits will accrue through successful implementation. Most important, operations management and staff must understand and agree to the benefits to be derived so that they will see the change as necessary and act on it. Change is difficult for both individuals and organizations. In this context, it is usually necessary for the auditors to discuss their recommendations and proposed changes with operations personnel before issuing their report—usually during the field work phase—to motivate them to take corrective action.

(e) Inclusion of All Attributes

The auditors' well-developed audit findings should not only include every attribute, but should also be written so that each attribute is clearly distinguishable from the others. The audit report readers will then have no difficulty understanding what was found, what the auditors think about what was found, why it happened, what the effect is, and how the auditors believe it should be corrected. When audit findings are reported with one or more of the attributes missing, the reader almost always raises questions. For no matter how skillful the auditors are as writers, if they do not adequately cover every attribute while the audit work is in process, they will have problems when writing the report. Examples of reporting audit findings are shown in Figures 6.2 and 6.3.

FIGURE 6.2. Reporting audit findings: Product design change reviews.

Condition: (What was found by the operational auditor)
Once a product design review change is approved for implementation by senior management, the Engineering Department is to start work immediately on redesigning the product specifications for manufacturing and purchasing. At the same time, the Sales Department is to start actively selling the product with the new design change to customers. Based on our analysis of all 148 product design changes worked on by the Engineering Department during the last year, we found it took a minimum of 52 days, an average of 68 days, and a maximum of 146 days to complete these changes.

Criteria: (What it should be)
The Example Company attempts to operate on an integrated basis; whereby the Engineering Department, Manufacturing Department, Purchasing Department, and Sales Department work together to coordinate product changes with sales forecasts, production schedules, and purchase commitments. Accordingly, company policy states that all such product design changes must be completed and approved for production within 25 days from initiation of the approved design change.

Cause: (Why it has happened)
The Engineering Department was not meeting its product design change schedule because it lacked the necessary information from other departments such as sales, manufacturing, and purchasing as well as top management. In addition, the Engineering Department assigned only two full time and one part time employee (out of a staff of 12) to work on these product design changes. Although this level of personnel was sufficient three years

FIGURE 6.2. *(Continued)*

ago when design changes were less than 50 for the year, at present these individuals are not able to support the present level of 148 changes for the year. And there is no effective system for scheduling, monitoring, and controlling these design changes so as to detect scheduling bottlenecks, time delays, and slippage for remedial action to be taken.

Effect: (What has resulted)
The impact of not meeting the 25 day schedule for product design changes has resulted in chaos between sales forecasting and production scheduling. Our analysis of new customer orders related to the 32 major product design changes in the past year disclosed that over $300,000 in sales were canceled prior to or during actual production. In addition, for those customers who did not cancel their orders, actual shipments were made between 45 to 80 days beyond promised delivery dates resulting in greatly decreased customer satisfaction.

Also, as a result of rushing these product design changes into production in many cases, returned goods were found to be 22% of total sales as opposed to a more normal 6% for all other products shipped. Although the overall impact could not be quantifiably measured, this situation also caused great disruption in the production scheduling and control, manufacturing process, inventory control, and the purchasing function.

Recommendation: (What would you recommend to correct this situation?)
The Engineering Department should establish a routing and approval schedule for all product design changes to include Sales, Manufacturing, Purchasing and any other appropriate functions or individuals. This insures desired integration between all affected parties, as well as complete and accurate data for the Engineering Department to process the desired product design change. As the workload of product design changes is not consistent throughout the year, it is difficult to permanently assign any number of engineers to this function. We recommend that all 12 engineers be cross trained to work on these product design changes, so that the greatest flexibility is achieved in meeting necessary commitments. In addition, temporary peakload situations need to be taken into account where the present level of engineering personnel is insufficient to meet product design change requirements. Consideration should be given to more flexible project scheduling, the use of per diem engineering assistance, appropriate project delays, and so on.

Since not all product design changes are of the same nature and extent, the application of a standard 25 day period for completion and approval is not really workable. A more realistic approach would be to schedule each product design change using effective engineering scheduling techniques based on a system of project priority assignments and available resources. What is most important is the adherence to the agreed upon schedule and proper integration and communication with the other parties affected such as Sales, Manufacturing, and Purchasing.

FIGURE 6.3. Reporting audit findings: Purchasing department renovations.

Condition: (What was found by the operational auditor)
An approved plan for the comprehensive renovation of the Purchasing Department facilities has been part of the last three years approved organizational plan and related budget. However, in each of these three years, Purchasing Department management has been able to divert these budgeted funds via approved budget change requests to their normal operating requirements. As a result, these needed renovations have still not been started.

Criteria: (What it should be)
Proper planning calls for effective priority setting of goals and objectives and resource allocation. If the renovations are an agreed upon priority amongst management and adequate resources were allocated for successful accomplishment for the past three years, then proper accountability expects the project to be done. By diverting these funds for normal operating purposes, management erodes the entire organizational planning and budget system.

Cause: (Why it has happened)
Management has implemented planning procedures. However, adequate control systems have not been implemented that insure plan completion. Once organizational and departmental plans and related budgets are agreed upon by top management, plan implementation becomes the responsibility of each operating department. There is no overall mechanism in effect to control all departmental plans from an organization standpoint. Each department is then free to make whatever changes they desire on an almost automatic basis.

Effect: (What has resulted)
As a result of the current lack of monitoring and control of the organizational and departmental planning system, the Purchasing Department has been able to divert the funds earmarked for facility renovations to their normal operations for the past three years. The funds needed for these renovations have increased from $220,000 to over $340,000 over the three year period. In addition, since the renovations have not been made, the deficiencies that would have been corrected are continuing, resulting in unnecessary on-going operating expenditures of approximately $120,000 per year.

Recommendation: (What would you recommend to correct this situation?)
Planning systems and procedures should be revised to include proper monitoring and control systems. Such controls should prevent arbitrary planning and budget changes. Responsibility and authority should be delegated to an independent work unit to coordinate the implementation and reporting of results of organizational and departmental plans.

The renovation of Purchasing Department facilities should be accomplished. This is an approved and agreed upon project with economic and operational justification. Proper project control procedures should be established to insure successful project completion.

6.7 ABCs OF EFFECTIVE REPORT WRITING

For the audit team to produce more effective reports, it sometimes helps to think in terms of the ABCs of effective report writing, as follows:

1. *Accuracy.* The auditors should be accurate in presenting facts, spelling, punctuation, grammar, and usage. Accurate description of problems, conditions, and situations is an absolute necessity. If management is to rely on the information given by the audit team, it must be accurate in all respects. The auditors cannot shade the facts or manipulate them to their unfair advantage. If they do, they shake management's faith in their reporting.

2. *Brevity.* The auditors should strive for brevity, using the short, concrete word and the short, simple sentence. Their report should be exactly the right length—long enough to cover the subject, short enough to be interesting. Lengthy narratives and long paragraphs are to be avoided; listings and tabulations should be used instead.

3. *Confidence.* The auditors should be confident that they have something of value to say. If they are—and this is basic to an effective report—then they must say it confidently, positively, and sincerely, as well as simply and directly.

4. *Defense.* As the saying goes, there are two sides to every story, so the auditors should be sure to present management's defense and reaction to their findings and recommendations. Failure to present management reactions detracts from the value of the report to management and wastes time. Management may agree with the auditors' findings and conclusions in whole or in part, or may totally disagree.

5. *Explain.* The auditors must explain, interpret, and describe, since many times facts have to be interpreted for management. Tabulations, charts, and graphs may present the overall picture, but the auditors have to tell management what the facts mean.

6. *Format.* In presenting the audit report, there is the conflict between formatting it in "free style," based on the creativity of the auditors, or using a strict formula in which the auditors fill in the spaces. A recommended middle ground is to define some basic directions, but to avoid strict standardization. Figure 6.4 illustrates a sample report format of this kind.

FIGURE 6.4. Sample report format.

Mr. John Q. Reader
ABC Department

Dear Mr. Reader:

This "Guide" has been prepared to simplify the task of writing and to standardize the format of operational audit reports. It has been prepared in the format of an actual report.

In many ways, the introductory paragraph is the most important part of the report. It is the first thing the reader sees. The reader's reaction to these first few sentences determines whether the reader cares to read further. The auditors must prepare the report in a manner that motivates the reader to accept and implement their recommendations.

MAJOR SIDE HEADS

The major side heads signify the major divisions. They are started at the margin, in capital letters and underlined. Major side heads are never numbered.

Minor Side Heads
This is an illustration of how to use minor side heads.

A Second Minor Side Head.
When minor side heads are used, it is mandatory to have at least two under a major side head. Note that the minor side head is indented five spaces, underscored, and in upper and lower case.

Another Minor Side Head
Frequent use of major and minor side heads has several advantages, namely,
- They help the writer to outline the significant major and minor findings, conclusions, and recommendations for each section of the report before he or she begins to write the report.
- They assist the reader in quickly locating major and minor subjects in the report.

TWO TYPES OF REPORTS

There are two types of operational audit reports: the letter report and the regular report.

1. The *letter report* is designed to be used when the subject matter requires only a few pages of discussion. As a general rule, it should not be used if the report will be more than five pages, contains exhibits or numerous appendices, covers a complex subject, or contains a group of different ideas or topics.

6.7 ABCs OF EFFECTIVE REPORT WRITING

FIGURE 6.4. *(Continued)*

2. The *regular report* contains the introductory letter, in the form that you are presently reading, plus a table of contents and several report sections, each covering a major subject.

LISTINGS AND TABULATIONS

Listings (see "Two Types of Reports") and tabulations (see "Another Minor Side Head") can be used. Note that the items are single-spaced but have a double space between items. Listings are numbered. Tabulations are preceded either by a "bullet" (•) or a dash (—).

REPORT DATE

The report is dated as of the date it is delivered to operations management as a final product. It is, however, a good practice to provide a draft of the report beforehand and to include management's and staff's comments in the final report.

PAGE NUMBERS

The first page of the letter report or introductory letter is not numbered. Succeeding pages are numbered in the upper right-hand corner (Page 2, 3, etc.).

For the long or regular report, the first and succeeding pages of the sections are numbered in Roman numerals-Arabic numerals (I-1, I-2, etc.).

CONTENTS

Contents of the letter report or introductory letter will have the following typical major heads:

Background
Scope of Our Review
Objectives
Our Approach (how you made the study)
Summary of Findings and Recommendations
Concluding Paragraph (expressing your appreciation)

In both the letter report and the regular report the section "Summary of Findings and Recommendations" would include a brief description of the auditors' findings and related recommendations. The reporting of all of the attributes (statement of condition, criteria, cause, effect, and recommendation) directly associated with these findings have either been submitted and reviewed with management previously and/or can be included as an appendix with the report.

In the long regular report this section in the introductory letter would be called "Summary of Findings and Recommendations," and only the major or significant findings and recommendations would be included. A final sen-

REPORTING PHASE

FIGURE 6.4. *(Continued)*

tence would be added which would indicate that details of the major recommendations, plus all other findings and recommendations, are located in the following sections of the report, such as:

  I. PURCHASING UNIT PROCEDURES
 II. VENDOR RELATIONS AND ANALYSIS
III. STANDARD SPECIFICATIONS UNIT
 IV. COST TO PROCESS A PURCHASE ORDER
  V. SHIPPING AND RECEIVING OPERATIONS
 VI. PROPOSED INTEGRATED COMPUTER SYSTEM

* * * * * * *

At the close of every report, it is suggested to include a comment regarding the cooperation (or lack of cooperation) of the audited organization's staff and to state that the audit team can be contacted for any additional information relative to the findings in the report. Remember, another important purpose of the operational audit report is to acquire additional or follow-up work and to convince management of the merits and benefits versus cost of having other operational audits performed by the audit organization.

TABLE OF CONTENTS

I. ORGANIZATION AND MANAGEMENT	I-1
How to Organize	I-2
Existing Organization	I-3
Pyramid Type	I-4
Communication	I-4
Personnel	I-5
II. PURCHASING PROCEDURES	II-1
III. VENDOR RELATIONS AND ANALYSIS	III-1
IV. STANDARD SPECIFICATIONS UNIT	IV-1
V. COST TO PROCESS A PURCHASE ORDER	V-1
VI. SHIPPING AND RECEIVING OPERATIONS	VI-1
VII. PROPOSED INTEGRATED COMPUTER SYSTEM	VII-1
APPENDIX AND EXHIBITS	
SUMMARY OF MAJOR FINDINGS AND RECOMMENDATIONS	A
OTHER AREAS FOR REVIEW	B
DETAILED FINDINGS AND RECOMMENDATIONS	C

6.8 SAMPLE REPORTS

FIGURE 6.4. *(Continued)*

I. SECTION HEAD

The introductory paragraph introduces the reader to the section. From this introduction the reader should learn what this section is about.

Note that each section has a section heading, which is centered in upper case and underlined. Each section should be prefixed with a Roman numeral (as in "I" above), followed by a very brief, descriptive, interesting subject heading.

MAJOR SIDE HEAD

The long report should extensively use major side heads and minor side heads.

TABLE OF CONTENTS

The table of contents of the report is comparable to the table of contents of a book. It lists every section head, major side head, and minor side head in the report. The purpose of the table is to help the reader find a topic in the report. It also gives the reader a summary of the organization of the report and the topics covered.

The table of contents is prepared after the report has been completed. It is placed between the introductory letter and the first major section.

6.8 SAMPLE REPORTS

Strict standardization is not recommended for operational audit report formats. However, without some basic directions, there would be as many variations of reports as there are operational auditors. The suggested sample report format shown in Figure 6.4 can be used effectively by operational auditors—intact or with their own modifications.

Figure 6.4 describes these two types of reports, the letter report and the regular report, as follows:

1. The *Letter Report,* or short report, is used when the subject matter requires only a few pages. As a general rule, it should not be used if the report will be more than five pages, contains exhibits or numerous appendices, covers a complex subject, or contains a group of different ideas or topics.

2. The *Regular Report,* or long report, is used for more lengthy reporting, particulary when a number of different areas or subjects are covered.

REPORTING PHASE

It typically contains an introductory letter, plus a table of contents and several report sections, each covering a major subject or area.

A sample letter report and a sample regular report for the Example Company Purchasing Department case study materials covered in preceding chapters are presented in Figures 6.5 and 6.6. These sample audit reports contain many of the elements discussed and recommended for good operational audit report writing. These materials should be reviewed and then used as a guide for preparing operational audit reports.

Note that in the letter report there is a "Summary of Findings and Recommendations" section, which gives a general description of each finding and the estimated savings. The detailed audit findings have either been presented previously, or are documented separately or included as an appendix to the report. In the regular report introductory letter, the "Summary of Findings and Recommendations" section merely references the audit findings and states the total amount of savings. The major findings are then summarized by section, as referenced in the table of contents. Attachment A to the report is a "Summary of Major Findings and Recommendations," which provides a capsulized view or scoreboard for management. Attachment B, "Other Areas for Review" describes nonmajor areas noted by the auditors on which management can either take action on their own or enlist the audit team to help them (see Figure 6.6).

6.8 SAMPLE REPORTS

FIGURE 6.5. Sample operational audit letter report.

July 8, 19XX

Mr. George Worthington
Vice President - Operations
The Example Company
Example Boulevard
Example, XX 99999

Dear Mr. Worthington:

Reider Associates is pleased to submit this report to the Example Company relative to our findings and conclusions as a result of our review and analysis of Purchasing Department procedures. During the course of this consulting engagement, we:

1. Analyzed present purchasing procedures.
2. Assisted the Example Company personnel in implementing our recommendations of an immediate and short-term nature.
3. Documented the methodology for implementing long-term improvements.
4. Identified areas of personnel staffing economies in conjunction with recommended efficiencies of operations.

Background

Prior to our review, the Example Company Purchasing Department work unit consisted of 16 employees associated with the following functions:

- Purchasing Supervisor
- (7) Buyer II's
- (4) Buyer I's
- Clerk-Stenographer
- Clerical Supervisor
- (2) Clerk-Typists

The Example Company senior management has been aware of the need for an operational review and analysis of Purchasing Unit procedures. While the scope of purchasing activities has greatly expanded in response to changing internal and external requirements, basic procedures have remained relatively stable. Additional procedures have been implemented solely to address specific situations. Accordingly, this method of operation has produced an operating environment characterized by individualized procedures that do not always efficiently meet purchasing operating and reporting needs. In recognition of this need, the Example Company management engaged Reider Associates to assist them in performing an operational audit of Purchasing Unit procedures.

FIGURE 6.5. *(Continued)*

Scope of our Review

For the purpose of identifying areas for improvements, our analysis of present Purchasing Unit procedures included the following tasks:

1. *Personnel Interviews*

   Met with Purchasing Department management and Purchasing Unit operations personnel to analyze present operating procedures and associated areas for improvement, as well as to determine future requirements. These discussions and reviews provided us with a working knowledge of:
   - Present operating procedures.
   - Timing and flow of current data.
   - Problem areas, particularly the critical ones.
   - Coordination and related reporting and communication networks between departments.
   - Information requirements, present and future needs.

2. *Functional Activities*

   Review of systems and procedures presently required to perform such purchasing-oriented functions as:
   - Purchasing Department organization structure and related functional job descriptions, including responsibility and authority relationships.
   - Purchasing Department planning systems, including the establishment of goals, objectives, and detail plans; and the integration of such plans with overall organizational planning systems.
   - Personnel practices including employee hiring, orientation, training, evaluation, promotion, and firing.
   - Purchasing Department policies and operating procedures.

Objectives

The objectives of this engagement were to identify the work being performed by Purchasing Unit personnel in order to formulate future operational requirements, as well as to make observations and recommendations as to the manner in which immediate and short-term improvements could be realized. The principal focus of our efforts was toward developing operating procedures which would provide optimum efficiencies in meeting the Example Company's requirements.

Our Approach

Our approach to reviewing Purchasing Unit operating procedures involved an analysis of operations according to the existing organization structure. Accordingly, we divided our review into the Purchasing Unit functional activity areas:

- Purchasing supervision.
- Buying and vendor relations.
- Purchase requisition and purchase order processing.

6.8 SAMPLE REPORTS

FIGURE 6.5. *(Continued)*

- Open purchase order control and expediting.
- Internal record keeping.
- Purchasing information system.

At the conclusion of each of the above stages of analysis, we prepared a review of findings and recommendations which were submitted to appropriate Example Company management and operations personnel in oral presentations, together with written documentation. Accordingly, these presentation materials are not being included in this report. Basically, our review of findings discussed present deficiencies, suggested methods of improvement, and identified areas where economies and efficiencies could be achieved immediately or as a result of additional work efforts.

Summary of Findings and Recommendations

We are summarizing our major findings below for your review. The details of each finding have been submitted under separate cover for your information. We believe that should you implement all of these recommendations, the Example Company could realize an estimated annual savings of $410,000.

1. *Purchase Requisition Procedures*

   Purchase requisitions are not prenumbered and effectively controlled, resulting in instances in which items are ordered more than once or in which needed materials or services go unordered. Based on our analysis of this situation, we believe you can realize at least $120,000 in annual savings, as well as maintain more effective controls as to purchasing only those items that are necessary.

2. *Budgetary Controls*

   Purchase requisitions are not being checked against approved plans and budgets, resulting in purchases being processed for many items that exceed budgetary approvals. There is a combined problem in this situation: ineffective planning and budget procedures (using static rather than flexible budgeting) and the lack of budgetary controls. We analyzed this situation and found that an estimated annual savings of $80,000 could be realized through the elimination of unnecessary purchases.

3. *Buyer Function*

   The buying function is presently performed by (7) Buyer II's, and (4) Buyer I's. We analyzed their functions and found that the work load is distributed by commodities. Accordingly, there is uneven distribution of the work load as to vendor relations and negotiations, processing of purchases, etc. By distributing work based on activity levels, you should be able to eliminate at least four of these positions, resulting in an estimated annual savings of $164,000, without sacrificing the effectiveness of operations.

REPORTING PHASE

FIGURE 6.5. *(Continued)*

4. *Value Analysis Program*
    A "value analysis" program does not exist whereby purchasing analyzes the items to be purchased to determine if less expensive items can be used to meet the same needs. Based on a limited review of 120 selected items, we found that more than $46,000 could have been saved through the use of such a value analysis program. The total savings that could be realized from a full value analysis program would, of course, be much greater than this.

* * * * *

We appreciate the courtesies and cooperation extended to us by Example Company personnel during the course of this engagement. We are, of course, prepared to discuss any aspects of this engagement or specific items mentioned in this report with you, should you so desire. In addition, we are available to provide additional consultative assistance in the operational review of other functional areas, as well as to work with you in the implementation of recommendations mentioned in this report. We appreciate the opportunity to assist Example Company management in accomplishing the results of this operational review engagement and look forward to continued good relations between Reider Associates and the Example Company.

Very truly yours,

Harry Reider, President
REIDER ASSOCIATES

6.8 SAMPLE REPORTS

FIGURE 6.6. Sample operational audit regular report.

July 8, 19XX

Mr. George Worthington
Vice President - Operations
The Example Company
Example Boulevard
Example, XX 99999

Dear Mr. Worthington:

Reider Associates is pleased to submit this report to the Example Company relative to our findings and conclusions as a result of our review and analysis of Purchasing Department activities. During the course of this consulting engagement, we:

1. Analyzed present systems and methods.
2. Conceptualized new manual and computerized procedures.
3. Identified those areas not susceptible to mechanization.
4. Assisted the Example Company personnel in implementing our recommendations of an immediate and short-term nature.
5. Documented the methodology for implementing long-term improvements.
6. Instituted a system for setting project priorities and monitoring progress on an actual versus scheduled basis.
7. Identified areas of personnel staffing economies in conjunction with recommended efficiencies of operations.

Background

Prior to our review, the Example Company Purchasing Department consisted of 23 employees, associated with the following functions:

Purchasing Unit
- Purchasing Supervisor
- (7) Buyer II's
- (4) Buyer I's
- Clerk-Stenographer
- Clerical Supervisor
- (2) Clerk-Typists

Standard Specifications Unit
- Standard Specifications Supervisor
- (2) Procurement Technicians
- (2) Management Trainees
- Clerk-Stenographer
- Clerk

The Example Company senior management has been aware of the need for a comprehensive operational review and analysis of Purchasing Department

FIGURE 6.6. *(Continued)*

management and operating systems and methods. While the scope of purchasing activities has greatly expanded in response to changing internal and external requirements, basic manual and mechanized systems and procedures have remained relatively stable. Additional procedures have been implemented solely to address specific situations. Accordingly, this method of operation has produced an operating environment characterized by individualized systems that do not always make efficient use of common data to meet purchasing operating and reporting needs in the most economical and efficient manner. In recognition of this need, the Example Company management engaged Reider Associates to assist them in making (1) a detailed review and analysis of Purchasing Department operations, (2) a study of personnel efficiencies, (3) a definition of data processing requirements, and in (4) developing an implementation priority list and schedule to achieve desired results.

Scope of our Review

For the purpose of identifying areas for improvements, our analysis of present Purchasing Department systems and methods included the following tasks:

1. *Personnel Interviews*

   Met with Purchasing Department management and operations personnel to analyze present operating systems and procedures and associated areas for improvement, as well as to determine future requirements. These discussions and reviews provided us with a working knowledge of:
   - Present operating procedures - manual and computerized.
   - Source document forms and their use.
   - Timing and flow of current data.
   - Problem areas, particularly those critical to future data processing.
   - Coordination and related reporting and communication networks between departments.
   - Information requirements, present and future needs.

2. *Functional Activities*

   Reviewed systems and procedures presently required to perform such purchasing-oriented functions as:
   - Purchasing Department organization structure and related functional job descriptions, including responsibility and authority relationships.
   - Purchasing Department planning systems, including the establishment of goals, objectives, and detail plans, and the integration of such plans with overall organizational planning systems.
   - Personnel practices, including employee hiring, orientation, training, evaluation, promotion, and firing.
   - Purchasing Department policies and operating procedures related to areas such as:
     - Forecasting commodity and service needs.
     - Vendor relations and analysis.

6.8 SAMPLE REPORTS

FIGURE 6.6. *(Continued)*

- Purchasing specifications development and use.
- Purchase approval and requisition procedures.
- Purchase order processing and control.
- Open purchase order follow-up and control.
- Purchased items receipt controls.
- Purchasing information system.
- Electronic data processing procedures.

Objectives

The objectives of this engagement were to identify the work being performed by Purchasing Department personnel in order to formulate future operational requirements, as well as to make observations and recommendations as to the manner in which immediate and short-term improvements could be realized. The principal focus of our efforts was toward developing an approach for an integrated system that would provide optimum efficiencies in meeting the Example Company's requirements. Such an integrated system would provide for (1) a purchasing information and control system within internal and external purchasing guidelines, which would provide all necessary data for proper record keeping, analysis, and control of all purchase requisitions and orders, and (2) a meaningful planning and control system for purchasing management, operational analysis, evaluation, and general control. Accordingly, an additional objective was to define methods that would enhance the effectiveness of purchasing operations and staff by providing personnel at all levels with more timely information to enable them to make improved management and operational decisions.

Our Approach

Our approach to reviewing purchasing operations involved an analysis of operations according to the existing organization structure. Accordingly, we divided our review into the existing purchasing functional activity areas:

- Purchasing supervision.
- Buying and vendor relations.
- Purchase requisition and purchase order processing.
- Open purchase order control and expediting.
- Internal record keeping.
- Purchasing information system.
- Purchasing specifications.

At the conclusion of each of the above stages of analysis, we prepared a review of findings and recommendations, which were submitted to appropriate Example Company management and operations personnel in oral presentations, together with written documentation. Accordingly, these presentation materials are not being included in this report. Basically, our review of findings discussed present deficiencies, suggested methods of improvement, and

FIGURE 6.6. *(Continued)*

identified areas where economies and efficiencies could be achieved immediately or as a result of additional work efforts.

In addition, we presented a conceptualized plan for an integrated purchasing operating and information computer system that was designed to meet Example Company's requirements as determined through our operational review and analysis. The proposed system would include all present purchasing-oriented manual and computer applications effectively integrated with:

- Manufacturing control systems; including production and inventory control procedures.
- Cost accounting systems.
- General ledger accounting system, particularly the budget and accounts payable modules.

Such an integrated computer system would use common data sources, many of which exist presently, to efficiently update the system.

Summary of Findings and Recommendations

We are summarizing our major findings in the following sections of this report for your review. The details of each finding have been submitted under separate cover for your information. We believe that should you implement all of these recommendations, the Example Company could realize an estimated annual savings of $1,775,000. We are also attaching a list of other findings identified during the course of our review that we believe should be brought to your attention for remedial action to achieve increased economies, efficiencies, and effectiveness of results in the purchasing-related areas.

*   *   *   *   *

We appreciate the courtesies and cooperation extended to us by Example Company personnel during the course of this engagement. We are, of course, prepared to discuss any aspects of this engagement or specific items mentioned in this report with you, should you so desire. In addition, we are available to provide additional consultative assistance in the operational review of other functional areas, as well as to work with you in the implementation of recommendations mentioned in this report. We appreciate the opportunity to assist Example Company management in accomplishing the results of this operational review engagement and look forward to continued good relations between Reider Associates and the Example Company.

Very truly yours,

Harry Reider, President
REIDER ASSOCIATES

Attachments

6.8 SAMPLE REPORTS

FIGURE 6.6. *(Continued)*

THE EXAMPLE COMPANY
PURCHASING DIVISION OPERATIONAL AUDIT REPORT
TABLE OF CONTENTS

	Page
I. PURCHASING UNIT PROCEDURES	I-1
1. Purchase Requisition Procedures	I-1
2. Budgetary Controls	I-1
3. Buyer Function	I-1
4. Open Purchase Order Control	I-2
5. Competitive Bidding Procedures	I-2
6. Value Analysis Program	I-2
II. VENDOR RELATIONS AND ANALYSIS	II-1
1. Dealing with Same Vendors	II-1
2. Vendor Analysis	II-1
3. Leased Car Procedures	II-1
III. STANDARD SPECIFICATIONS UNIT	III-1
1. Staffing Requirements	III-1
2. Reporting Relationships	III-1
IV. COST TO PROCESS A PURCHASE ORDER	IV-1
1. Present Purchase Order Costs	IV-1
2. Purchases Under $200	IV-1
V. SHIPPING AND RECEIVING OPERATIONS	V-1
1. Shipping Procedures	V-1
2. Receiving Procedures	V-1
3. Palletized Shipments and Receipts	V-1
VI. PROPOSED INTEGRATED COMPUTER SYSTEM	VI-1
Proposed Computerization	VI-1
Additional Personnel	VI-1
Computer Processing Priorities	VI-1
Computer Equipment Requirements	VI-2
ATTACHMENTS	
Summary of Major Findings and Recommendations	A
Other Areas for Review	B

FIGURE 6.6. *(Continued)*

I. PURCHASING UNIT PROCEDURES — Page I-1

We reviewed operating procedures of the Purchasing Unit to identify those areas of deficiency where positive improvements could be made in terms of economy, efficiency, and effectiveness.

The following major areas for operational improvement were noted for your review:

1. *Purchase Requisition Procedures*

    Purchase requisitions are not prenumbered and effectively controlled, resulting in instances in which items are ordered more than once or in which needed materials or services go unordered. Based on our analysis of this situation, we believe that you can realize at least $120,000 in annual savings, as well as maintain more effective controls as to purchasing only necessary items by using such controls.

2. *Budgetary Controls*

    Purchase requisitions are not being checked against approved plans and budgets. Accordingly, purchases are being processed for many items within the company, which are known to exceed existing budgetary approvals. There is a combined problem in this situation: ineffective organizational planning and budget procedures (using static rather than flexible budgeting), together with the lack of budgetary controls at the time of purchase requisitioning. We analyzed this situation and found that an estimated annual savings of $80,000 could be realized through the elimination of unnecessary purchases. In addition, with the implementation of effective planning and budgetary systems, you should realize other monetary and operational benefits.

3. *Buyer Function*

    The buying function is presently performed by (7) Buyer II's, and (4) Buyer I's. We analyzed their functions and found that the work load is distributed by commodities. Accordingly, there is uneven distribution of the work load as to vendor relations and negotiations, processing of purchases, etc. By distributing work based on activity levels, you should be able to eliminate at least four of these positions, resulting in an estimated annual savings of $164,000, without sacrificing the effectiveness of operations.

4. *Open Purchase Order Control*

    The control over open purchase orders is presently being accomplished on a manual basis. Purchase order copies are used as the control mechanism. We found that there are approximately 1,200 open purchase orders at any one time, so that this has become a difficult task for the one Clerk-Stenographer to handle on a manual basis. Our proposed computerized system will eliminate this problem by providing mechanized control over

6.8 SAMPLE REPORTS

FIGURE 6.6. *(Continued)*

the expediting of open purchases, resulting in an increased degree of on-time vendor deliveries. We estimate that the present large number of late deliveries is costing you more than $245,000 annually in canceled customer orders and manufacturing delays and stoppages.

5. *Competitive Bidding Procedures*

    Although your present purchasing procedures state that competitive bidding procedures must be used for each purchase over $2,000 and at least annually for repetitively ordered items, we found such procedures rarely applied. Based on our analysis, we estimate that you could save a minimum of $342,000 by effectively exercising such bidding procedures.

6. *Value Analysis Program*

    A "value analysis" program does not exist, whereby purchasing analyzes the items to be purchased to determine whether less expensive items can be used to meet the same needs. Based on a limited review of 120 selected items, we found that more than $46,000 could have been saved through the use of such a value analysis program. The total savings that could be realized from a full value analysis program would, of course, be much greater than this.

FIGURE 6.6. *(Continued)*

II. VENDOR RELATIONS AND ANALYSIS   Page II-1

As part of our operational review of Purchasing Department functions and activities, we analyzed those systems and procedures related to vendor relations. Our major findings and recommendations are summarized below:

1. *Dealing with Same Vendors*

    We found a predominant practice of habitually dealing with the same vendors. Although this makes it easier for the buyers to perform their functions, it is a costly practice from the standpoint of achieving the best possible pricing. On this basis, we found that it is costing the company an estimated annual amount of more than $224,000 for the purchase of manufacturing raw materials. This does not include all other purchases.

2. *Vendor Analysis*

    Vendor analysis is not presently being performed in an effective manner, considering such aspects as price, quality of goods, services delivered, and timeliness of deliveries. This is presently accomplished on an exception basis, as the result of a specific complaint. However, we found no evidence of effective vendor action or of any vendor being replaced as a result of such actions. Although we could not quantify the cost of such inefficient procedures, as adequate records do not exist, we have documented for you a number of such incidences in previous reporting.

3. *Leased Car Procedures*

    We analyzed the procedures used by the Buyer II responsible for negotiating and assigning leased cars to employees. We found that for the 87 cars being leased, 24 were being used insufficiently to justify the lease payment. In addition, we found 37 other employees who presently use their own cars and are reimbursed at 28 cents per mile, whereby the actual reimbursements exceed the cost of leasing. The reassignment of these leased cars, based on actual usage, will result in an annual savings of more than $44,000 per year.

6.8 SAMPLE REPORTS

FIGURE 6.6. *(Continued)*

III. STANDARD SPECIFICATIONS UNIT Page III-1

The Standards Specifications Unit is responsible for maintaining the detailed specifications as to what to purchase. As this is an extremely critical function, particularly for the Example Company manufacturing operations, we included a review of its activities in our operational audit. Our major findings and recommendations are presented below.

1. *Staffing Requirements*

   The Standard Specifications Unit was originally established when the Example Company first started in business more than 12 years ago. At that time, purchasing specifications were required for all production materials, which needed to be developed from engineering bils of material. The staffing level of one Supervisor, (4) Procurement Technicians, and (2) Clerical Support personnel was established at that time. The same positions still exist, although two Procurement Technician jobs are being done by Management Trainees. However, at this point, there are very few new products requiring new purchasing specifications, and the unit is primarily responsible for maintaining existing specifications. Based on these present requirements and our analysis of existing systems and procedures, we believe that you can accomplish the present level of activity with one Procurement Technician and one Clerical person. This should result in the displacement of five employees, for an estimated annual savings of more than $150,000.

2. *Reporting Relationship*

   Based on the above proposed reorganization of the Standard Specifications Unit, we believe that the revised unit of two employees can report directly to the Purchasing Supervisor, resulting in increased control and efficiency within the unit.

FIGURE 6.6. *(Continued)*

IV. COST TO PROCESS A PURCHASE ORDER   Page IV-1

As part of our operational audit we determined that it was advisable to establish appropriate policies relative to the amount of a purchase that should be processed by the central Purchasing Department. To arrive at what this amount should realistically be, we calculated the present cost to process a purchase order. Our findings are stated below.

1. *Present Purchase Order Processing Costs*

    We determined that it presently costs approximately $51 to process a purchase order. This cost has not been calculated since you first started operations more than 12 years ago, when it was calculated to be $11.80. Based on this calculation and your policy that purchase orders should not be issued where the cost to process the purchase is greater than 25% of the value of the purchase, your rule has been that all purchases over $50 go through the Purchasing Department. However, based on our calculation of $51 to process a purchase order and your 25%-of-value policy, we believe that all purchases under $200 should circumvent the purchasing system.

2. *Purchases Under $200*

    We analyzed present purchases and found that 23.5% of all purchase orders were for $200 or less. We estimated that it costs about $216,903 to process these purchases. We believe you can realize an annual savings of more than $160,000, as well as increase the efficiency of the Purchasing Department, by having all purchases under $200 processed as petty cash or direct purchases.

6.8 SAMPLE REPORTS

FIGURE 6.6. *(Continued)*

V. SHIPPING AND RECEIVING OPERATIONS   Page V-1

During the course of our operational review of Purchasing Department operations, we identified some major operational deficiencies in the shipping and receiving areas. Based on our review of these areas with you, it was mutually agreed that we should spend the necessary time to analyze these operations. Our findings in these areas are presented below.

1. *Shipping Procedures*

    Our analysis of shipping procedures disclosed that you are presently storing finished goods on pallets in your warehouse. However, at the time of shipping, you use forklifts to take the items to the shipping area. Work crews then unload the pallets by hand onto trucks or railcars. We were told that this policy was instituted owing to the large number of pallets lost in shipment in the past. We contacted your 12 major customers (accounting for more than 80% of total sales) and found that 10 of them would be willing to provide pallets to you.

2. *Receiving Procedures*

    Receiving procedures were found to be working in just the opposite way, whereby your major suppliers are shipping unpalletized. Your receiving personnel then have to remove the goods from the trucks or railcars and place them on pallets for the forklift operators to store them in the raw material warehouse. We checked with your four major suppliers and found that each of them would be willing to palletize your shipments if you would provide in-transit pallets.

3. *Palletized Shipments and Receipts*

    The net cost savings of revising shipping and receiving procedures, as described above, is estimated at more than $200,000 annually. In addition, the use of palletized shipments and receipts for other customers and suppliers should result in even greater annual savings.

FIGURE 6.6. *(Continued)*

VI. PROPOSED INTEGRATED COMPUTER SYSTEM   Page VI-1

The computerized integrated purchasing control and management reporting system that we are proposing involves a communications process in which data are recorded initially, and revised as needed, in order to support management and staff decisions for planning, operating, and controlling purchasing operations. Our conceptual design attempts to maximize the use of common data to satisfy the information requirements of the Example Company staff at various levels. It attempts to strike an economic balance between the value of the information to be carried and the cost of operating the system. Accordingly, our objective is not simply to mechanize, but to design an effective computerization plan that will provide the Example Company purchasing personnel with the necessary data to manage and operate.

1. *Proposed Computerization*

    Proposed computerization will also afford the opportunity for additional personnel cost savings in the purchasing, inventory control, and warehousing functions. Accordingly, Example Company management should review future departmental and personnel functions and responsibilities for possible eliminations, combining, shifting, and downgrading. A personnel plan should be developed to coordinate procedural changes with personnel requirements on an ongoing basis as changes are implemented.

2. *Additional Personnel*

    We believe that to successfully implement the proposed computer systems in a timely manner, in addition to simultaneously completing our other data processing-related recommendations, will require at least one additional experienced computer programmer to be hired.

3. *Computer Processing Priorities*

    We also believe that the most efficient and practical course of action for Example Company management to take, with regard to computer processing, is to establish the following priorities:

    - Implement our recommended purchasing function improvements, based on the priorities previously established.
    - Simultaneously program and implement the production and inventory control systems presently being designed.
    - System design and program the proposed integrated purchasing computer system as described.

Computer Equipment Requirements

We believe that the present computer system is capable of performing the processing described above. Present computer usage of approximately 50 hours a month is relatively low at present and can be appreciably increased with minimal impact on overall data processing operations. Additionally, manual control functions should be reduced, providing for a streamlining of operations. After the recommendations described above have successfully been accomplished and are operational, Example Company management should reappraise computer equipment needs with respect to total processing.

6.8 SAMPLE REPORTS

FIGURE 6.6. *(Continued)*

THE EXAMPLE COMPANY
SUMMARY OF MAJOR FINDINGS
AND RECOMMENDATIONS

Attachment A
A-1

Description	Estimated Annual Savings
1. *Purchasing Procedures*	
a. Purchase requisition controls	$ 120,000
b. Purchasing/budgetary controls	80,000
c. Redistribution of buyers' work loads	164,000
d. Control over open purchase orders	245,000
e. Competitive bidding procedures	342,000
f. Value analysis program	46,000*
2. *Vendor Relations and Analysis*	
a. Dealing with same vendors	224,000**
b. Vendor analysis	Can't quantify
c. Employee leased cars	44,000
3. *Standard Specifications Unit*	
a. Personnel displacement	150,000
b. Reporting to Purchasing Supervisor	—
4. *Cost to Process a Purchase Order*	
a. Purchases over $200	—
b. Purchases under $200	160,000
5. *Shipping and Receiving Operations*	
a. Shipping procedures	—
b. Receiving procedures	—
c. Revised shipping/receiving procedures	200,000
Total Estimated Annual Savings	$1,775,000

* Based on a limited review. Total annual savings should be much greater.
** Includes manufacturing raw materials only.

FIGURE 6.6. *(Continued)*

THE EXAMPLE COMPANY   Attachment B
OTHER AREAS FOR REVIEW   B-1

Based on the work performed during our operational review of the Purchasing Department, we identified additional operational areas that we believe should be brought to your attention for further review and analysis. These additional areas include:

1. Organizational planning and related systems. We found that presently the Example Company operates on a reactive basis, that is, in response to specific situations and crises. Steps should be taken to implement effective planning techniques which encompass:
   - Sophisticated sales forecast procedures that allow management to determine the related production requirements based on planned customer demand.
   - Effective production scheduling systems that provide for controlling manufacturing operations based on planned customer orders rather than on inventory demands.
   - Formal planning procedures that would include organizational and departmental goals, objectives, and detail plans, as well as an effective reporting and control system to ensure compliance to agreed-upon plans.
   - Development and implementation of departmental and work unit budgets that use established plans as their basis and are reported on a flexible basis as related to activity levels.
2. Review and analysis of organizational structure directed toward making the organization more responsive to current demands. Areas to look at could include reporting relationships, responsibility/authority relationships, management/supervisory assignments, work load distributions, etc. For example, based on our review of the Purchasing Department, we suggest you review the following areas:
   - Purchasing Department reporting to the Vice President of Operations; under the direct supervision of a Purchasing Supervisor.
   - Functions, responsibilities, and authority of staff positions such as Market Analyst and Administrative Analyst.
   - Use of clerical staff such as two Clerk-Stenographers reporting to the Vice President of Operations, four clerical staff in the Purchasing Department, two clerks in the Standards Specifications Unit, and three in the Inventory Control Unit.
   - Work units such as Inspection, Inventory Control, and Warehouse reporting to the same individual as the purchasing function—the Vice President of Operations.

6.8 SAMPLE REPORTS

FIGURE 6.6. *(Continued)*

3. Review of personnel practices related to hiring, orientation, training, evaluation, promotion, and firing. We found no policies or procedures related to these personnel practices in existence at the Example Company. Accordingly, such practices are implemented by individual managers/supervisors based on their own criteria and expertise. Accordingly, in all of these areas, procedures are weak and inconsistent, resulting in employee confusion, improperly trained staff and management, loss of qualified personnel, and retention of undesirable employees.
4. Review of operating systems and procedures so as to perform necessary functions in the most economical and efficient manner without sacrificing expected results. For instance, our review of Purchasing Department functions identified operational areas for positive improvements, such as the following:
    - Well-defined organization structure with defined responsibilities and authority relationships.
    - Agreed-upon goals, objectives, and detail plans.
    - Accurate and up-to-date position descriptions.
    - Effective personnel practices to ensure well-qualified staff.
    - Workable and practical operating policies and procedures.
    - Integrated management and operating information system.
    - Use of efficient operating techniques, such as:
        - Traveling purchase requisitions.
        - Blanket purchase orders.
        - Integration of manufacturing and vendor deliveries.
        - Vendor analysis as to price, quality, and timeliness.
        - Competitive bidding procedures.
        - Value analysis program.
5. More efficient use and integration of data processing techniques with actual operations. You have had your computer system operational for more than 8 years; however, you are still performing manually many functions that lend themselves to effective computerization. A major reason for this is the lack of direction over data processing activities by top management. Accordingly, data processing personnel are presently maintaining those systems that were originally designed and implemented with the help of outside consultants at the time the computer system was installed. Accordingly, you are using these resources minimally, although there is sufficient personnel and equipment capacity within your organization to achieve maximum use. Our recommended integrated purchasing system is an excellent first step. However, other areas should be looked at as well, such as sales forecasting, production scheduling, production control, inventory control, and billing and collections.

6.9 CONCLUSION

The purpose of this chapter is to present principles and techniques for effectively preparing operational audit reports and presenting them to operations management and staff. Operational audit reporting can be accomplished in either an informal or a formal manner. The actual reporting can be oral, written, or a combination of both.

The operational audit report communicates the results of the operational audit work to the intended recipients. The principal objectives of the audit report are to provide useful and timely information on significant operational deficiencies, and to recommend operational improvements.

The reporting phase provides the auditors with an opportunity to obtain management and staff's undivided attention and prove to them the benefits of operational auditing and the auditors' related expertise. While the final report marks the official close of the present operational audit, it is also an effective vehicle for selling the concept of operational auditing for additional reviews. Moreover, if the reporting is done effectively, the auditors will not only be able to communicate the results of this operational audit and persuade management to take the proper corrective action, but may also be able to sell management on the benefits of additional operational audits. Each successful operational audit should develop the demand for the next one.

Another purpose of this chapter is to increase the knowledge and understanding of effective operational audit reporting principles and techniques. In relation to the operational audit reporting phase, the operational audit report should be viewed as more a summary of operational audit results than a postaudit call to action. To be most effective, the audit findings and recommendations should have been presented to and accepted by management as the audit team proceeded through the audit. It must be remembered that the primary goal of the audit team is to assist in improving operations as expeditiously as possible as a helping agent or catalyst, and not to hold back until the final report so as to receive personal recognition for the audit organization.

6.10 AFTERWORD

This guide to operational auditing has addressed various concerns relating to the phases of operational auditing:

1. Planning the operational audit,

6.10 AFTERWORD

2. Developing the audit program,
3. Performing field work steps,
4. Developing audit findings and recommendations, and
5. Reporting the results of the audit.

The techniques presented should be of particular interest and value to those who are presently or are desirous of providing operational audit services as external auditors or consultants for clients, as well as to those who provide such operational audit services internally for specific work areas or for others within their organizations.

Because of the unique characteristics of individual firms or internal organizations, the materials covered and the situations presented may not all apply directly to every specific situation. Each reader should, therefore, use his or her own professional judgment as to which suggestions and recommendations to use in a given situation. However, the adoption of the systems and procedures covered in this guide should help in the development of effective operational audit practices thus effecting more economical, efficient, and effective operations.

Index

A

Accounting objectives, 14
Accounting records, controls review, 57
Accounting system, internal control structure, 55
Accounts receivable ratios, 80–81
Accuracy, reporting, 238, 249
Acid-test ratio, 77–78
Activity ratios, 80
Adequacy of support, reporting, 238
Administrative and operational controls review, 57–58
Administrative controls, planning, 56–58
Agenda, interviewing, 153
AICPA (American Institute of Certified Public Accountants), 4, 11, 54
AICPA Committee on Operational and Management Auditing, 4
AICPA Committee on Relations with the GAO, 4
Alternative criteria, 206
American Institute of Certified Public Accountants (AICPA), 4, 11, 54
Analytical evidence, 197
Approach, to development of audit findings, 215, 218–220
Asset turnover ratio, 82
Assignment of staff, audit program, 125–126
Attributes:
   development of audit findings, 203–214
   evidence, 197
Audit programs, 21
   planning phase, 58, 61–65
Audit reports, see Reporting
Audits:
   defined, 8
   performing, 41–42
Audit findings, development of, see Development of audit findings
Audit work plans, 111

B

Bar charts, 85–86
Benefits:
   operational auditing, 16–19
   operational audit program, 106–107
Borrowed standard, 208
Brevity, reporting, 249
Budgets, for operational auditing, 24–25

C

Calendars, audit program, 131
Cause, audit findings, 209–211, 214, 245
Clarity and simplicity, reporting, 240
Closing interview, 159
Common-size statements, 73–84
Communication between management levels, 19
Comparative analysis, 207–208
Comparisons, financial statement analysis, 66–72

INDEX

Competence, evidence, 197
Compliance component, auditing, 13
Computer-auditing, 110
Conciseness, in reporting, 240
Condition statements, 214
Confidence, in reporting, 249
"Consideration of the Internal Control Structure in a Financial Statement Audit", SAS 55 (AICPA), 54
Constructiveness of tone, in reporting, 241
Control environment, internal control structure, 54–55
Controllers, 173
Control procedures, internal control structure, 55–56
Convincingness, reporting, 238–239
Cost of operations, 6
Cost reduction, 17
CPAs, 2
Criteria:
   development of audit findings, 205–209, 214, 245
   standards, 206
Critical areas, identification of, 86–87
   audit reports examination, 53
   key activities, 52
   management reports use, 53
   physical inspection of activities, 53
   planning phase, 111
   responsible personnel, 54
Current ratio, 77

D

Data collection, findings development, 202
Data gathering, engagement, 29
Debt to assets ratio, 79
Debt to equity ratio, 78–79
Defense, reporting, 249
Development, operational audit program, 108–109
Development of audit findings, 222–226
   approach to, 215, 218–220
   attributes, 203–214
   cause, 209–211
   criteria, 205–209
   effect, 211–212, 213–214
   identification of attributes, 215–218
   introduction, 201–202
   recommendations, 212, 226–229

   statement of condition, 203–205
Development procedures, 111–112
Dispatchers, 173
Documentary evidence, 197
Duplication of effort, 149–150

E

Economy component, 13–14
Effect:
   development of audit findings, 211–212, 213–214, 245
   reporting, 245
Effective interviewing, 50
Effective listening, 158–159
Effectiveness, 5-7, 14
Efficiency, 4-5, 6, 13–14
80/20 rule, 46
Engagement, 11
Engagement budget, 119–125
Engagement control, 131, 136, 138–142
Engagement development
   data gathering, 29
   evaluate situation, 29
   operational auditing, 26–44
   proposal letter, 29, 32–41
   recognize and define problem, 26
Evaluation, 19
   development of audit findings, 202
   engagement development, 29
Evidence:
   attributes, 197
   field work phase, 197–198
   types, 197
   in workpapers, 198
Explanations, reporting, 249
External auditors, 2

F

Field work, 21
   evidence, 197–198
   factors in reaching conclusions, 149–150
   introduction, 147–148
   job responsibilities questionnaire, 186–191
   layout flowchart, 172–173, 179–180
   performance versus plans, 194
   personnel functions and responsibilities, 186
   recommendations, 148–149

systems flowchart, 160, 166–172, 174–178
techniques, 151–184, 193–194
tests of transactions, 193–194
workpapers, 194–197
Financial auditing versus, operational auditing, 9–10
Financial component, auditing, 13
Financial data, planning, 51
Financial information on organizations, planning, 48–49
Financial objectives, 14
Financial statement analysis:
common-size statements, 73–84
comparisons, 66–72
planning phase, 58, 65–71
trend percentages, 72–73
Findings and recommendations, 21
Format, reporting, 249
Functions to audit, 22–24
criteria for determining, 22–23
operational auditing, 22–24
planning phase, 90
Function understanding, planning phase, 91

G

Gantt charts, 131, 132
GAO (U.S. General Accounting Office), 3
Goals, organizational, identifying, 17–18
Graphics use, planning phase, 84–86
Gross profit margin, 83

H

Hierarchical pyramids, 173
Horizontal analysis, 66

I

Identification, workpapers, 195–196
Identification of critical problem areas, planning phase, 52–54, 86–87
Identifying attributes, development of audit findings, 215–218
Improvement areas, 16–17
Improvement in policies, procedures, 18

Improvement opportunities, engagement, 11
Inclusion of all attributes, 246
Income improvement, 17
In-depth operational audits, 20
Information-gathering, planning phase, 47–50, 88
Information needed, planning phase, 47–50
Information sources, planning phase:
financial data, 51
operating and management reports, 51
organizational data, 50–51
physical inspection, 51–52
policies and procedures, 51
Information systems, administrative and operational controls review, 57–58
Initial survey, 25–26
Institute of Internal Auditors, 4
Interest coverage ratio, 79–80
Interim reporting, 233–234
Internal auditors, 2
Internal controls, adequacy of, 14–15
Internal control structure:
accounting system, 55
environment, 54–55
procedures, 55–56
Internal reports, 57–58
Interviewing, field work, 151, 152, 153–160
agenda, 153
closing interview, 159
effective listening, 158–159
note recording, 159–160
note taking, 158
questioning procedures, 158
sample interview, 160, 161–165
scheduling, 153, 155–156
Inventory turnover ratio, 81–82
Isolates, 173

J

Job responsibilities questionnaire, field work, 186–191
Key activities identification, 52

L

Laws and regulations, planning phase, 47–48

INDEX

Layout flowchart, 172–173, 179–180
Leasing insurance costs, 43–44
Legal requirements compliance, 19
Letter reports, 250, 253, 255–258
Leverage ratios, 78–80
Line charts, 85–86
Liquidity ratios, 77
Long-term solvency, 78–80

M

Management, of operational audit program, 126–130
Management information and reports, 49
Management's use of reports, 51, 53
Management's use of standards, 149
Methods of operation, 6

N

Net profit margin, 82–83
Note recording, interviewing, 158–160

O

Objectives, operational auditing, 14–15
Objectivity and perspective, 239–240
Operating methods and procedures, planning phase, 49
Operating reports, planning phase, 51
Operational Audit Engagements (AICPA), 4, 11
Operational auditing:
  benefits, 16–19
  budget for, 24–25
  components, 11–14
  defined, 7–8
  economy, 4, 6
  effectiveness, 5–7
  efficiency, 4–5, 6
  engagement development, 26–44
  versus financial, 9–10
  functions to audit, 22–24
  initial survey, 25–26
  introduction, 1–3
  objectives, 14–15, 89
  phases, 20–21
  reasons for, 10–11
  scope, 89
  standards, 3–4
  terminology, 8–9

Operational audit program:
  assignment of staff, 125-126
  benefits, 106–107
  development, 108–109, 111–112
  engagement budget, 119–125
  engagement control, 131, 136, 138–142
  introduction, 105–106
  management, 126–130
  sample program, 112–118
  schedule control, 130–131
  standards, 107–108
  work steps, 109–111
Operational controls, planning, 56–58
Operational deficiency, 209
Operational results, 15
Operational viewpoints, 2
Oral reporting, 234–235
Organization, 241–242
  administrative and operational controls review, 57
Organizational chart review, planning phase, 91, 98, 99
Organizational data, planning phase, 50–51
Organizational efficiency, 15
Organizational goals, identifying, 17–18
Organizational philosophy, planning phase, 88-89
Organizational pyramids, 173
Organization structure, 18

P

Performance assessment, engagement, 11, 19
Performance ratios, 80–84
Performance standards, 57
Performance versus plans, field work, 194
Personnel:
  capability, 149
  functions and responsibilities, 186
  selected to manage operational audit, 126–128
Phases, operational auditing, 20–21
Philosophy, organizational, 88–89
Physical evidence, 197
Physical inspection, planning phase, 51–53
Pie charts, 85

INDEX

Planning phase, 20, 87-103, 90-103
   administrative and operational controls, 56-58
   audit program, 58, 61-65
   critical areas, identification of, 52-54, 86-87
   financial statement analysis, 58, 65-71
   functions, 90, 91
   graphics, use of, 84-86
   information gathering, 47-50, 88
   information sources, 50-52
   internal control structure, 54-56
   introduction, 45-46
   objectives, 89
   organizational chart review, 91, 98, 99
   organizational philosophy, 88-89
   scope, 89
Policies and procedures, planning phase, 51, 57
Positiveness, 241-242
Preliminary operational audits, 20
Problem areas, planning phase, 49-50, 86-87
Procedural compliance, 15
Procedures, 18
Profitability ratios, 82-83
Profit center, 42
Proposal letter, engagement, 29, 32-41

Q

Questioning procedures, interviewing, 158
Quick (acid-test) ratio, 77-78

R

Ratio, change, and trend analysis, 181-184
Recommendations, 214, 245
   development, 212, 226-229
   field work, 148-149
   for improvement, engagement, 11
Regular reports, 251, 253-254, 259-273
Relevance, evidence, 197
Reporting, 21, 242-248
   characteristics of, 236-242
   critical problem area identification, 53
   effective, 249-253
   interim, 233-234
   introduction, 231-233
   oral, 234-235
   sample reports, 250-273
   written reports, 235-236
Responsible personnel, 54
Results of operation, 6
Return on assets (ROA), 84
Return on equity (ROE), 84
Return on investment (ROI), 83-84
Review, defined, 8
Risk areas, 111
ROA (return on assets), 84
ROE (return on equity), 84
ROI (return on investment), 83-84

S

SAS 55, "Consideration of the Internal Control Structure in a Financial Statement Audit" (AICPA), 54
Scheduling:
   control, 130-131
   interviewing, 153, 155-156
Significance, good reporting, 236-237
Skills required for work steps, 125
Staff assignment, audit program, 125-126
Standard for Audit of Governmental Organizations, Programs, Activities, and Functions (AICPA), 3
Standards:
   operational auditing, 3-4
   operational audit program, 107-108
   performance, 57
   use by management, 149
Standards for the Professional Practice of Internal Auditing (AICPA), 4
Statement of condition, 244
   development of audit findings, 203-205
Sufficiency, evidence, 197
Survey form, 26, 27-29
Systems flowchart, field work, 160, 166-172, 174-178

T

Table of contents, workpapers, 196-197

INDEX

Techniques, field work phase, 151–184, 193–194
Terminology, operational auditing, 8–9
Testimonial evidence, 197
Test of reasonableness, 208–209
Tests of transactions, field work, 193–194
Timeliness, good reporting, 237–238
Trend percentages, financial statement analysis, 72–73

U

U.S. General Accounting Office (GAO), 3
Usefulness, good reporting, 237–238

V

Violations of good principles forms, 58, 59–60

W

Working capital, 77
Workpapers:
  evidence in, 198
  field work phase, 194–197
  identification, 195–196
  table of contents, 196–197
  use, 195
Work plans, audit, 111
Work steps, operational audit program, 109–111
Written instruction, 149
Written reports, 235–236

Y

Yellow book, 3